Spreading the Barcode

Personal Remembrances of an IBM Salesman at the time the Company entered the Cash Register Business and got those Universal Product Codes on all the products we now purchase

Personal Experiences of Bill Selmeier

Original 2008

Copyright © 2008 by William P. Selmeier

All rights reserved. No part of this book may be used
or reproduced by any means, graphic, electronic, or
mechanical, including photocopying, recording, taping
or by any information storage retrieval system without
the written permission of the author, except for brief quotations.

ISBN: 978-0-578-02417-2

This page intentionally left blank

To honor all those IBM manuals I read over the years containing this same message

Before the U.P.C. Barcode checkout used electromechanical cash registers.

The barcode that changed it all

After the U.P.C. Barcode checkouts look different

Preface

Son, this is your dad's story. You came along later in life so we weren't able to be friends at this earlier time. Remember when you read this that I was much closer to your current age than to my own age now. This account is about a time when the world was possibly simpler and just waiting to be changed. I would have a blast doing my part in it. There are books about how the U.P.C. Barcode came to be. This book is slightly different. It is more about how it felt to be there and participate in making it happen at the time, almost a week by week chronology. This is about my experience, typical or atypical as it may be, of being an IBM employee in the 1970s. It was a different time and it was a different IBM.

I had the unbelievably great opportunity to work in the group that helped create the U.P.C. Barcode Symbol, and influence people so that all those little bars showed up on packaged goods products, perishable products and essentially everything that you buy today. The U.P.C. Barcode and the expanded information gathering that it fostered became the initial foundation of most consumer marketing today. As a group there are hundreds of people who contributed inside and outside of IBM. We had little realization of its impact at the time. We did things that literally changed the way the world shopped. Over a decade afterwards when I was on the Shinkansen, the Japanese Bullet Train, from Tokyo to Oyama the on board food service came through the car and they were scanning the U.P.C. symbol. It suddenly struck me just what had been accomplished. Half way around the world in 1990, here was somebody using something I had helped to start eighteen years earlier.

But there are more observations than just some of the details getting the U.P.C. started. This book is a history about moving into different jobs. Entering any job, I'm not very effective. Hardly anyone is. It takes time to be effective, but if you invest your passion in it and go out each day and execute, you learn how to do it better and better until you do it well. Persistence often trumps simple smarts.

This book is non-fiction; an autobiography of a little over eight years of my life, but it is not a detailed scholarly treatise about a major industry transition. It's more personal. We deeply felt the change. We participated in it. This is more of a week by week log. I was not the management making all the decisions that others followed. I was a worker, the doer, but I was in an environment where our managers encouraged us to follow our own intuition, to find our own approaches to the tasks. I hope you see how committed to success people felt in a great corporation at such a time of incredible opportunity. Consciously or unconsciously I think most of us felt we were changing things. That was our role.

Page ii Spreading the Barcode

We were continuously motivated. If you wonder how anyone could remember all that is written in this book, I didn't. I stumbled on my copies of my expense reports buried in the back of a filing cabinet drawer. They define the "When," "Where," and "Why" for many of my activities. In my garage I stumbled on old pocket organizers from the same period. And some of the conversations had such impact at the time that I simply still remember them.

I was incredibly fortunate as a new IBM salesman to have been assigned to IBM's Kroger Corporate sales team, the Grocery Food Chain that took the leadership role in automating store checkout using optical scanning, and then, following that, to have participated and lived through the roll-out of the IBM 3660 Supermarket System, the first commercially available system dedicated to using the U.P.C. Barcode. This was a technology that ended up having a worldwide impact. But more than that, I was fortunate to have worked in and near the IBM field force at the time when that company's mission was about changing the world - pioneering new applications and expanding computer technology. A big part of our job was simply educating our customers and prospects on what was possible. At that time most industries were still pretty green when it came to using computers. Education was the principal marketing approach.

In addition to just providing some detail on where U.P.C. scanning started and how it came to be everywhere, I hope I can share a little of how it felt to be in a company that saw opportunities in almost every direction it looked. For that reason the story will actually start with the time I joined IBM. But to clarify my personal objectives then maybe I should state my perspective at that time. In college, a fraternity brother had suggested I read "Sincerely Willis Wade" a fictional book about how an Industrial Engineer saves several corporations by being the "change agent" moving them into more profitable businesses. I was enrolled in the Industrial Engineering program. Although I never actually worked for corporations of the type described in the book, ever since reading it, I saw myself as the "change agent."

This was also at a time when IBM would celebrate the "wild duck." IBM encouraged productive individualism. They wanted each employee to think individually and attempt new avenues in creative uses of computing. Although there were and still are many jokes about a rigid IBM dress code of a dark suit, rep tie, and Florsheim Imperial shoes. Your clothes don't constrain you, your thinking does. We were encouraged to find new ways to explain what might be possible with computers. There were no confining constraints. People who see dress as a constraint miss the real point which is creative thinking. Creative thinking comes from your head not what you wear.

This was a time when most of the world still did not understand what a computer could actually do or how it would be applied. Other IBM Marketing Representatives from that era, or the current, may see the experiences related here as typical of their experiences or not. By chance I ran into Dr.

Henry Steele a PhD Mathematician who worked to develop uses for in-store information, about a decade after I departed Raleigh, North Carolina. He was still working in the Raleigh Store Systems Market Support Center. When I asked him how things there were going, he replied that things were "good but different. There no longer is that feeling that we are on a mission like it was when you were there."

In some ways I was much luckier than others in being assigned to a customer in the grocery industry during its major transition to automated checkout. But, in those days the introduction of computers made most industries transitional. I've recently met several current IBMers and when they hear which years I had spent in IBM they often exclaim, "Ah, the Golden years!" And they truly were.

I hope this is a fun book about some pretty fun times - hard working, but still fun. For this was the time that the annual Diebold Study told us only 2-3% of corporate expenses went to Information Processing and less than 3% of the population had any hands-on contact with computers. To have actual hands on experience in those days meant that you either worked for a company that made computers or in a medium to large sized company's data processing department. Small companies did not have data processing departments or computers. Ninety seven to ninety eight percent of the world only saw computers in advertising, TV or movies or read about them and discussed them around the water cooler. Maybe they could see one by standing outside the glass wall of a corporate data center. For most people who had any interface with the computer, it was through a fan-folded printout delivered to their desk or some input form they completed and sent to the key punch department. But, a growing corporate awareness of the data centers value to the company, its vulnerability increased concerns for its security and often made the corporate data center go behind thicker walls. At that time companies set aside thousands of square feet to house their main frame computer. It was a far different world then than the current one full of laptops, PDA Cell phones, and home PCs.

A word about technical accuracy: I stand behind the details about the events that I personally observed or actually managed. But in all honesty 25 to 35 years have elapsed since these events occurred. I still have some retained artifacts that helped to validate historical detail and some friends have been most helpful on a few of the details. But it would be highly unlikely that some detail isn't misreported after all these years. Hopefully it will be a less important detail. Next, there is some technical Jargon. To minimize its confusion, a Glossary was added at the back of the book. Lastly, I remember that during those first 30 days I was in Raleigh NC, Larry Goodwin and Ralph Converse must have said a half dozen times, "This is such an incredible experience. We gotta write a book about it!" Well, guys, I'm going to try and do that now.

This page intentionally left blank

Acknowledgement

Nothing, not even your own tale, gets done without a lot of help from others around you. I am deeply indebted to many people in putting this together. Ed Salonus, my partner in Cincinnati reviewed the first few chapters, Art Cornwell, a friend since the second grade and an author himself, provided many, many valuable insights, Bill Carey, my first manager in Raleigh was most helpful and reviewed the events reported in this book, my brother, Dick Selmeier, took his critical marketing eye to it, and Fred Altomare, a fellow voyager in the road to establishing automated checkout benefits as an industry educator in IBM's Distribution Industry Education Center, all have made great comments. Margaret Williams, a friend from recent years, did an exceptional job of reviewing the manuscript for grammar and punctuation. Even George Laurer, the actual inventor of the U.P.C. barcode has read the manuscript and provided input. If anything is still amiss, it falls on my shoulders to have created the error.

I appreciate the help of the Computer History Museum in Mountain View, CA where I have spent many enjoyable days volunteering and was able to scan a number of slides I'd saved over the years to incorporate them in this book.

I also must recognize the patience of my wife, Leslie, who endured at least two years of over fifty out-of-town business trips per year and three more years with only slightly less trips. Through it all she still was willing to sometimes drive me to the airport and pick me up on the return. She also performed the final edit to put all those commas in the right places. And to my son, Craig, to whom this book is addressed, for his help in providing the picture layout on the outside front cover

This page intentionally left blank

Table of Contents

Preface..i
Acknowledgement..v
Chapter 1 My First Days at IBM..1
Chapter 2 Into the Territory..17
Chapter 3 Designing New Relationships..............................43
Chapter 4 Living New Relationships....................................57
Chapter 5 Raleigh at the Start...75
Chapter 6 IBM Supermarket System Announced................97
Chapter 7 Uncovering the Challenges...............................119
Chapter 8 First Steps in the Real World............................157
Chapter 9 Launching the IBM 3661 - a Baby Brother........179
Chapter 10 Revitalizing the Market....................................201
Chapter 11 Store and Forward Expanding the Market......251
Chapter 12 Moving On...267
Chapter 13 Epilogue..271
Glossary..275
Index..281

Chapter 1 My First Days at IBM

Entering IBM

"We're going to drag them, kicking, screaming, and yelling, into the 20th century." It was one of our favorite observations about selling computers in the 1970s. Not everyone but certainly many of us sometimes felt as if we were on a mission. That may sound a little arrogant and self centered today, but we were all extremely fortunate to have participated in what was to become the widening commercial thrust of the information age. It was at this time that computers went from being unique machines built for little understood special purposes to becoming an accepted part of the infrastructure of all business. Workers did not have a machine on their desktop, yet... But more and more of the information they used came from the company's computer, probably on dirty carbon smudged paper printouts 132 print positions wide, and much of the work they produced went into their company's computer, probably on a key-punched 80 column card.

Our story is going to start on February 17th, 1969, the day I joined IBM. That was really a very special period in the history of IBM, a special time in the evolution of electronic technology and a turning point in white collar work and maybe for all of society. To most people then, computers were still a "black magic." People knew computers could do what is trivial today but at the time were incredible computations. But, few understood even the simplest of concepts about how this was accomplished and what the impact of it could be. Computers were just big boxes you put facts and numeric values into and somehow reports on the amount of sales, merchandising costs, corporate profits, and how far you were behind on your project even more magically came out.

The consequence of this was that most people did not grasp where computing capability could or would be successfully applied. In the 1960s less than 3% of the population had first-hand contact with computers i.e. had either a job working for a company that made computers or worked in the data processing department of a company that used computers. Even fewer of them got close enough to a computer to actually touch it. Mostly people read about them, saw something on television, or looked through the glass window that showed off the data center. This window vantage point was still common but becoming less so even in those days. Computers were magical things that did amazing feats of computation, processed the corporation's orders, tracked the finances, paid the employees, and generated reports that initially were fairly crude but became increasingly more understandable to managers making decisions about how things would be done in the future. Companies were starting to be more concerned about keeping them physically secure than showing them off.

Page 2   Spreading the Barcode

IBM was flush from successfully completing what was arguably the biggest product gamble of the company's life. It replaced a legacy variety of computers engineered for specific application areas, e.g. financial processing, large scale scientific research, small scale scientific research, or manufacturing management, with a single family of general purpose computers, the IBM System/360. The company and its employees were in a magical place. The priorities apparent to me and thousands others were 1) convert customers using existing IBM 7000 series and 1400 series computers to a computer in the S/360 family, 2) dramatically expand the number of companies using computers, and 3) convert companies using other than IBM computers to the appropriate IBM computers. By the time I arrived at IBM, priority 1 was largely accomplished but was still the focus in the mandatory introductory training classes. Priority 2 had achieved significant results but was really still just starting. For many companies their first computer was a System 360 Model 30 or Model 40. In the larger companies, Priority 3 had also racked up some impressive results with companies buying into the broad family of computers concept. IBM was rapidly becoming the de facto computer company. To pick up company reports you were sent to the "IBM room." Often people in corporations talked about the computer printouts as the IBM reports.

As a company IBM was consumed by the desire to grow and strictly disciplined itself in its focus on this. As an information product company, it took its own medicine. It collected information about its customers, its competitors, everything and almost anything that would help its employees to understand the market for computers, and give itself the opportunity to grow more. But this tale is not going to be just a litany of what happened in IBM or what happened to get the U.P.C. birthed into the world. Hopefully it will also more relate to how it felt to be part of this process. A very special feeling!

I came to IBM from Procter & Gamble, another very professional and disciplined company. This provided a number of advantages which helped me to focus and achieve things at IBM that would have a lasting impact. Most new hires to the company were just out of college, coming out of the military service, or for other reasons they were experiencing their first real full time work environment. I had come from a company that stressed organization, focus, and a business-like rationale for problem-solving, a good environment for marketing computers.

My IBM memories begin in Bill Pendl's office that first day. Bill was an interesting character. He was medium height with a tendency to the stocky side. But he was not out of shape. He was an avid tennis player. More significant he frequently had a little curl to his mouth indicating he had something interesting to say. Sometimes that smile made you wonder what prank had just been pulled, and when he spoke he might draw out the words to increase the suspense.

Chapter 1 First Days at IBM   Page 3

Bill Pendl hired me on February 17, 1969 into the Cincinnati, IBM Branch Office 096, which was then located at 2830 Victory Parkway.. Since my previous job had been in P&G's Advertising Personnel Department and P&G was a prominent IBM customer in Cincinnati, every step of the job change proceeded cautiously and strictly "by the numbers." In January 1969, I went through a series of interviews with various Marketing and Systems Engineering Managers in the Cincinnati branch culminating in an interview on January 16th with Art Feige, the Branch Manager of Branch 096.. At the end of the month the hiring Manager, Bill Pendl, informally outlined that IBM would be interested in hiring me, but only if it would not create any problems between P&G and IBM. IBM would not make an offer in writing until I had notified P&G that I had initiated employment conversations with IBM, that IBM appeared to be interested, and P&G had the opportunity to make a counter offer. If P&G countered, IBM would withdraw.

But in IBM and P&G employees frequently left to work elsewhere. Both companies were recognized as breeding companies for their industries. I understood that there would be no counter offer, but the procedures to ensure no one would be surprised had to be followed. I went back from the mid day meeting and asked to see my boss, Dave Warnier. A few minutes later when I verbally gave him my two weeks notice, he asked me three questions: "Was there anything he could say that would change my mind?" I told him no and he said that he'd expected that would be the case. Inside P&G you better have made up your mind before you brought up the subject of resigning. I was in a personnel function and knew that well. He expected that I would have asked and answered all the questions within myself before actually coming to him. "Was this something I really wanted?" and "Would I be entering the department from which IBM commonly finds its CEO?" Since the answer to both of those questions was "yes," he wished me well and said he'd take care of notifying the other parts of Procter & Gamble that needed to be told. With that I called Bill Pendl, told him that P&G had been notified and gave him the substance of my conversation with Dave. Bill Pendl was pleased that it had gone well and indicated an offer letter would be sent to my home address. It arrived in a day or two and I returned with it to the IBM Branch Office, signed the acceptance line in their presence, and picked Monday, February 17th 1969 to be the start date.

Leaving P&G

I had transferred into P&G's Advertising Personnel less than six months earlier after several years in the Industrial Engineering Division and IED needed to be told. I got a call from Phil Willard, the last Associate Director of IED that I had worked for to confirm that it was true.

A large part of my job was to go to campuses and do the initial selection for Brand Advertising groups. We had scheduled people ahead so when I notified P&G of my intent to go to IBM, I still had scheduled visits to campuses. Dave Warnier was willing to cover some of the commitments, but manpower was stretched and so he asked me if I felt I could still go to Michigan State and represent P&G Advertising on Wednesday in my last week with P&G. Of course I could. P&G was a great place for many people. Just for me, I felt that I would be better fit at IBM. P&G could change their products but their products were fairly traditional consumer goods like soap, paper, toilet goods, etc. I did not think P&G would ever sell computers. IBM's products would change the world.

On Friday, my last day at P&G, I had to fill out paperwork for terminating health benefit programs, retirement plans, etc. (Man, I didn't know I was giving up that much retirement!) Dave casually mentioned that coincidentally he and his wife would be going to the Symphony on Saturday evening with Russ Fitzgerald, the IBM District Manager and Art Feige's boss. Dave said he'd put in a "good word" for me. On Saturday evening, true to his word, Dave casually mentioned to Russ Fitzgerald, "By the way you're getting a good guy on Monday. He worked for me." That was enough to set off alarms in Russ' head. Upon getting home, Russ woke up Art Feige to ask him if he was certain that P&G was OK with this hiring. Art woke up Bill Pendl with the same question. Bill did not wake me up but called me later on Sunday to reconfirm that there would be no problems. Monday I called Dave Warnier at P&G from IBM and got his side of the chronology. IBM was very, very careful of the customer interface.

IBM First Day

A significant memory from that first day of completing hiring/payroll forms was Bill Pendl's presentation of a small card to me. Without making light of it in any way, Bill handed me a card that listed the three basic beliefs of the IBM Corporation and asked that I carry it with me:

- Respect for the Individual,
- The best possible customer service, and
- Accomplish everything in a superior fashion.

The directness and genuineness with which it was presented made an impact on me and I pretty much kept those thoughts in my mind for the whole time I was employed by the IBM Corporation.

Often when you first join the company, you'd be paired up with some more experienced employee, take on a small project, and start absorbing what is required from what he is doing. But at IBM you went to school. My start date was timed so that later that day I started Computer Systems Training or CST, a program which educated students about IBM products and the market for computers. On that first day Bill also cautioned me that he could understand that as a professional hire rather than a "recent college grad" hire, I might feel that I did not need to go to all those classes IBM had for recent college graduates to learn about computers and the business world. I might want to be excused. "Don't even ask, you're going to go," he told me.

CST Class

Conveniently, the school was taught one floor up from the local office in the same building, immersed in the business environment of the real world. The IBM building on Victory Parkway included the education center, data center, Data Processing Branch Office, Office Products office, Field Engineering, and everything else. The business environment of IBM actually had an interesting blending of school-like structures, mixed in with real business activity. They taught a variety of programs to educate workers, both in general education, and in job-specific skills. This was, perhaps, an excellent way to gradually adapt newly-out-of-college recruits into the environment of

CST Class Picture at Entrance to Victory Parkway IBM Building

the real world. Having already had work experience in a company that did business with IBM; I was fortunately a step ahead of the game. At P&G I had been a part of the PL/1 Beta test program IBM ran, which helped me to be somewhat familiar with the programming languages covered in CST. My P&G experience made me quite assured in IBM's initial class. I was elected class president the first week of CST.

Spreading the Barcode

The very fast paced and competitive work environment at P&G, made the work pace of the class feel more relaxed. In the end I graduated number one in the class. This helped me feel very much at home and maybe too confident in my abilities when I was ready to begin facing the world as an IBMer, the point when I needed to make the decision on what specific job to assume after CST.

But, I felt my election as class President bothered two Southern California recruits fresh out of college. Perhaps it was a cultural thing. I looked too intense coming from the P&G training and culture. They were not yet as focused, and likely were less comfortable around highly focused people. It wasn't that I didn't enjoy a gab session, but I probably was more concerned that something got done A challenge many intense people have is to not raise the fear factor in those more laid back or less confident in what they themselves are doing.

Most of the class stayed at the Alms Hotel, a hotel with economical double room accommodations. It was right around the corner from the IBM building at Taft and Victory Parkway. Three students in the class were from Cincinnati and therefore lived at home. In the basement of the Alms hotel was the man who was starting a foosball game manufacturing business, and was desperately trying to increase the popularity of the game – thus there were several foosball tables around the hotel basement that people could play with.

Classroom training was fairly straightforward. The first part of training was essentially 'what is a computer?' – what are the hardware elements e.g. the Central Processing Unit, Console, Disk Drive, Tape Drive, Card Reader and Punch, Printer that can be a part of it? What are "E" and "I" time? The class manager, George Lortz, told us the five methods of man-machine communications: the card reader, console keyboard, tape drive, and disk drive. Someone in the class piped up 'That's only four.' George's response was: "Right! The 5th method is to walk up to the machine, place both hands on either side of the IBM 2311disk unit, and say 'Machine... if you don't do it this time, I'm going to kick you.' " Everyone laughed. He'd sucked us all in.

But the best reaction was saved for when he tried to explain how the IBM 2321 Data Cell operated. The Data Cell was an early concept of mass storage where information was written in high density on short strips of tape stored in groups of hundreds held straight by gravity alone. IBM wasn't that far from the days of processing cards through unit record machines, but the thought of little metal fingers pulling out hanging pieces of tape, wrapping them around a read head and successfully returning them to hang between other tapes in the storage area, brought the class to an uproar. It seemed very close to pushing on a noodle.

We also got a brief introduction to programming by writing simple programs in PL/1, COBOL, RPG, and Assembler programming languages. The programs were tested on the System 360 Model 40 in the Data Center on the first floor. I remember being happy when we were given the PL/1 task because I had participated in a beta test group when PL/1 was being announced 2 - 3 years earlier. That experience had taught me much more about PL/1 than what could be covered in the one or two days spent on it in CST.

After 6 weeks of class everyone went back to their Branch for a week or two. At this time I got assigned to help an experienced salesman develop a demonstration as part of a sales effort for selling IBM 2260 display terminals for data entry to replace keypunching the information. He was using a simple little demonstration program that would put up card images on the screen where prospects could key in input like it was a real application. I wrote the configuration cards that would create the demo. The Marketing Representative (salesman) would talk to his "inside salesman" at the customer and come back and tell me what the customer really wanted to see so that I could change and add it to the presentation. IBMers always sought out "inside salesman." This is where I think I first learned about the concept of "inside salesman" or the person who is inside the customer organization and really wants you to win. These people can be relied upon to tell you what were the real obstacles to the sale and often strategize on how to overcome them. For a new hire this was great experience. When the "Inside Salesman" came to the office to preview the demonstration, I was significantly interacting with a real customer on a significant sales opportunity, pretty much on my own after being employed for about 7 weeks. After this, I went back to second session of CST.

The first session of CST had been about learning the technology. The second was about learning how to position and sell the technology. We had many trial sales calls in this second session. A major thrust was to try to convince customers about the advantages of a multi-program environment. Prior to the IBM System/360 it was common for a computer to only run one program at a time. We prepared an education presentation to teach people what multi-programming was. I took a set of three blocks of different lengths and painted each a different color on one side, and black on the other. When I came to this presentation, I put the blocks together, the black side forward, and explained how old IBM machines could only run one thing at once. If they wanted to run just one program (flipping one block over), the other space was wasted. But with the new machines (flipping the other blocks over), they could run each different color at the same time, not wasting processing power and time. A silly visual, but it really surprised and pleased the instructor. I never used the blocks with a real customer.

After CST

At the end of CST, Bill Pendl welcomed me back to the branch with "Maybe you'd like to go sell something." I felt fairly on top of the world at the time,

Page 8   Spreading the Barcode

albeit IBM was about to rethink its entire process of dealing with customers. Bill gave me a list of people I could go call on. One of them was American Printing. I hoped and expected this would go quite well, but it did not go well at all. It was a very humbling experience. The man at American Printing let me talk to him, but I felt I had no persuasive effect on him whatsoever. The meeting was 45 minutes of nothing, essentially. I still wanted to be a salesman, but clearly I had more to learn.

First my expectations were all wrong. It's simple to see now but selling computers was not at all like the other kinds of selling that I'd previously observed, e.g. automotive sales, department store selling or grocery selling. Selling an IBM computer was a very large price sale. Sales campaigns went on for months. Three months were the short ones. The more common cycle on a large account could be nine months to a year. My CST experiences had been but bits and pieces of the total fabric.

And only for the smallest of prospects was it a single man effort. The IBM Marketing Representative's main job was to orchestrate the activities of sales resources such as System Engineers, Industry Specialists, regional topical experts, Customer Executive Education, symposiums, other IBM people, and possibly some non-IBM people into a sales campaign symphony that educated the customer on the value of IBM's products and the need for them in his business.

New sales recruits here had a choice between two different jobs - Systems Engineer, or Marketing Representative. At that time, a Systems Engineer was directly responsible for implementing the technical aspects of a marketing effort by consulting, educating, demonstrating, anticipating problems, and sometimes even programming IBM products with respective clients. Their compensation was one hundred percent salary, which remained static despite whichever job they were assigned. Marketing Representatives directly assumed responsibility for the success of any sales project, discovering the client's needs, with technical input from the Systems Engineer, determining the product solution and coordinating or providing the sales effort required to close business. Their compensation was part salary and part commission. At that time a Marketing Representatives salary portion would be roughly 80% the salary of an equivalent Systems Engineer. The rest of their paycheck was earned through commission on sales of equipment. Therefore, they accepted some risk with regards to their earnings. But if they exceeded their quota, their bonus would more than make up the difference between the Systems Engineering and Marketing Representatives base salary. It was a choice between security or ambition. Most Marketing Representatives made more money than if they had been one hundred percent salary but they had to accept the risk that if they didn't make enough sales, they would make less.

Of the three people hired about the same time and in my CST class, I was the last to be called into Bill Pendl's office after CST. The first two had been asked if they wished to become Marketing Representatives or System Engineers and both had replied they would prefer to be Systems Engineers, and be paid 100% on the salary. When I entered, Bill started with, "So, I assume you'd like to be a Systems Engineer as well?" I looked at him, and replied "If you make me a Systems Engineer, it'll be my last day with the company." Pendl laughed then smiled. This was what he wanted to hear. It meant I would be sent to Chicago for systems training in marketing and then to Sales School. It meant I had shown additional ambition, and that I wanted to reach as far as possible. And so, shortly thereafter, my second series of IBM training courses began.

Systems Design School

The second course for Marketing Reps and Systems Engineers was Systems Design School. It was an interesting time to be there, both in IBM and in this country. It was during this time that Neil Armstrong made his landing on the moon, and Americans developed an attitude of expecting more things to be possible. One day the class was excused half a day allowing the IBMers to watch the astronauts ride down Michigan Avenue in front of packed sidewalks. All in all though, this was but one of many vivid experiences I had while in Chicago.

I could look out the window of the classroom we used and see the SRA building across the street. My dad had worked in curriculum development in public school administration. I remember him talking about SRA tests and textbooks. IBM had purchased SRA and I felt somehow connected sitting in that classroom, looking at the building across the street that housed a company my dad had interacted with.

The hotel at 14 West Elm Street where we stayed for our time at Systems Design School was of memorable low quality. Although IBM was a quality institution, it paid attention to expenses and did not splurge on its new employees by providing five star accommodations during training. I made an observation about this to an education manager early on in my career at IBM, which may or may not have had a lasting impact on the opinions he held and passed on with regards to me. One experience partly explains my feelings about these accommodations. One Thursday morning the 14 West Elm's elevator's carpeting felt mushy.. We later learned that a body had been dumped in the elevator during the night and ignored by hotel staff.

Introduction to Kroger

Upon returning from Systems Design School Bill Pendl wanted to know what kind of territory I would like. I was willing to take any territory that he thought I'd do well in. He felt that because of my background I should be on a large account. In Cincinnati that meant the specific account might be Cincinnati Milling Machine, Kroger, Federated Department Stores, Cincinnati Bell or

Page 10   Spreading the Barcode

maybe an insurance or financial company. Procter & Gamble was not an option. I again deferred to him, so he chose to keep me in his unit and get me involved with the Kroger Team. I joined Gordon Vick, Joe Bischoff and others on the Kroger Team

Kroger's Cincinnati Headquarters

At the time Kroger was a five billion dollar grocery retailer, the third largest food chain in the country after Safeway and A&P, and also the most advanced in using computers. Kroger had two System 360 Model 50s installed at their headquarters in Cincinnati which communicated over 2400 baud communication lines to 24 different warehouses each with an IBM 1401 or sometimes a System 360 Model 20. These remote machines principally acted as remote job entry stations for the machines at Headquarters. Kroger operated a $5 billion corporation where all the operational information was transmitted on twenty-four 2400 baud communication lines.

The main application that drove everything in data processing was Order Picking. Stores had ASR 33 Teletypes in their back rooms which they mostly used to type up their orders for more merchandise and other data like work hours, bank deposits etc.

ASR33 Teletype similar to those used in each Kroger Store to send orders and other store level information. Courtesy of the Computer History Museum.

onto paper tape. The tape was then left in the paper tape read station of the ASR 33 to be polled by their division. Using Teletype ASR 35s, a more rugged teletype, information workers in the division manually dialed all the stores and read the paper tapes that were waiting in their readers onto paper tapes on the ASR35s at the Divisional office. Then through off-line equipment, information on that paper tape was converted to 80 column cards which were then read by the IBM 1401 or

System 360 Model 20 and transmitted to the on-line System 360 Model 50 in Cincinnati.

The on-line machine in Cincinnati would spool off miscellaneous information for various daily or weekly batch runs, but if the data was a store's order, it was processed immediately in a different section of the on-line machine's internal memory. This memory contained the warehouse layouts for each of the 24 Kroger Divisions. Warehouse picking documents were created within minutes and sent back to the division to go to the warehouse to prepare shipments to the stores. In Cincinnati the same data about each store's orders were spun off and set aside for the weekly financial reporting cycle. The other System 360 Model 50 was there to do the batch jobs and would become the on-line system should there be any failure in the active on-line system. Kroger computer operators could manually shift the teleprocessing and picking application from one machine to the other in a matter of a few minutes. This was the largest and most sophisticated information processing environment in the grocery industry at the time. In the late 1960s Kroger Food Stores was able to have a full set of company financials from the store level rolled up to the company as a whole with as much detail as you wanted by 9:00 am on Monday morning of each week. This amazed the rest of the industry and Kroger entertained visits from other chains, for example Safeway, the nation's largest grocery chain, about Kroger's integrated systems.

Accomplishing this level of computing centralization in a $4-5 billion dollar business using only 2400 baud communication lines was an incredible feat in 1969. It required powerful and likely application specific compression routines on the communication lines, which is why there were computers at both ends. Common remote job entry terminals were not sufficiently configurable. And IBM had invested a lot of Systems Engineering talent to assist in designing and possibly coding some of the sending and receiving programs. It was very leading edge in 1969. A team of extremely talented Kroger systems people had coded the whole thing with IBM's assistance. And as we so often saw, after it was operational, this customer team decided to go off and commercialize the concept someplace where they had a larger ownership stake in the financial rewards. The departing group attached itself to a group of Ohio State professors consulting in the hardware store industry and became known as Management Horizons. As Kroger worked to replace and grow its internal systems competency, IBM had a key role to play as the people who had been there, helped create the systems and were still there to help to assist and educate others coming into the task.

This perhaps is a practical example of what justified that commonly quoted statement: "No one was ever fired for buying IBM equipment." IBM built good equipment, but where IBM really came through was in standing by the customer. When Kroger's key systems staff essentially left Kroger all within a short time of each other, IBM systems engineers increased the time they spent at the Kroger building and filled the void by getting more involved on any critical system issue. There always seemed to be experienced IBM Systems Engineers in the Kroger building during normal working hours. If a problem arose, one of these IBM Systems Engineers stepped up to resolve it. Kroger was working to replace the resigned people, and IBM systems engineers jumped in to fill the gap in the interim.

At that time however I personally had no idea what application those machines ran. As the prospective new member of the team, I went with the more experienced team members to "learn the ropes." Kroger maintained an office for its IBM representatives in the programming area. Most of what I did at that time was get introduced to people others felt I should know and find ways to be helpful while I waited for my turn in Sales School. There had been a recent departure of a sales team member who had worked closely with Kroger's Drugstore Division, SuperX Drugs, at that time the third largest drug chain in the United States behind Walgreen and Eckerd. Initially I was targeted to fill in his coverage area, so I was introduced to Ron Adams, the CFO for SuperX. Ron was a tall, thin, soft-spoken executive and a very thoughtful man. He had a comfortable way of leaning back in his chair during a conversation and he rarely expressed any impatience with how the conversation was moving along.

When I first met him he had recently attended an Executive Class in Poughkeepsie. As it turned out, the IBM jet was available for his return flight. During the flight the pilot had invited Ron and the other guests, one by one, into the cockpit. Ron had really enjoyed that and since I was a private pilot we just naturally had lots to talk about in addition to business. Over the years Ron and I had many interesting conversations on philosophies of business, new retailing ideas, new health care technologies, and more. Ron could be counted on to suggest an interesting thing to see, or offer you one of the new Vitamin E pills with the comment, "This will become as big as Vitamin C." He enjoyed exploring new ideas.

IBM Unbundling

There were more reasons for my spending time around the Kroger building. On June 23rd 1969, IBM restructured its relationship with its customers in what became known as "unbundling." Prior to that announcement there would commonly have been two or more Marketing Representatives and three or more Systems Engineers around the Kroger building each week keeping up with what was going on, talking about additional uses of computers or changes to the configuration and even showing them how their own applications were coded and worked. "Unbundling" in late June 1969 changed IBM products. The Kroger Team, as we were known ranged from 5 to 7 people at any point in time who were mostly experienced Systems Engineers. Before June 23rd everything you needed, like software, educational assistance, systems engineering assistance, and other things necessary to make your computer operational, were included when you paid the monthly rental or even if you had purchased and were likely to purchase more. After unbundling, computer hardware, major software (except for the Operating System which was still included in the price of the computer), Systems Engineering time spent helping you install or apply software, and education designed to help you use or install IBM products were all separately priced. Marketing education like an Executive Class was still free.

As a Marketing Representative in training, I could go down to Kroger, but management in the Branch Office warned Systems Engineers like Joe Bischoff, who for the past two years had spent 30-50% of his life working with teleprocessing issues in the Kroger building, that he could not even enter 1014 Vine Street without already having a signed Purchase Order placed for his services. Customers, including Kroger, were in shock and IBM Branches were confused and watching everything they did. A lively banter between Kroger and IBM the week before the announcement went to a stillness as what had been five guys visiting every day dropped to one or two guys. A big part of pushing me into Kroger could have been motivated by a need to fill the silence.

The effect in the Branch Office was interesting too. In those days the one branch office in Cincinnati was a large bull pen arrangement covering the entire second floor at 2830 Victory Parkway. On the second floor you could almost walk from the offices on one end of the building to the offices on the other end of the building on top of the Marketing Representatives' and Systems Engineers' desks without touching the floor. Prior to Unbundling it would be unusual to see people at more than about 10% of the desks at any given time. Everyone was out with prospects and customers. For the second half of 1969 it was common to see people at 50-70 % of the desks.

It was a very big change and was the kind of change I'd seen coming prior to joining IBM when a chance conversation with an IBM recruiter divulged that IBM believed it needed every college graduate off every campus to handle its growth. To me that meant this was the time to join IBM and be on more of an equal footing with everyone already there. IBM was going to be forced to change its business model.

The branch office was changing in physical ways. When I joined every IBM field marketing person from every division – Data Processing, Office Products, Service Bureau, and Information Records were on the second floor. Bill Pendl's office was down past all the manager's offices along the front of the building and far up line of offices along the end of the building. These were the offices that didn't have doors. I was sitting in his office more than one afternoon when Art Feige, the branch manager, would pop his head in with a question. Bill would answer it and then with a smile ask Art, "Would you mind closing the door on your way out?" Art would just jerk his head with a little frustration and leave. "I just looove to do that to him," Bill usually explained after Art had gone. He'd have that little smile on his face. It was Bill's way of reminding Art of the value he brought to the group.

IBM Sales School

Bill Pendl was pushing to get me into a sales school class as early as possible. There was a big marketing effort to upgrade Kroger from the two System 360 Model 50s to a System 360 MP65, a more powerful machine with additional availability benefits. Bill told me he wanted me on quota before that order came in so that I could participate in the crediting of the business and earn my first 100% Club award. Bill Pendl felt the additional horsepower of the System 360 Model 65 over a Model 50 was valuable to Kroger, but more significant would be the nearly instant switchover for the on-line warehouse picking application to the other processor, if there was a hardware problem. That made it an irresistible proposal to a company as dependent on teleprocessing applications as Kroger was. A recent lead salesman on the Kroger team had been promoted to a position in the Poughkeepsie Sales School, so Bill was working multiple channels to get me a slot. It wasn't very long after completing my Chicago education before I was in Poughkeepsie starting sales school.

Sixty to seventy of us in the two week Sales School class stayed at the Red Bull Inn in Poughkeepsie in the early fall of 1969. I remember course work on learning the Sales Process from opening remarks, initial benefits statement, trial close, handling objections, to the final close. It was taught to us by the six or seven instructors, each of which had successfully used it themselves and would reference their real life experiences whenever relevant. I remember lots of discussion on time and territory management techniques. I remember reference selling. I remember a mock presentation on why it's important to have Sales Schools. I remember a lot of video equipment. Many of the exercise call scenarios were video taped and then reviewed with instructors afterwards for the good, the bad, and the really ugly. I remember baseballs. If you had a particularly good practice call, you got a ball thrown to you with "PRO" written on it.

I remember learning about CARS, the competitive tracking system. If you noticed any competitive equipment in your account, you documented it in CARS. When you had a competitive challenge, you documented it in CARS. CARS was where everything other than IBM equipment was tracked and history was built up about what strategy worked in competitively challenging situations.

I remember one instructor's "War Story" about eternal liability. Every IBM sales person in a branch office territory was compensated in part for how the value of IBM equipment in their customer's possession increased - measured in equivalent monthly rent. In fact that change in value was split between two points, one at the time when the customer was really completely sold on purchasing it and second at the time it was actually installed at the customer's location. If the new product purchase replaced something from IBM, it didn't matter how or when the prior equipment had been acquired or what real monthly revenue it still provided. IBM compensated the Marketing Representatives on the net change in value not the total amount of the new equipment. If something was newly rented replaced something purchased years earlier which because of technology advances, was less capable but priced higher earlier, the quota person could see a net minus to their measurements. The instructor had been on the Chrysler Motors account and his first commissionable transaction was to eat the loss of an IBM Vertical Sorter on month to month rental that had been installed in 1933 more than 30 years earlier.

I remember learning about IBM Marketing Practices. An IBM lawyer, actually from my own alma mater's law school, spent several hours briefing us on IBM marketing practices – mostly the "thou shalt nots." The one instruction I really enjoyed was, "IBM Marketing Representatives are not to ask the customer a question when they already know the answer!" That certainly didn't jibe with my observation of TV Courtrooms, so I asked him, "If I know that that Univac printer doesn't have a high speed skip on it and that will slow down the customer's check printing, I can't say, 'Does the Univac printer have a high speed skip?'" He replied, "Absolutely not! If you bring it up as a question, you are misrepresenting what you really know." "Wow," I had to reply, "Perry Mason would never ask a question he didn't already know the answer to." The rest of the class began questioning it too and the speaker took a brief glance at the door as if he was measuring the number of steps. I can't guarantee I never asked a question I already had the answer to, but it wouldn't have been often.

I also remember Buck Rogers, then President of IBM's Data Processing Division, the IBM sales arm for computers. Buck came up from White Plains to give the closing sales school talk and send us out as full Marketing Representatives for IBM. What a great speaker. I couldn't tell you what his points were anymore, but I was very proud to represent IBM after he spoke.

Page 16   Spreading the Barcode

Chapter 2 Into the Territory

Deeper into Kroger

Back from Sales School after being ranked fourth in my class, I was "on quota" and now devoted full time to learning the ins and outs of Kroger. I met the data processing programming group supervisors in the Kroger building; I called on the CFOs of SuperX - Kroger's Drug Store chain and Kroger Processed Foods - the manufacturing arm that made much of Kroger brand products. Visiting Kroger Processed Foods in the geological basin on the west side of downtown Cincinnati was an eclectic treat if you liked the smell of coffee and food seasonings and other grocery odors mixed together.

Within a few days Ron Walker, then Director of Data Processing for Kroger, the man in the corner office responsible for everything having to do with computers, stopped by the IBM cubicle to speak with Gordon Vick, my teammate. Ron was an exceptionally intelligent and analytical person who was also very polite. Medium height and build he had some aspects of that "accounting image" but it would be wrong to stereotype him as an accountant. He had an intuitive sense of financial value and that drove his approach to looking at all proposals. In effect, he was a senior executive well before his time. He looked for business value, not simple purchase price. Over and above his business judgment was an exceptional set of principles on how to conduct business and great personal ethics. He spoke with crispness in his words that hinted at the precision of his thought. Ron dressed in a business suit and usually had his coat on, even when working hours at his desk. But every once and a while, as was characteristic of the early '70s, Ron would come in wearing an apricot colored shirt and a wide pink tie under his dark blue suit.

Like many executives in large corporations in Cincinnati, Ron realized the need to participate in community activities. Ron was very active in Scouting. "I need a favor and maybe there is someone at IBM that would be interested." he began. I'm on the Dan Beard Boy Scout Council and we're looking for help in setting up new Cub Scout Packs and Boy Scout Troops at organizations that want to sponsor them. Is there anyone you can think of at IBM that would be interested in helping us do this?" Looking a little quizzical Gordon Vick, a strong technical person replied "Oh jeez Ron, let me see...." Gordon appeared to be reviewing the branch personnel in his mind. This was almost déjà vu from my P&G experience.

Page 18   Spreading the Barcode

Stan Schrotel Chief of Kroger Security and I washing the car of the United Appeal worker who had the highest attainment in my District.

At one point while at P&G, my management had suggested it would be in my professional interest to run a United Appeal District which I did. They also provided me with Peter Keane, a P&G ex-advertising manager to help as a behind the scenes co-district manager. That was the year that Jack Strubbe, a Senior Vice President of Kroger was the General Chairman. UA Districts had three separate components: a campaign to raise money from businesses and their employees, a campaign to raise money from the general public and a targeted campaign to wealthy individuals known as Special Gifts. In a stroke of genius Peter Keane suggested I recruit Stan Schrotel, Kroger's Security Director the ex Cincinnati Chief of Police who had been on the cover of Life Magazine as "America's Top Cop," for my District's Special Gifts portion. Stan knew all the lawyers that were overseeing the estates of wealthy widows in the district and we made the District's targets there.

With this in my UA history in mind I immediately jumped in and offered my services to Ron. Ron was appreciative and told me that if I could find more people, I should. I could imagine that I had just helped Ron fulfill a promise he had probably made to some other business leader who also volunteered his time to the scouts. All of these organizations depended on business managers from many companies to donate their time and human networking skills to make things happen. If Peter Keane as my UA coach had taught me anything, it was that everything depended on the human network. As an IBMer I was very interested in joining that kind of a network, and initially you did that by volunteering to help in some way. Ron gave me the name of a contact within the council that would help with my orientation and tell me where I was needed.

Help from P&G

Thinking about Ron's suggestion that I find other people, Michael Caver, a friend from Advertising Personnel at Procter & Gamble came to mind. I called him, told him I might have an opportunity for him and we arranged a lunch. When he arrived at the lunch, Dave Warnier, my old boss, was with him. Dave joked he wasn't too interested in losing any additional people to IBM and was pleased we were only talking about the Scouts. He gave his blessing and Mike agreed to help with the Cub Scouts. We each spent about 3-4 nights talking with people at a school and several churches interested in hosting a Cub Scout Pack or Scout Troop. A very small effort for the good will it created between Ron and me.

Marketing in the '70's

When you joined IBM in the late 60s you went through a blizzard of schools. CST, Systems Design and Sales School were the regular standard schools. But at the start of the 1970s IBM possibly sensed more challenging economic times. They responded by creating another school which all Marketing Representatives would attend within the first few months of 1970 called "Marketing in the '70s." Bill Pendl wanted me in the beta test of that school to be held in Chicago the first week in December 1969. I went and it was an interesting experience. For one thing, Spike Bietzel, IBM's VP of Sales, audited the class. IBM salesmen still within their first year of employment don't often get to meet the Vice President of Sales. I remember talking with him briefly and asked how many sales people IBM had in the USA. He replied with a specific number close to five thousand "give or take a few." I replied, "Well that seems pretty close." But he quipped back, "Not close enough for me. I don't understand why I can't know that number exactly any time I ask for it." Executives in IBM were probably much less tolerant of not having exact information than executives in other companies.

The "Marketing in the '70s" course was designed to give IBM Marketing Representatives the perspective of a corporate CEO. We had lectures on corporate accounting, financial measurements, their significance and goal setting. We played a business computer game where we competed in groups of four against the other groups in the class giving input once or twice each day about prices for several products, manufacturing quantities, research investment, and marketing investment.

But the most interesting event connected with that class came later in the following spring when Gordon Vick took his turn to attend. Kroger had been switching from a picking document that looked similar to an invoice to a sheet of adhesive labels where the warehousemen walked the warehouse and stuck a label to the case of items ordered by the store which then went on a pallet. Because Kroger so fully utilized the communications lines, any change like this had to be carefully tested before being implemented or the on-line capacity might not be enough to keep up with real time. It was possible that special compression / decompression code running in the regional computer at the warehouse may need adjustment for this new procedure. Cutovers from shipping documents to labels were made near the end of the week when warehouse to store shipments would be less and Kroger staff could have the weekend to fix any problems. It was still risky. After several successful prior conversions, Kroger scheduled a large division's conversion to shipping labels the week Gordon Vick was at school.

Gordon had been one of the SEs to initially help Kroger create their on-line environment. Later he converted to being a salesman.

Kroger had problems with this particular conversion. The compressed label images created in the headquarters System 360 Mod 50s were not getting decompressed correctly in the regional machine. Unknown to me at the time, Kroger's data processing staff called around and actually reached Gordon in Chicago at the end of his session of "Marketing in the Seventies" to plea for his help. Gordon intuitively reverted to his native Systems Engineering mode and told them his return flight was leaving in a few hours and he'd stop by Kroger's offices as soon as he got back.

He did stop and he fixed their problem. That resulted in Gordon and I being invited into a closed door meeting the following Monday afternoon with the Marketing Manager, Bill Pendl, and the SE Manager, Sam Hitchings. It started with Bill Pendl telling Gordon that he was close to being fired for violating IBM marketing practices when he helped Kroger on a non-contract, non-fee basis. Gordon didn't back down one bit and challenged Pendl to define, "What is the business of the IBM Company?" Which Gordon also answered, "To make customers successful using IBM computers!" There were a lot of "You better be careful!s" thrown around on both sides. I started to jump in once on my partner's behalf and was immediately told, "Once more and you're outta here!" It was a very heated discussion designed to impress Gordon and I with how serious IBM was that consulting activity was now only done for a chargeable fee. IBM would be enforcing their marketing rules. Our intent was to impress them with how we saw a commitment to not let the customer fail as the dominant objective in any business relationship. I don't remember who won. Both sides thought they had made their points, but of course it was clear to everyone that the managers could terminate a salesman's employment for providing, support consulting, on his own even if not for the salesman's personal gain. There would be no marketing samples in consulting.

Kroger Relations

The prior incident is indicative of the reasons that Kroger Data Processing loved Gordon Vick. His low-key soft-spoken presence was visible all around the data processing area, especially in the most technical systems area. Gordon was simply Gordon and would talk about the details of almost

Chapter 2 Into the Territory   Page 21

anything he knew about with anyone at any level that cared to discuss it. He might talk with Ron Walker for an hour about how some part of a computer worked and then be asked a similar question by lowest ranking programmer and spend an hour or more explaining it to him. Kroger had a blind programmer whom they assigned to a cubical next to the IBM cubical, so we saw him a lot. He had a special print train for the IBM 1403 printer that could print Braille. We'd pass him walking up the aisle with his white cane, print train and Braille printout of the instructions. One time he realized that Gordon was in the aisle and he had a question. Gordon talked with Rob for 15-20 minutes before Rob went off happily with his answer. Gordon turned around, walked into the cubical and said to me, "You know, I don't think Rob does any productive work for Kroger at all. It takes all of his time to make the Braille tools work." But Gordon willingly spent the 15-20 minutes talking with Rob.

When it came to figuring configuration upgrades out as to what was best for Kroger, Gordon had no equal. So the role of extending IBM's presence outside of Data Processing fell to me. In addition to my assigned responsibility for interfacing with Kroger manufacturing and SuperX drugs, I tried to meet other Kroger managers to learn more about Kroger's culture and any challenges they had. As IBMers, we looked for the business challenges our customers saw as the best place for our business opportunities. Most IBM Marketing Representatives focused on their customer's Data Processing needs like changes to configurations, education for new staff, system performance upgrades and the like. I was probably a little different in that I focused more on searching out new applications at Kroger where Data Processing could be applied but had not been thought of yet. This was what the Industrial Engineering Division at P&G had done. Gordon was good at working inside the data processing department. I was good at working with the other management. That required some coordination, but may have resulted in better coverage for IBM.

SuperX Third Party Script Scanning

A prior member of IBM's Kroger team, someone before me, had convinced SuperX drugs to optically read input for third party prescriptions refunds requested from insurance companies. I learned from conversations with Ron Adams that collecting the money from the insurance companies was a big problem. Pharmacists in the more than 800 SuperX drug stores filled the prescriptions. Increasingly instead of paying for the prescription with cash, the customer was presenting some identification from a third party insurance company associated with their labor union or a corporation. In these cases the information was noted and forwarded to SuperX Headquarters in Cincinnati. At the headquarters they had submission forms for all the plans and most of the forms were unique for each plan. Clerical staff laboriously typed up the submissions for reimbursement. All this took time. But more important the insurance companies could be very picky that every "t" was crossed in the exact manner they specified. When there was an error on the form, the insurance company rejected it and returned it to SuperX. SuperX found that months were going by before claims were paid which tied up a large part of their assets.

The concept behind optically scanning the input was to speed up getting the data into a system after the form came from the store and to use computer programming to reduce the numbers of errors getting flagged by the insurance carriers and returned to be corrected by SuperX. Instead of typing up the forms directly, the SuperX headquarter clerical staff hand wrote the information on special white forms with light blue blocks to indicate where the information was to go. The handwriting had to be good and the clerical staff had training sessions to teach them just how to make each number and letter. An IBM 1270 Optical Scanner was installed in Kroger's Data Center. It was a large machine about 10-12 feet long, 6 feet tall and 4 feet deep. The application would have worked had optical character recognition been a little more tolerant of the handwriting. Even with an operator standing at the machine to correct questionable reads when the machine had problems reading a form, the error rate was so high SuperX never got the benefit. The machine was discontinued after a few months. The technology wasn't there yet, and the problem was getting bigger because more and more prescriptions were being paid by third party insurance carriers.

Introduction to Kroger Processed Foods

Kroger Processed Foods always smelled good, particularly if you liked coffee. They had a System 360 Model 20 which connected on a leased line to the headquarters downtown. But their applications were very different from the regional Food Store applications and they ran more applications work locally than other sites. Almost all, if not all, of their programming was still done by the central staff in the Kroger Building downtown and mostly ran on the main machines. Unfortunately, that usually meant not with the same priority as a Kroger Food Store Division. Their Controller was highly partial to NCR. Once I remember his comment that he felt the applications would work better if the S/360 Model 20 used "Rod Memory" a short stick of ferrite alternative to the doughnut shaped circular ferrite core memory in IBM machines. NCR ran TV commercials showing little rods that were the memory in their machines. I suspect his comment wasn't that applications on NCR machines were better than those on IBM (although I'm sure he believed that too.) He may really have believed that straight ferrites made for better program code.

One day he suggested we take a plant tour and picked the Kroger Candy Plant in northern Cincinnati. Kroger had the second largest candy plant in the USA only slightly smaller than a plant Brach's had constructed. On the day of the tour Gary Doyle, who was another IBM Kroger team member, and I showed up at the plant and began to walk through with the Kroger

Chapter 2 Into the Territory   Page 23

Manufacturing Controller. It was a very large plant comprised of many, many production lines. The Controller led the way through a maze of rooms and small conveyor belts and then began sampling off each of the lines commenting on the quality of the candy. It was like a wine sampling only with chocolates. But after several hours of sampling orange slices and chocolate turtles in succession my stomach told me I'd had enough. As we got to the end of the tour, the Controller suggested we also go through the Kroger Dairy about a quarter mile away. Unless you've experienced it yourself, it's hard to imagine how bad cottage cheese manufacturing looks to a stomach full of orange slices and chocolate turtles.

Major Tape Reconfiguration on S/360 Model 50's

The Kroger headquarters configuration was two System 360 Model 50 mainframe computers each with 512K bytes of memory –the maximum amount of core memory possible on that machine, an IBM 2916 switch to connect and switch the telecommunications controllers, card readers and printers to the correct System 360 machine should the system that was on-line to the regional warehouses fail, eight tape drives and lot's of disk storage. The disks were wired to be shared between the on-line Model 50 talking to the 24 Kroger Divisions on leased lines and the Model 50 batch machines, but the tape drives were not. Gordon had convinced Kroger of the advantages of pooling the two separate batches of 8 tape drives into a single pool of 16 so that up to 14 drives might be used concurrently on the batch machine. The conversion was to take place over the Friday through Sunday three day July 4th holiday since the Kroger staff at the regional warehouses and the rest of headquarters would not be working. To make the change IBM had to interconnect the tape storage control units which meant the field engineers needed to have both System 360 machines.

Kroger wrapped up work on Thursday night and let the IBM Field Engineers in later in the evening for what was hoped to be a quick install. I got a call from one of the Field Engineers at 10:30am the following morning saying I'd better come down. "My customer" was getting very upset. There had been problems, the change didn't work, they tried to roll back by removing the change, resetting everything as it had been before and couldn't. They were already into the standard IBM Field Engineering service escalation procedures so that branch office specialists and district people were already there on site and they were close to calling for regional specialists, but mostly they had called me because Harry Jordan, the Kroger Operations Manager, had come in and looked very upset. The FEs had first tried to call Gordon Vick, but couldn't reach him.

I was down at the Kroger Building in less than 30 minutes. After a quick update on the status from one of the Field Engineers, I asked Harry to have some coffee with me. His face was already turning red. Harry was about fifty years old and quite excitable. His job at Kroger was to keep the data

Spreading the Barcode

processing equipment producing in a timely manner the warehouse documents and reports and whatever other information Kroger management asked for. He took his job very seriously and was quick to push back at anything that he perceived would threaten the results that Kroger management expected from him. Looking me straight in the eye Harry said, "I know I have to be careful about getting in the way and actually slowing things down. I don't want to do that, but you have to understand that we must be operational before the week starts. Now what do you know about when this will be working again. I have to know."

For just a split second I thought about my response. Then in as calm a voice as I could find I told him, "Harry we are having a problem. And more than that, right now they don't yet know why we are having a problem." Harry started to interrupt but I went on, "Harry you know that IBM is going to use everything it has to get this fixed. You recognize some of these Field Engineers. They are most of the regular Kroger Field Engineers. They are all here. They know how important it is to have this center operational when work starts next week. Harry jumped in with "Before next week? We must have reports by the start of next week that haven't been run yet."

"OK," I continued, "right now we have specialists from the branch office and our district office out in Montgomery already in the computer room. They are already calling the plant. If we need to, we will fly people in from the Regional office in Chicago or the plant where the equipment is engineered. We are going to do whatever it takes to fix the problem and get the new switch configuration installed."

"Bill, I'll try and stay out of their hair, but I'm not leaving the building and whatever you learn, you gotta come and tell me as soon as you know. This is the Kroger Company and you have to understand we are depending on you and your company to do our work. I'll be around my office," he concluded.

"I'd expect that, and I will be here also. I'll let you know anything significant." and I walked back to the computer room where the Field Engineers were working. I hadn't told Harry that when they initially tried to remove the change to make the systems work as before, they couldn't. Right now it was either forward or the graveyard. I located the senior FE on the Kroger team to tell him about my conversation with Harry and learned from him they had made no progress in the past hour. It was going to be a very long weekend. The Field Engineer told me they probably wouldn't fly anyone from the Regional staff in Chicago since they could accomplish all the input that could be provided from there over the telephone. The next step would be to increase the plant level involvement, but plant people were also many hours away by plane.

I wanted to keep Harry occupied enough so the FEs could do their job and part of that was keeping him feeling he was informed on the status of things.

I'd spend 20-40 minutes in the computer room basically observing, drinking that terrible gritty coffee that vending machines dispensed for ten cents into a paper cup, and wondering how long this could go on. Then I'd go walk around the offices to try and keep track of where Harry was. I'm sure I offered my services to the Field Engineers to help them in any way I could, and I'm sure they told me just keeping Harry occupied so they could work the problem was the most help I could provide. The problem dragged on. Harry only left the building for short time periods, which meant I didn't leave. Friday turned into Saturday and by Saturday afternoon, the Field Engineers still couldn't identify exactly what was broken. We had the regular Field Engineers, the branch specialists, the district specialists, and we were talking on the phone to the plant specialists and the problem was still a mystery.

By late on Saturday afternoon, I felt it was time to do some contingency planning. What would we do if the machines were not operational by Sunday evening? The only thing I could think of was to see if P&G would help out their customer. I talked with Harry to tell him that despite everything, it looked like we needed to find a back up machine. I could see if Procter & Gamble would make their machine available. Even though it was a System 360 Model 65 machine, Kroger's batch programs should run on it. He called the key players inside Kroger, Ron Walker and the Systems Support people. I talked with my manager, Bill Pendl and updated him on the situation. Bill Pendl called his counterpart that handled P&G who then called someone on the account team who then called someone appropriate on the P&G staff. Of course they agreed to make their System 360 Model 65 available to Kroger. I briefed Harry that we had P&G's agreement and he called in Dick Kunz from Kroger's technical staff who modified the Kroger operating systems to work on the P&G System 360 Model 65 configuration.

Around 9 or 10 PM on Saturday night one of the P&G System supervisors opened the door and let about three Kroger data processing people and me into P&G's headquarters on Sixth Street and their computer room and then stayed with us. He would be of assistance if needed while Dick Kunz tried to get the Kroger configuration to operate on P&G's machine. I know they tried to configure it several ways, but it never really would boot up on the machine. After a few hours of trying everything that anyone could think of we threw in the towel, packed everything up and returned to the Kroger building. It was a long, frustrating, and unproductive night. Outside of showing that IBM could get one customer to help out another, it had been a bust.

Fortunately on Sunday the Field Engineers discovered the problem. I think they called it an "open land pattern" a tiny hairline crack in a computer logic circuit board probably the consequence of thermal expansion and contraction that occurred when the machine was shut down after operating for months. Kroger got their machines back with the new larger switching capability in place and did their normal batch processing in time to have their Monday morning reports available as usual. I went home as soon as I heard things were working and went to bed. This kind of around the clock attention was typical of IBM and probably elsewhere in the industry in those days.

Introduction to Kroger Industrial Engineering

It wasn't too many weeks later that I learned I really wanted to get to know people in Industrial Engineering at Kroger. They were doing the new and most interesting things that would change Kroger in the future. I had an Industrial Engineering degree from college and had started with the Industrial Engineering Division at P&G. I thought I could relate to what they did. Someone told me the Director was Bob Cottrell. When I called him, he enthusiastically agreed to a meeting.

Bob welcomed me with a broad smile and a, "Hi, nice to meet you. What can I do for you?" He wasn't particularly large and had sort of an academic style about him that matched his soft voice. I reviewed that I was an IBM Marketing Representative assigned to the Kroger account. As we got into discussions he was very candid and complete about their project to create an electronic improvement to checkout. I was careful to advise him that I should not learn about any information proprietary to other vendors and he indicated he would respect that but he clearly wanted more contact with IBM. I had to check, since IBM had strict rules against deceptively viewing a competitor's proprietary information.

"Before you leave I want you to meet the people most involved in the checkout project." and he walked me out to the outer office where Dave Keyser and Dick Blair sat at desks in a bullpen arrangement. At the same time he motioned for Bob Sloat to come out of his office and join us. "These are the people who are actually doing the work of creating a scanning checkout." he said as he walked me to the desks. We all shook hands.

Sloat was the most outgoing; to the point of being gregarious. "If you have some time I can go over some things about what we are doing?" I jumped at the opportunity and Bob Sloat walked me into his office. Keyser and Blair followed and sat or stood (there were only 3 chairs) as Bob and I talked. "Kroger has shown that optically reading a package at the checkout is the most productive method of checking out our customers. We've done a fair amount of laboratory work and we're about to commit for a full store test where every customer's cart is scanned at the checkout."

"Well without going into any thing that is proprietary to some other company, how do you optically scan a cart?" I asked because I wasn't yet smart about what was feasible and practical and what wasn't.

"We don't scan the whole cart. Customers put their items on the checkstand and we scan each item individually. I'm familiar with how IBMers fear disclosures of competitive information." (Not really true, but IBM was careful to acquire it under appropriate circumstances.) "But what I'm saying here will be very public very soon. We plan to make this a very public experiment with lots of press. You need to hear this and pay attention. If we pick another company to be our in-store vendor, they will become the prime choice for equipment in the division offices. All those IBM computers in our divisions will go away. They won't be staying around" That sort of talk raises any marketing persons attention, but I did wonder who was going to write that very specialized compression/decompression code that was necessary to get the work transferred in time between the headquarters data center and the regional data center.

"Well let's go back to where things stand now and see what we can accomplish," I continued. "Understand I am just your local marketing contact. Basically I want to keep you happy and satisfy your needs, Probably because that is my perspective, I don't get to make decisions like the ones we're discussing now. But, I do carry the torch for you and I'm personally very interested in doing that. Also, of course, I have to operate within the rules IBM lays out, but let's see what we can do." Bob was not displeased with that response.

Sloat pulled out a diagram showing a conveyer belt ending up at a steel plate with a single horizontal narrow slit through the middle of the plate. "This is what we believe is the right kind of checkout. An electric eye looks up at the package. The checker can use both hands to pull items across the slit and put them in the customer's bag sitting on a shelf right in front of her. There will a symbol of concentric rings on every package that encodes its identity."

"Don't tell me details, if they're proprietary." I replied.

"It isn't," he rejoined, "It's being used because it speeds up checkout. With a concentric ring symbol the electric eye can see it and read it no matter which direction the package orientation comes from. To be productive the checker has to be able to use both hands and not spend time to make sure the package is facing the right way for scanning. We can take you to our laboratory sometime if you'd like."

"OK, I replied. Say, I've head about some special cash register keyboards that are tuned to the checker's hands so they can touch-key?"

"You mean ESIS." Bob replied showing a little disdain. "You have to remember the checker is still only using one hand to move the items because the other has to stay on the keyboard. They don't have a chance against our two handed approach. You know we want to talk to companies. We've been working with RCA and they've been very helpful, but both they and we understand that this whole effort won't happen if they are the only company making the equipment. RCA wants us to talk with other companies."

"We talked with IBM before...."

"Yup, I'm aware of that," I interjected.

"Well RCA has been very good, more responsive than you guys. We tried to talk with NCR, but that's very difficult. We worked with Sylvania a while back but that can't go farther. (At this point I decided not to ask him why the Sylvania relationship was ended, believing it would not be significant.) This isn't a new project. We've been at this awhile and I think we've discovered and proven just about everything we need to, to go ahead."

"OK," I started. "I think I want to go check some things inside IBM now. I very much appreciate the time you spent here. I don't know where this will lead. I have to go find out. But I will be staying in touch with you. Even though I don't know when I'll be back, I don't think it will be long from now." And I left to find Gordon Vick for some more background.

Kroger was very comfortable with creating its own path at the checkout. They had earlier stopped using NCR cash registers, preferring to go with Anker registers because the equipment operated with one less key depression for each item ring. Now they wanted to eliminate the keying for everything but exception transactions like voids or taking the tender at the end of the order.

When I caught up with Gordon Vick I learned that this project had been going on for about four years. Early in the project Kroger had approached IBM and IBM was not willing to spend resources on it in 1967. The Kroger people had teamed for awhile with Sylvania and now with RCA. IBM's Industry Marketing was well aware of this and they acted as the interface between Marketing Representatives in the field and Development in the Laboratories. I called Ed Igler in DPD headquarters to tell him about the experience. He told me I was coming to his next Industry class. Everyone on the Kroger team was aware of what was happening in the industry. Back on January 21st I had subscribed to Progressive Grocer, Super Marketing and Supermarket News. We each had our own subscriptions which carried a story in every issue about the on-going effort to develop a Universal Product Code. At this point the discussion was about establishing the code, the symbol would come later.

IBM Industry Classes

IBM held industry meetings at least once every year for sales people to share experiences about selling to their accounts, updating everyone on interesting applications and learning IBM directions that might affect them. The key sessions I attended were the grocery oriented meetings run by Ed Igler, the Supermarket Industry Consultant and the Drug Store oriented meetings run by Bob Costello, the Drug Store Industry Consultant.

The supermarket meetings usually took place in Chicago. Since we were the largest accounts with IBM equipment installed, I usually roomed with Ed Spiller, the Safeway account manager, which made for interesting discussions. You might suspect that we talked about events in our accounts or what application expansion we were each working on, but that was only partly true. He had transferred or immigrated to the US from South Africa where as an IBM salesman he had called on diamond mines. He had the greatest tales about calls within the mines, something you could only do infrequently because of the high powered x-ray procedures you had to pass through entering and leaving. I was informed about the details of the very stringent examination process you undergo whenever you leave the mining area. And on one visit flying to a mine in a remote location, IBM gave him some gold coins to buy his freedom from the natives in case the small Cessna they used to get there happened to go down. It didn't and he gave the coins back.

The main purpose of these classes was to share application experiences between accounts. One got a good feeling for the industry from listening to the various marketing representatives talk about the new applications their customers were developing. In this first class that I attended, the discussion was mostly about inventory control at the warehouse level and a program designed to optimize store profits called Cosmos. Cosmos sought to optimize store profits by adjusting shelf allocations based on demand and the item's gross profit.

Several salesmen reported on their customer's progress in implementing Direct Store Delivery accounting systems. Direct Store Delivery is the category of vendors that drive their truck up to the store each day and unload bread, beer, cookies, crackers, potato chips soft drinks and dairy products. About thirty percent of the merchandise the store sold didn't arrive from the chain's own warehouse, but came on the vendors' direct store delivery trucks. The question here is who's doing the checks and balances on what is actually delivered and how thorough is the recording of what arrived? Before electronic cash registers, it wasn't possible to separate out the sales of DSD merchandise from the merchandise from the company's own warehouse. Putting in a DSD system increased the discipline in getting accurate information on what was actually delivered to the store.

Ed Igler would also update everyone about Industry trends and the Universal Product Code. The U.P.C. was certainly known to everyone and a great topic during informal bull sessions. But there was nothing yet for most chains to act on. Formally, there was little for us to talk about. We Marketing Representatives at Ed's meeting speculated about which competitors would enter the electronic cash register market. But food chains were still primarily buying an NCR class 22, or 24 type machine or a Class 5 electro-mechanical cash register for special situations beyond our understanding. The only departments that stores recorded sales into were Grocery, Meat and Produce unless they used the more expensive Class 5 register.

Some discussions occurred on the topic of portable data collection. I learned that Kroger had pioneered their use a few years earlier with a large clunky keyboard (IBM 1907 which looked like a 1950's style comptometer) on the top of a shopping cart and a lead-acid battery on the bottom of the cart which was pushed around the store. But by the time I joined the team those had been discarded in favor of carrying around store order forms and then keying the order to paper tape on the ASR Teletype 33 in the back room of the store.

System 370 Announcement

In 1970 IBM announced the System 370. This first announcement wasn't the same scale as had occurred for the System 360. It was only for two of the models: the System 370 Model 155 and the System 370 Model 165. These were positioned as upgraded versions of the IBM/360 Model 50 and Model 65. After feeling we had come so close to convincing Kroger that they should have replaced the two purchased System 360 Model 50s with a System 360 MP65, branch office management identified Kroger to be a likely prospect for a S/370 Model 155. I think we initially looked at it much like one looks at buying next year's car model: it's just what you do to keep up to date. The System 370 focused heavily on RAS, Reliability, Availability and Serviceability which was a key selling point at announcement. These machines would have better up time, better performance, and less required maintenance. They would keep running in situations where a System 360 would simply stop. For example, where the System 360 had parity checking on its memory and if it detected that a single bit in core had changed, it stopped operation and registered an error. The System 370, using semiconductor memory, also had a special algorithm that could correct that single bit error. And even better it could detect if two bits flipped where the System 360's parity check would presume everything was still OK. In short, the customer would get more usable hours from a System 370 than the prior generation machines.

A few days before the official Announcement Day all the DPD Marketing Representatives and Systems Engineers went through a day long introduction training class and our customers received an invitation to a 10:00 am presentation in the Ballroom at the Hilton. Gordon Vick and Joe Bischoff, one of the Systems Engineers focused on Kroger's communication software, developed a System 370 configuration to propose to them. This is when I discovered that Gordon had Kroger letterhead stationary in his desk drawer.

"Where did you get that?" I asked?

"I've always had it. Ron Walker's secretary gave it to me." he replied with a smile.

"Does Ron know?"

Gordon was really smiling now. "Sure, Bill. This is your first big announcement. These are fun. We'll type up a letter addressed to us with

Chapter 2 Into the Territory   Page 31

everything Kroger needs to order. Then they just need to sign it so we can get a slot in the first day orders." Bill Pendl, the Marketing Manager and Sam Hitchings, the SE Manager oversaw the whole process to ensure everything got included that needed to be.

In IBM, orders were prioritized according to the time they were received at the Branch Office. There was a time stamp machine on one of the administrative desks that you always took your order letter to first. This was a way of making the delivery sequence fair for all customers, except on big announcement days it wasn't so fair. Lots of orders were going to be received. Why should a customer with offices next door to the branch get an earlier order entry time than one 15 miles away? So, any orders received on the announcement day were customarily assigned a random position within all the other orders received on announcement day at a lottery that took place a few days later. After the first day, orders were generally time stamped and assigned a date after all the first day orders.

To make sure their customer got into the first day lottery, many salesman asked for and were given a few sheets of the customer's letterhead stationary. The salesperson would type up a letter from the customer to himself outlining a reasonably accurate configuration of the equipment the customer would eventually like to install. After the formal announcement the salesperson would review it with the customer. If the customer showed interest, the customer would sign the letter the salesperson had prepared and the salesperson would bring it back to the office to be accepted by IBM. Initially only the actual announcement day was the first day, but as the market expanded and announcements became more complex the "first day" might really be a week or even up to a month long. Generally depending on how many systems were ordered, a preliminary shipment date would be assigned within a few days to a few weeks after the close of the time considered to be the "first day."

On the day of the announcement we met the Kroger Data Processing Management team at the announcement hotel, Ron Walker, the Director of MIS; Jerry Drew, the Systems Manager; and Jim Ficken, the Applications Manager. After an hour long program everyone commented on what an impressive announcement it was and Gordon wandered off with Ron Walker to review the letter. Gary Doyle, Joe Bischoff and I went back to the branch office on Victory Parkway. Gordon didn't come back until about 4 pm and he looked unhappy.

We had a huddle in Bill Pendl's office, Gary, Joe, Gordon, Sam, Gary, me, and of course Bill Pendl.

"What did Ron say?" Bischoff blurted out.

"Wait, wait, let's do this professionally," Pendl said as he took control. "What was Ron's reaction?"

Gordon replied, "Well he looked at the letter and took a few moments to look at it in detail. Then he wanted to know what capabilities I thought they had for Kroger that Kroger couldn't already do with the machines they already had. So I started to review the capabilities and growth potential."

"Did you tell him how much more memory there would be for the on-line system?" Bischoff pleaded.

"Did you tell him there would be less scheduled maintenance?" Hitchings asked.

"Well, sure," Gordon defended. "But he...."

This banter or inquisition went on for about twenty minutes until Pendl summed it up, stretching out every word, "Well, I'll tell you what's going on. Ron, you know he's a smart guy and even though we wouldn't credit anything on an order signed on announcement day, he probably knows that if he signs that letter it will look to the other people in Kroger like he's just taking the impulsive path. He probably wants to let a few days go by and then he can sign it and it will look like it was his decision and he didn't get pushed around by the vendor. It'd be the smart thing to do. We're going to get this one, never worry. Kroger's gotta be running out of gas. We got the best proposal for them. Right, Gordon?"

IBM Business Crediting Practices

Pendl's comment about not crediting the order referred to the marketing judgment principally made by the Marketing Manager as to when a customer's order for equipment was truly a serious order in the customer's view. IBM did not require the customer to write firm specifications in the letter to put a machine on order. A simple piece of paper signed by the customer indicating the customer's interest in acquiring a machine or entire system would suffice. The IBM Marketing Representative was responsible for completely defining products or services being ordered right down to the color of the side panels, voltages, keyboard format, etc. Customers didn't have to overly concern themselves with detail specifications. Their IBM representatives would figure that out.

The other side of that was that IBM did not hold the customer liable to accept things ordered. Many IBM salesmen would ask their customer to place a "position order," to put something on order to get onto the delivery schedule just in case the reason for the order became real. Customers understanding that there was no hard obligation for what they were ordering were more likely to place an order which gave the sales team time to finish selling the new application that required the equipment being ordered.

IBM understood that making it this easy to place an order meant there would be a lot of orders that might be mostly just a gleam in the eye of the customer. But getting a no risk piece of paper onto an IBM site meant there would be time for the marketing people to work to convince the customer that they really wanted it. To protect against the possibility of misrepresenting IBM's real sales with these still uncertain orders, IBM accepted the orders, put it into the production schedule at a time far, far out in months, but credit for the sale was withheld from the Marketing Representatives, Marketing Managers, et al until the Marketing Manager judged that the order was solid and the customer was serious about getting the equipment. Branch Office management separately determined if the order had really been sold or was just there to keep the customer's foot in the door. Many orders, in fact maybe most orders, were entered "un-credited" and would only become orders for commission purposes when local management understood that the customer had a serious interest in the ordered item. At that time management credited the order or considered it a "firm order" and the most economical monthly rental value of the equipment was added towards the Marketing Representative's sales quota attainment.

And there were additional checkpoints. Having an order, or part of an order credited, gave the IBM Corporation more confidence that the equipment was really sold, but not enough to start manufacturing. There was a separate check event called Production Schedule Confirmation, usually four to ten months before the scheduled ship time when the Marketing Representative would take a letter to the customer documenting the exact configuration on order and the expected ship date. If the customer at that time was planning to accept the equipment, he signed the letter and IBM manufacturing received a confirmation for building the machine. The customer was still no more liable for accepting the equipment than before, but any significant modifications to the configuration after this date would cause re-work charges to be applied to the branch office where the order originated. Branch Offices took this very seriously and consequently made certain they understood how committed the customer was to accepting the shipment as then configured. I can't think of a single instance where a customer signed the PSC letter and subsequently canceled the equipment. I can believe it happened, but not very often.

Only if the equipment on order was actually shipped and then not accepted, would IBM bill the customer for the shipping costs. I never heard of that happening. Theoretically the customer could refuse it at his door and only be liable for shipping charges. But once there the Field Engineers worked quickly to get the product installed. Once they indicated the product was installed, the customer then was liable for the invoiced amount. If the customer wanted to give it back to IBM after that, it was considered a discontinuance.

Selling the Upgrade

Gordon Vick led the campaign with the technical comparisons and carried forward all the talking points that had been used for the MP65 proposal.

Page 34   Spreading the Barcode

Gordon spent a lot of time talking with Jerry Drew the Systems Manager for Kroger Data Processing to convince him of how much more advantageous a System 370 was than their existing System 360s. While future growth was much greater with the S/370, Kroger also had the feeling, "if it ain't broke, why fix it?" We needed a compelling reason. In hindsight, it's fair to say we did not spend enough time dealing with the fact that Kroger had purchased both those System 360 Model 50 machines. Consequently the monthly cost in actual cash flow was only the maintenance charge to IBM, not a regular rental cost. For accounting purposes the customer added a monthly depreciation of the previously purchased asset to his considerations. It is likely if they went for the System 370 Model 155s, they would have purchased them too. We didn't have much information on the other demands for capital within Kroger at that time.

Handling the "purchased equipment" factor could be interesting within Kroger. If you were talking to the executive or financial groups in Kroger they understood that depreciation was an accounting mechanism used to spread out the effect of large amounts of cash leaving Kroger for a major purchase, like a mainframe computer and its peripherals, over the period of time that the asset might be used. These numbers can be adjusted taking into effect the tax consequence for the right proposition that might affect the amount of real dollars leaving the company each month. But at the operational level within Kroger, MIS viewed depreciation on purchased equipment as an out-of-pocket very real cost.

Later on there was an interesting sales presentation Gary Doyle made to the operational management proposing IBM 3420 tape drives to replace the existing 1600 bpi High Density (at the time) IBM 2420 tape drives. Gordon and I watched it unfold. Kroger had sixteen IBM 2420 tape drives on rent from IBM that connected through tape control units they had purchased from IBM with the purchased System 360 Model 50s. Gary was proposing a one for one replacement of an IBM 3420 which included its own control capabilities and cost about five dollars less a month to rent with each IBM 2420. The real reason we were making the proposal was to proactively reduce the threat of any future competitive battle with Telex who made cheaper tape drives that connected to purchased IBM 2803 control units.

The first reaction Gary got from data processing management was "If you're going to get less money from Kroger each month, why are you proposing this? What are you not telling us?" It was not uncommon for operational people to think this way

Gary just responded that he thought it was in their best interest. They no longer needed to include the IBM 2803 tape control units in their operation and they saved money at the same time. Well that set off a flurry of interest on what should be done with the purchased IBM control units.

Chapter 2 Into the Territory   Page 35

Gary responded it didn't matter what they did. They could sell them or just push them in the corner. The Kroger data processing people's response to the first question was they couldn't sell them because they were not totally written off yet. Today they probably know that it just required an accounting entry to be resolved but then it was an impossible hurdle. Their response to the second alternative was that they couldn't possibly have an asset that wasn't being fully utilized.

By now Gary was looking a little incredulously at the group and Gordon and I were keeping our mouths shut and letting him handle it. The next description of the proposition bordered on insulting. Gary went to a board in the conference room and drew a tall building down low pronouncing that that was Kroger in Cincinnati's downtown basin. Then up high he drew a small building and identified it as IBM up on the hills that surrounded the downtown. There was a line in between representing the road we came down when we came to Kroger followed by two rectangles near the road, one just a little smaller. These were identified as the monthly checks Kroger wrote to IBM without the proposed change or with the proposed change. "Every month you're going to send a smaller check to IBM," Gary explained.

Someone asked again about the unused IBM 2803 tape controllers Kroger owned and Gary responded, "It doesn't make any difference what you do with them. It's still going to be less cost to Kroger each month. You could push them through the wall and let them crash on Vine Street and it would make no difference."

Well that was truly the wrong suggestion. Things went verbally ballistic. Harry Jordan, the Operations Manager exclaimed, "You can't just go around destroying Kroger property!" All rationality had been lost. The new replacement as Director of MIS, himself also an ex-divisional controller, jumped up and took the magic marker from Gary announcing he was going to teach us Accounting 101 as he started drawing what accountants refer to as "T" accounts on the board.

The cause was lost. When we broke up Gordon had some other things to do and Gary and I left to return to the IBM branch office (up on the hill in Gary's diagram). As we hit the sidewalk, Gary turned to me saying, "Did you understand anything about what was going on?" I replied that he and I had missed that section in Sales School where they talked about avoiding verbal land mines.

One idea for additional justification for our System 370 proposal was to run a gigantic Kroger Food Processing job inside of Kroger. It was a large linear programming model that Kroger paid the University of Cincinnati to run on their System 360 Model 65 computer with 1.5 Megabytes of LCS extra memory or Large Core Storage. The job could not be run in any reasonable time on the System 360 Model 50, but it might be processed on a System 370 Model 155. In support of this we scheduled some benchmark time at the

Page 36   Spreading the Barcode

IBM System 370 demonstration facility in Poughkeepsie, NY. Chuck Stapleton, the Management Science Director, and systems staff person, and I flew to Poughkeepsie with a copy of their program and the data pack for the Candy Plant Linear Program. The program which had run over 24 hours on the Model 65 before it was completed was done in about four and a half hours on the System 370 Model 155. That looked good, but there was an available System 370 Model 165 just sitting there in the demonstration facility.

I couldn't resist. "Hey, let's just see what this Model 165 machine can do." I said encouraging them on. And they were curious. So we loaded the program and let it start. Within a few minutes the CRT console on the S/370 Model 165 reported a successful ECC correction in its memory. ECC was a system microcode that trapped any single bit error on values coming out of main memory and corrected them as well as detecting any two bit errors and halting the machine. Being the salesman, I was quick to point out how we had been saved from what would have been a machine check and hard stop failure on Kroger's System 360 Model 50 machine in Cincinnati. The single bit error on the System 360 Model 50 would have been detected and the machine would have stopped.

Then the message popped up again and I was a little surprised but still positive on the machine's capability. When it appeared a third time, I decided it didn't need to be commented on anymore. System 360 machines used core memory, made up of small donuts of ferrite that could be magnetized clockwise or counterclockwise to indicate a 0 or a 1. Core memory was a very stable technology that had been around since MIT built the Whirlwind in the early 1950's. The new System 370 used semiconductor memory, new technology, less expensive and quite obviously not as stable as core memory.

But the Candy Plant job did run to a successful conclusion in just a little over 30 minutes of wall clock time on that big machine.

This added to the justification, but still not enough to convince Kroger to replace the System 360 Model 50's. In that tightly managed operational environment it was very difficult to convince management to perturb the operations. The upside of each proposition just didn't exceed the downside risk of perturbing their environment. But Kroger was spending more and more dollars on timesharing services to support the management science applications. They could see installing a third S/360 Model 50 to provide on-line timesharing in-house and potentially be useful in a large scale failure easier than upgrading the existing two machines to a duplex S/370 Model 155. So Gordon sold them on a third S/360 Model 50.

Changes to Branch Personnel

Art Feige retired and we got a new branch manager. Art had been the classic IBM Branch Manager, a pillar in the community and active in the Salvation Army. He was the sort of person you'd think had met and talked with Tom Watson Jr.'s dad sometime in the past. I'm sure he had been focused on a career when he was younger, but at this point he was only focused on doing a good job with IBM in Cincinnati. He was coming to the end of the trail and already saw the barn. You could be proud to say you had worked for him.

SuperX Photo Processing Plant

SuperX Drug soon extended their service business by opening a photo processing plant on the west side of Cincinnati that required a billing computer. Ron Adams asked me to see him and provided a few operating requirements. It was small enough and had totally separate and unique application requirements. We proposed the recently announced System/3 as it was the lowest cost solution and we believed the new System/3 small card format fit into the photographic processing requirements better. Normally Kroger's Data Processing placed all equipment orders for installation any where in the corporation but this time Ron Adams, the SuperX CFO, ordered the machine. This was very unusual. During a review of the configuration I wondered if Ron would break with the tradition of Kroger red computers and go with a blue color. He chose Kodak yellow to match the photo processing equipment and made it the only yellow computer I ever sold.

It also taught me a lesson over the next year. The initial sale was for a batch oriented RPG controlled computer that did the job. A year and a half later we proposed a more efficient procedure using terminals at the end of the photo processing lines to capture the information instead of taking things in batches and keypunching customer and store information, but we couldn't get agreement from SuperX because the length of time before the savings benefit equaled the additional investment or payback period was too long. Ron simply told me, you should have proposed this a year ago and it would have sailed through as part of the initial order. Making changes later needed incremental justification and was much harder.

Kroger Industrial Engineering Scanning Development

I talked with Bob Sloat and his team looking at scanning checkouts every 3 to 4 weeks. Bob introduced me to the people from RCA during one of the early visits. In all honesty we looked at each other a little warily but we both appreciated that the other was there. It was an agreeable meeting. Although they joked that they didn't want IBM to get any store level business from Kroger, they felt that either NCR or IBM had to be in the scanning checkout electronic business if the whole effort was to look real to the world. On my

Spreading the Barcode

second or third visit Bob started talking about checkstand design. He felt the design of a new checkout counter was central to getting productivity gains from electronic optical scanning of a symbol.

Kroger quickly discounted the productivity gains reported by Jewel Tea using the Nuclear Data ESIS system. Nuclear Data was a small high tech startup in Schaumberg/Rolling Hills Illinois. They were getting a lot of positive trade press in 1970 from their joint development of a key entry system with a keyboard optimized for checkout. First they used a 10 key pad in place of the traditional bank of keys from 0 to 9 in each digit's position. Next they installed the keys at different heights ranging from about a quarter of an inch off the machines surface up to almost an inch. There were at least three different key heights and this provided the checker with excellent tactile orientation. The checker could feel the proper key without looking at the register. Next they were one of the first to use Item Codes for frequently purchased produce items. ESIS systems had a store controller, so item codes added an accuracy and pricing consistency to the price of included items. They also automated the cash tendering process, calculating change due and generally improving the accuracy of checkout.

But to Kroger optical scanning freed up both hands to handle merchandise and that was going to be fundamentally more productive than any optimization of only one hand. The cashier still used her left hand to move the merchandise. And not only was the item ring up more productive, but the bagger had been eliminated from the process. The procedure had gone from "ring" the item and then "bag" the item to "ring and bag" the item using two hands in one step. Bob told me about a checkstand distributor who was also an NFL official on weekends. The distributor was providing NFL game tickets for the game where he officiated to one of Kroger's top executives for him and his kid to see a professional football game somewhere every weekend. Bob sent me out to his offices in a Cincinnati suburb where there was a model of the new type of checkstand. It was higher than existing checkstands and the checker stood at the end of the counter belt instead of at the side. A lot of work had been done measuring checkout speeds with different size checkers and different height counters. The best compromise seemed to be 38 inches high.

Most important in their eyes was the need for an omni-directional symbol. Any requirement to orient the package before the symbol could be read dropped productivity, sometimes dramatically. So, they favored a circular symbol which became known as the bulls-eye. This is the symbol RCA eventually proposed to the Symbol Selection Process. I had my own subscription to Supermarket News and hardly a week went by without news on the progress of changing how checkout would be done. Discussing the news with the Kroger Industrial Engineering team was great fun since I essentially was talking with some of the people who were being reported on in the trade press. You got additional insights that way.

Cincinnati Mill in the Cash Register Business?

I'd look at anything that came along related to cash registers. I remember we saw a press article that the Cincinnati Mill was looking at making a cash register which they called "George." Cincinnati Mill was an interesting IBM customer at the time. They fully saw the coming age of computer controlled machines, although I don't believe there were any in their product line back in 1970 and 1971. And they were a good IBM mainframe customer. There was an expectation that they would be competing against IBM when they finally had computerized manufacturing automation equipment. After all, IBM was selling BOMP or Bill of Material Processing and clearly was interested in all things informational on the plant floor. Cincinnati Mill understandably considered that to be their domain and they isolated the IBM Marketing Representatives and Systems Engineers to the front office part of their facility. Field Engineers were permitted in engineering and other areas to service equipment. That always confused us, because I know almost all IBM salesmen and most IBM systems engineers could look right at your secret circuit and understand nothing about it. We were much more software oriented. Field Engineers, though, could understand what your circuit did.

George, the cash register, was being field tested at a fast food restaurant about five miles from the IBM office, so a group of us decided to have lunch there. When we arrived we found that the restaurant wasn't quite completed. We ate next door. After lunch we walked over to the building still being worked on and looked in through the windows. Beneath the counter was a machine reminiscent of a DEC PDP 8. Someone noticed that we were looking at it through the window and came over to see what we wanted. We identified ourselves as IBMers and said that we had heard about their new checkout system. We were told to "go away." I never went back, there wasn't anything I was gong to learn about my checkout environment or that would tell me more about the market.

I didn't understand the hardware circuits, but did understand the computer applications and their value. Sometime about then the cost of a desktop calculator fell below $100. I remember sitting with Gordon in our Kroger cubical and contemplating that I had to get one of those calculators. He just looked at me in amazement and asked me why I didn't just go over to the FEs service room, pick up a few abandoned circuit boards and make my own. He didn't think the FEs would mind. I just stared back in amazement. I was a salesman and couldn't begin to figure out how to do that.

Ron Walker Promotion

Ron Walker had recently moved up to the position of Kroger's Corporate Controller and was deeply involved in many Food Store activities. Ron was pretty good at bringing things to the bottom line. The Kroger buyers were quite proud of the money they had been making for Kroger by speculating on Orange Juice futures. The buyers couldn't resist taking a profit when the

Page 40   Spreading the Barcode

futures they purchased for delivery some time in the future, went up in price. They'd sell these on the market for a great profit. When they bragged about it, Ron confronted them with specific data like: On a January 8th you bought 12 thousand April Orange Juice futures at $43. In February you sold them at $49.50 making a profit of $78,000. And in April it cost Kroger to purchase for sale to customers $648,000 for that same Orange Juice or $132,000 more because we no longer owned the futures. The buyers were not heroes making money for the company. Their $78,000 profit was really a net cost of $54,000. Ron shared that experience with Gordon Vick as he was preparing to move from his second floor Data Processing office to his new top floor office as Kroger Corporate Controller.

IBM 100% Club

One of the experiences Gordon and I shared was a trip to the IBM 100% Club in May of 1971 in a private airplane. I was a private pilot and on occasion had taken Kroger data processing people up for an aerial view of their homes and other sights around Cincinnati. IBM, likely due to Tom Watson Jr's love of flying, had very favorable policies allowing employees to fly their own plane on company business. If you flew in a private aircraft, IBM would reimburse at the standard coach ticket price.

In 1971 the 100% Club for 1970 qualifiers was held in Denver. IBM private air transportation policies allowed me to fly Gordon, myself and Owen Higgens another SE in the branch from Cincinnati to Denver for the Club, then go on to see Indian ruins at Mesa Verde, then go to the Grand Canyon, then to Las Vegas, and finally return to Cincinnati. IBM reimbursed us for three round trip coach fares from Cincinnati to Denver so it cost us a net out-of-pocket transportation expense of 45 cents a passenger.

I was a member of a flying club at Blue Ash airport known as the "Flying Neutrons" which had six airplanes ranging from a Citabria for people that like to fly a stick and upside down, to a twin engine Piper Apache fully instrumented for instrument flying. But it was the well instrumented single engine Beech Bonanza V35 that was my choice for cross country flying. It had everything we would need, the ability to fly up to 18,000 feet, dual axis autopilot, true 185 mph at any altitude, retractable landing gear, but no oxygen delivery system. And at that time it only cost 10 cents per mile to fly including the fuel.

Gordon really enjoyed the trip, particularly the sight seeing. He loved the Grand Canyon, walking a short way down and exclaiming he was going to bring his toddler aged son back to hike to the bottom. In Las Vegas we benefited from a friend from Procter & Gamble, a secretary who had married an accountant who worked at the time on the Howard Hughes account. He graciously arranged for us to see a show, joining us between the shows and entertaining us with some of the exploits in the world of Howard Hughes Casinos. It was a great trip.

Page 42   Spreading the Barcode

Chapter 3 Designing New Relationships

Competition in Communications

In the late spring of 1971 our marketing team saw its most severe competitive threat since I'd been on the team. It centered on communications. Kroger regional computers at the warehouses, now down to about 22 as a consequence of selling off the Chicago division to Dominick's Food and closing another, mostly functioned as remote job entry stations for the main computer in Cincinnati. Keeping communications operational was central to staying in business. When the communications lines failed, fork lift truck drivers would run out of shipping labels to put on cases for shipment to stores. A few hours more and the truck drivers would start piling up in the warehouse yard because the previous trucks at the available doors could not be loaded. We understood that if we were down for three hours, about 200 people went home for the day. If that extended to six hours about 800 people were let go for the day. Eight to ten hour outages meant that deliveries didn't make it to the stores. People were scheduled to come in and stock store shelves when no stock was going to come. Nothing caused greater concern to Kroger's information processing people than losing their on-line communication capability. For this reason they were very cautious about making any changes to it.

Kroger had built their network early and they had to use the software and hardware tools available at the time. But in 1971 it was 3-5 years later and many new enhanced telecommunications capabilities with increased efficiencies had become available. Kroger's telecommunications was built using the first synchronous software IBM had, STRAM control software, but by 1971 Bi-Sync was the communications software in common use. When the Kroger network was initially built IBM only offered an IBM 2701 Telecommunications Control Unit for connecting the host computer to modems and then to the telephone lines. It handled only two lines at 2400 baud and rented for about $550 per month. It took 12 of them, one for backup, to handle Kroger's needs. By 1971 IBM had announced the 2703 which could handle more than 24 lines at that speed in a single chassis for less money but it required Bi-Sync and couldn't use STRAM software. The IBM sales team had already proposed to Kroger that it convert to an IBM 2703 to provide the most cost effective computing configuration, but Kroger rejected it, preferring to pay more and avoid the risk of perturbing their telecommunications environment.

Then in late spring of 1971 IBM announced the end of support service for STRAM. That meant that if a serious problem arose, only the local people would be available to solve it. It would be billed at an hourly rate and there would be no one at a plant engineering facility available to provide additional

Spreading the Barcode

help. When that news was delivered to Kroger, everyone knew we had to convert from STRAM to Bi-Sync. The IBM sales team dusted off the IBM 2703 proposal but, as anticipated, all the competitors showed up at the same time. The most challenging of them was Memorex's with its 1270 machine. It was deeply discounted compared to the IBM 2703. Standard IBM sales procedure in these situations is to gather as much information as we can and then return to the branch office to develop a plan to combat the competitive threat. Our management was made aware of it and they started contacting other resources. There was $13,000 of monthly revenue at stake and we didn't want to loose it. I believe the Memorex proposal was to do everything the IBM 2703 would have done for about one third the cost of the IBM 2703 which was already less than what Kroger was paying for the IBM 2701s, so Memorex bid three of their 1270s. There didn't appear to be any direct winning strategy based on IBM hardware configurations. But, a competitive situation is one of the things you never ignore within IBM.

A special resource, an ex-Field Engineering Manager from Raleigh, NC, called a National Thrust Coordinator for competitive communications situations flew in from Raleigh to look at our situation. I met him late in the afternoon, diagrammed our configuration, application flows and operating environment. Then we walked over to Kroger's offices and through the computer room. On the way to dinner he confessed, "You're going to go down in flames on this one, so now what we need is to make sure you don't go down without putting up a good fight. And I'll need you to come to Raleigh to preview a product that if it were announced, would give you a better chance at this battle." I did go to Raleigh several weeks later. That product became the IBM 3705. We didn't get any pricing information, but given the then current programming staff's reluctance to tweak the on-line system, I didn't see that it had a lot to offer us.

One of the other challenges at this time was that the most senior team member, Gordon Vick, one of the people who put this on-line environment together, was about to be promoted to a job in Raleigh working on something that was unannounced but most likely was a product for inside the store. He would be reporting to a manager named Bill Carey. Gordon strategized with us as best he could, but he would be elsewhere by the time anything happened. Branch management saw the competitive threat at Kroger as a major situation and they wanted an experienced competitive fighter on the team.

There was a recently re-hired salesman on the Armco Steel Account – then the fourth largest basic steel producer in the US. He also had experience as a customer. He had been re-hired to replace the then Account Manager on Armco who was about to move on. When that Account Manager did not move on, Ed Salonus joined the account team as Kroger's Account Manager. Gordon was promoted to Raleigh, NC.

Ed Salonus was short like Napoleon. And like Napoleon he was a leader. He had a take charge style but could be very collegial at the same time. He was a seasoned and smooth-operating street fighter when it was required and he always had on his gold rimmed glasses.

Intensive Planning Session

Then the District came up with a really novel suggestion. An IBM Branch Manager in the western US had developed a specialized market strategy development tool called an Intensive Planning Session. We were to become the fifth Intensive Planning Session handled by a new regional group out of Chicago. DPD had adopted it to fix big account challenges. Pendl called us in and told us we were all going to the Campbell House in Lexington KY for several weeks to think through how Kroger could benefit from IBM Data Processing. The whole team was to go, Pendl was to go, and Joe Bischoff one of the communications specialists assigned to Kroger before the Unbundling was to be included, Gary Doyle, Ed Salonus and I, all were to go. We asked about Gordon, but he was not to be included. So Sunday evening Joe Bischoff, Gary Doyle, Ed Salonus and I each drove down and checked into our own rooms with instructions to meet in a specified suite at 7:29 am the following morning.

At 7:29 am the next morning, the regional organizer, Fred Trembley, together with Bill Pendl, laid out the process for the Intensive Planning Session:

- We would do all the work in that room and we were not to leave the room unless the organizer gave permission, but room service had been told we had an open tab for anything we wanted (except alcohol).
- We could not call out from the room for information, but must depend on what we knew in our heads for all the exercises. This was to be our 100% focus. No checking up in the account or in the branch office. The front desk was instructed to get the organizer if there was a family emergency
- We would be given specific tasks to do by the organizer but he would only tell us one task at a time. We would not be told what was coming next or see any roadmap.
- We had to deal with existing IBM products and services. Nothing could be invented. Everything had to be in the current product sales manual. This was later relaxed as becomes apparent.
- We were there to develop a plan, but there would be only one plan. Contingency planning was not allowed.

Every so often Fred and Bill Pendl would be observing us from the adjacent room. Bill Pendl was living in the other part of the suite. If we had any

Page 46   Spreading the Barcode

questions we were to ask the organizer. He promised to keep the front desk aware of his location at all times.

Fred told us our first task was to put ourselves into the CEO of Kroger's shoes, become the CEO in our minds and ask "What are my main problems running this business?" At the time Kroger was really five relatively autonomous companies: Food Stores, Food Manufacturing, SuperX Drugs and some experiments with Family Centers (Mass Merchandiser) and a convenience store format, so we created 5 sets of challenges. I remember an unlimited supply of flip chart paper, masking tape, and magic markers. We wrote what we agreed upon on the charts and taped the charts to the walls. It took the better part of the day to get the challenges. Following that we were directed to prioritize the challenges in terms of their impact on the Kroger Company's business.

We ate breakfast and lunch in that room but we got an hour off for dinner in the Campbell House restaurant and then worked until after midnight that first day before Fred released us. So after a 17 hour marathon like that, Salonus and I headed for the bar. He was new to the team and we had to get to know each other less formally. Surprisingly the bar was packed, so after 20 minutes or so we both called it a night. We may have gone to the bar one other time during our stay. As the session continued we had the opportunity to learn a lot more about ourselves just talking in the suite.

Shortly after 7:29 am the next morning Fred explained our new task was to leave the CEO role and become an IBM salesman again. Using our knowledge of IBM products and capabilities, what could we offer to help solve the problems on the lists? As we worked on Kroger Food Stores problems, Fred relaxed the rule about not inventing a product. He told us that this was the only instance of this ever being allowed in an Intensive Planning Session, but since there might be a product for grocery stores in the near term future, we should consider it in our planning. For sure Bill Pendl had had some conversations with Fred. At the grocery store level we could consider in our planning an IBM system that might be announced in the future. None of us in the room had any details about what IBM development might actually be working on, so we had a clean slate.

We spent the first hour or two just talking about Kroger's stores and the Industrial Engineering Division's project. Fred, the organizer, made some really insightful comments at the start although he left shortly after this. We were discussing the impact of not having an in-store product. Kroger had pioneered several arcane data collection tools from IBM such as the IBM 1907, a big keyboard to media device contained in a grocery cart and running on a car battery, but we never had an appropriate system level product. The Kroger industrial engineers had told us that not being in the store level would mean that we would lose our equipment at the division warehouse level. Although none of us saw that as eminent, we did mention it as a consideration. Fred observed that losing the warehouse system wasn't really the issue. Kroger had over 1400 food stores and if a store system cost only $50,000, at Kroger that would be in excess of $70 million worth of business. The downside was nothing compared to the upside. That did focus us. Gary and then I, updated the others about my time spent with Cottrell and Sloat. But we were still just talking amongst ourselves to share information.

Since I had the most discussion with Kroger Industrial Engineering to that point, I took the lead in outlining the hypothetical in-store system. Putting a flip chart pad on the floor and grabbing a bunch of different colored magic markers, I got down and started drawing a system block diagram of checkout, cash control, replacement stock ordering, merchandising, direct store delivery, and labor scheduling. We then discussed how things would become available. In the first system only checkout and cash control would be there. Later ordering and direct store delivery would be added. The rest was in a third phase. It took 45 minutes to an hour to get it all laid out. At some point I was aware that Bill Pendl and Fred Trembley were standing in the doorway to Bill's bedroom watching but not saying a word.

Once the store system was completed we looked at how it tied into a changed Kroger division and corporate system. Everyone in the room contributed ideas above the store level. It took us about two days to define the proposed solutions for all the major Kroger operating units.

Somewhere along here we began to see some behavior change. We worked through the weekend, planning this for three of the five Kroger companies. Kroger Family Centers and their convenience store experiment didn't interest us much and it's interesting that Kroger did dispose of those companies within a few years. The 18 hour days were cut back to a more reasonable 12 hour day about our third day in Lexington. The process took much longer than it would appear to require on the surface. A lot of our time was spent providing other team members with details about the parts of Kroger that you were most familiar with. Joe Bischoff was king when it came to telecommunications and the history and challenges of its use at Kroger. I was the one that had spent time with Kroger's Industrial Engineering group, the people who were defining how Kroger stores would operate in the future.

But I also learned that Joe had pursued becoming a Jesuit priest and was an authority on the African Honey Bee. During our time at the Campbell House we learned many characteristics of the African Honey Bee, not to be confused with the African Killer Bee. Actually Joe looked much stronger, more muscular than the average priest. Although he was just slightly taller than medium height, he was built on a large frame and had well developed arms. Sometimes when talking, he'd speak in short bursts with a 3-5 second gap between phrases. But he was forceful in his beliefs as a good priest must be. Joe understood computer communications much better than the rest of us in the room.

Page 48 Spreading the Barcode

Ed Salonus was getting introduced to all of the details about Kroger but had good prior general experience with how executives made decisions and what would be required to be persuasive. Ed, as a Systems Engineer, had been hired away from IBM to become Director of MIS at Weirton Steel. IBM hired him back when the branch believed they needed him for Armco. Ed contributed several stories about how decisions were made at Weirton. Ed was short and sort of effervescent. You always knew Ed was in the room because he'd be organizing the activities. And he was comfortable with what executives did, since they were the types of people that were his colleagues at Weirton.

Unfortunately Gary Doyle got emotionally detached from the process somewhere during our first week and began to amuse himself by using matches to melt plastic cups into reasonably complex sculptures. Among several sculptures he managed to convert 3 or 4 plastic cups into a fairly good replica of a Bultaco which he explained was a very hot Spanish Motorcycle. There was also an Eiffel Tower. I really liked Gary. Although there was no question that he sometimes acted too young for his age, he had a natural pragmatic insight into things. I hope not, but this experience may have been the beginning of the end for him and he left the corporation a few months later.

After the proposed solutions had been identified and diagrammed or defined, Fred Trembley had us anticipate what objections Kroger might raise to our proposed solutions. Following this we developed the sales plan to present and get Kroger's commitment to implementing the proposed solutions, how to handle those objections i.e. identifying how a decision would be made and what it would take for our proposed solutions to be agreed upon by the Kroger executives who had the authority to approve the plan and make it happen.

But now 8 days have gone by and we've all been working in the same room for 12 hours a day. It's the morning of the 9th day. We have created proposals, we have identified how these proposals should be presented, anticipated the reactions and planned for how to resolve any objections. We must be done. We are really ready to go home. Then Fred showed up with the roll of butcher paper and lots of small blank System 3 cards. He hangs the butcher paper at eye level on three of the walls around the room and marks off about 18 months out on the paper. He has us write down any personal plans we had made for the next 18 months: vacations, Christmas holidays, IBM Schools, etc. on the cards and tape them on the butcher paper at the time for when they are scheduled. Then we go through all the planned events to sell these plans in the three large Kroger divisions, write them on the System 3 cards and tape them up where they have to occur to make the plan work. It was a 3 wall project planning Critical Path Method Chart.

I did like that he started this process with a warning. "Don't start with a call on the CEO. We are looking for a real plan. Who do you think gets to call on

Frank Cary – nobody! Develop real plans." It took the rest of that day and much of the morning of day 10 to finish this. And no contingency planning! If the plan fails, what do we do – we re-plan!

Late in the morning of day 10 after we had everything committed to cards on the butcher paper, Fred and Bill Pendl were walking around the room observing the results of our effort. Bischoff made a comment, "Well it's done. Now it's time to go home." Fred replied, "It'll be done and you'll go home when 'I' say it's done and not until. But he didn't have the hulk to back that up. Joe just whirled around, grabbed Fred by his upper arms and pinned him to the wall. I looked down and saw a good two and a half to three inches of air under the soles of Fred's shoes. While holding Fred in this position Joe continued, "Look we have solutions, we have a plan, and we know when and where we are going to execute the plan. There is nothing more to do here, but to go home and start executing the plan." I never knew that Jesuits could do that! Fred's eyes just bulged while Joe just let him slide gently down the wall to the floor. I don't remember Fred saying anything, but Pendl said he thought it was time to go and we packed up all our charts and butcher paper and went home. (When I happened to bump into Fred about five years later in Chicago, he still vividly remembered the Kroger Intensive Planning Session and his being lifted into the air.)

I had decided to stop shaving about the second or third day of the Intensive Planning Session, so I had a good growth by the time we got back. There was a Branch Office Meeting on the following Monday. The Branch Manager opened the meeting by welcoming the Kroger team back from its "retreat" and commenting that he didn't want to see that hair on Selmeier's face the following morning. He didn't. It was gone.

So what came out of the exercise? We didn't strictly follow the butcher paper road map. I think the butcher paper was rolled up and put in some closet, rarely to be viewed, but it totally changed my view of my relation with Kroger and its management. For better or for worse I became less intrigued by strictly Data Processing topics like tape switching units and the like and much more interested in things that would change the way people worked. The magic of the planning session wasn't the specific plan, it was the way it changed us, those that made the plan. From my perspective we thought on a different level after this exercise.

Checking the Plan

A comprehensive plan - that's a major deal in multi billion dollar corporations like Kroger and I was acutely aware that this plan had been developed in a closed environment, without customer participation, and by people who, with the exception of Joe Bischoff, had never worked through a major installation with Kroger. The first thing I wanted was input about the viability of the proposed plan from Gordon Vick, who was now in Raleigh.

It was close to the Fourth of July so arrangements were made for my wife and I to drive down and spend the holiday with the Vick's in Raleigh. I packed up all the charts and took them with me. After the rest of the family had retired on that first night, Gordon and I reviewed what the team had done. Gordon was mostly supportive. In fact he was so agreeable, I began to get uneasy. I began to ask should we have chosen "path a" or "path b" just to get some feedback and discussion. But he really had no glaring changes to suggest and mostly wanted to talk about how good living in Raleigh was and how much he liked the others in the group. So I felt good on the drive home.

That the Kroger team had gone through an Intensive Planning Session as well as our competitive situation was known throughout the IBM DPD distribution industries marketing organization. They wanted to see the outcome of the session, so a meeting was scheduled in the branch where Ed Igler from White Plains, Lyman Missimer from Chicago and several others came to see what we had done. They weren't there to evaluate the plan, just to learn what had resulted. They generally supported the proposed applications.

Taking the Plan to Kroger – Ron Walker

Both Ron Walker, now Corporate Controller of Kroger and Ron Adams, CFO of SuperX, were interested in what we had come up with. Independently we invited each to come down to offices in the IBM Education center in downtown Cincinnati to see what we had done.

Ron Walker was the toughest and likely the best customer I ever called on. He maintained a very professional relationship, never accepted gifts or lunches although he would take the IBM team to lunch at the more sophisticated Cincinnati Clubs. On separate occasions, Ron took the IBM sales team to the Queen City Club, frequented by Procter & Gamble executives, and to the Cincinnati Club. He would spend time explaining things to vendors, and expected only honest representations, candor, and integrity in return.

For this meeting Ron met us at IBM's new Education Center in downtown Cincinnati. He listened to everything and agreed with our problem statements, but much of our plan for Kroger Food Stores centered on an unannounced and unavailable product concept. I remember at one point in the discussion, Ron commented, "you need to learn more about how Gromarco accounting works." I think I simply replied, "OK" or "Yes." not wanting to appear too uninformed. When I subsequently searched accounting books for Gromarco, I found nothing. I didn't have a personal CPA at the time, but considered hiring one. No one in IBM was familiar with the term. About a year later while researching some companies for my own investing purposes, I stumbled on an entry identifying a Gromarco

Corporation, a company with stock owned by Kroger executives for the purpose of investing in buildings to lease to Kroger for grocery stores.

Taking the Plan to SuperX – Ron Adams

Ron Adams, SuperX's CFO, was also separately briefed at the IBM Education Center. The SuperX plan took into account SuperX's unique organization. Although they were the third largest drug chain in the country, SuperX operated no warehouses or distribution centers. Unique in the industry all orders were generated at store level and went directly to the vendors. When the merchandise arrived, a receiving document was sent to headquarters with the invoice to be paid from a central bank account. While this gave SuperX a lot of flexibility on where they opened and closed stores, it was very unusual for large organizations since there is less volume buying advantages.

Ron generally liked the plan we developed that helped them get control of the merchandise inventory processing from the start of the order flow instead of headquarters being on the end. He questioned what the next step should be to get the effort implemented. I was not comfortable just taking it to a Kroger DP development group. It would look too much like just an IBM sales proposal. I felt we needed a ground swell of user interest. So, we responded that this specific plan had been done in the vacuum of a hotel and we would all be better served if we re-did it with one of his people involved. He indicated he would support that when we were ready.

IBM Marketing Representatives often enjoyed very good relations with customer executives. Ron Adams and I had many informal conversations on whole ranges of topics. Once he suggested he and I might work together independently of Kroger or IBM on a music delivery system. His wife operated several franchised Hallmark Greeting Card stores. While in one of them it had struck him that recording companies forced customers to buy a bunch of songs they don't want just to get a few of the songs that they do want. Given the emerging cassette tape industry he was proposing we create and franchise Kiosks that would allow people to select from a library of songs and record customized cassette tapes with only the tunes they want to buy.

IBM 100% Club

Flying to the 1971 100% Club in the spring of 1972, again in the Bonanza, proved more eventful. This year the club was to be held in Los Angeles. Herb Rippe, then Account Manager on the Federated Department Store account was interested in going. Herb was a great person to have along since he was an amateur radio enthusiast, and a navigational ace. Herb had completed every Power Squadron and Coast Guard navigation course that existed and was qualified to sail and navigate anywhere on the globe. He

Spreading the Barcode

frequently was contracted by sailboat manufacturers to sail boats to their new owners. (During one weekend Herb was caught in a terrific storm on Lake Erie where about five boats were lost. Herb brought his crew and 40 foot yacht through, but not without some harrowing tales to tell.) Herb was proposing that we purchase a ferro-cement boat because it was so cost-effective. There would be some manufacturers in LA which he wanted to see during any free time at the club although his preference was for a yacht produced in South Korea. My only initial comment was that if it ever went down we'd know exactly where to go look for it later. But, Herb assured me, it was as safe as a fiberglass boat.

We convinced one of the SE Mangers, Clay Chapman, to join us in one direction, to LA, and Will Schwartz, a data entry specialist, to make the return trip although he would be dropped off in Rochester MN where he had recently been promoted to a marketing product management position.

The trip started with Herb and I in Cincinnati under a solid low full overcast sky. Since I was only VFR qualified in an airplane, we had to wait for the weather to clear. The plane was based at Blue Ash and unlike the year earlier, where I'd taken the plane to Lunken Airport to pick up Gordon and Owen, Herb went with me to Blue Ash. Blue Ash airport was an uncontrolled field. There was no tower and no flight service. You received your weather information by calling Lunken Airport from a phone in the Flying Neutrons Club room. We arrived at 9 am and called only to get bad news about weather. So we sat and talked for awhile and then called again. We called every 30 to 60 minutes throughout the morning with breakfast and coffee breaks in between. Late in the morning we saw a sucker hole, a place that you want to believe indicates it's clearing. We actually tried to see if we could get going and sneak out under the clouds. There were clear skies near Dayton just fifty miles north of us. But, that try was a very bad idea and we returned. Herb didn't offer any more advice on when we should leave. Then mid to late afternoon it started clearing and we were able to depart safely.

Clay was in St Louis with his family. We actually talked with him by phone two or three times to keep him aware of our situation. Our arrangement was to pick him up at a fixed base operator at Weiss Airport, a small airport on the southwest side of town. It was after 5 pm CST by the time we got there so I suggested we might just stay in St Louis that night and fly out in the morning. Clay made it clear that after sitting at the airport all day waiting for weather to clear in Cincinnati and explaining it all to his wife, we had to leave right then or he wouldn't be going.

So we left and spent the first night in Butler, MO a small town just before the Kansas border. We checked into this inexpensive motel which had two standard double beds. There were three of us. I have got to love Clay for saying, "Bill's the pilot. He gets his own bed."

Chapter 3 Designing New Relationships   Page 53

Early the next morning we were off to Mesa Verde for a look at Indian ruins and then the Grand Canyon. As we passed Ship Rock I got a chuckle when the Flight Service Station agent apologized for the poorer 90 mile visibility that day compared to their normal 125 mile visibility. Back in more industrialized Cincinnati, 15 miles visibility was very good and 25 miles was outstanding.

We spent two days in Las Vegas and saw a couple of shows. The other guys had to explain to me who Juliet Prowse was. Then we decided to see Bobby Darin's Midnight Show. Things started off right and Herb, Clay and I ended up sitting within 10 feet of the stage. But I was beat from all the extra flying and I started nodding off. All of a sudden I was fully conscious to hear Bobby Darin on the stage right in front of me, pointing at me, and yelling into the microphone, "Look at this, he's asleep in my show. This guy is sleeping!" I quickly decided I needed some fresh air and got out of the theater.

Then we went to San Diego. My flight instructor in the Flying Neutrons Flying Club in Cincinnati had suggested I go into Brown Field near the border, but the weather was closing to the south so we put down at Gillespie Field near El Cajon. On Sunday when it was time to fly up to Van Nuys where the plane would stay during the club, it was cloudy with a low ceiling again. We waited most of the morning but it was clearing very slowly. Finally I took a chance and flew a straight-out departure from runway 27. Before I knew it I was right over a large military airfield, Miramar, or what became known as the training base for Top Gun. I couldn't decide who to call. The military does not use the same tower frequencies as commercial fields. My radio doesn't reach their frequency. There was no activity on this Sunday morning, so I just kept flying and when I got to the coast I turned north for LA. (I hope there is a statute of limitations on over-flying military bases without a clearance.)

We crossed over LAX through something called a doughnut hole, a Visual Flight Rules space between 2500 and 7500 feet that VFR pilots could use to transit from north or south LA to the other side without having to talk to a controller on the ground. At Van Nuys, I found myself entering a landing pattern with eleven airplanes ahead of me. That's a few more airplanes than the maybe three to five common at Lunken Airport in Cincinnati. In the early '70's there were years when Van Nuys was one of the top 5 busiest airports in the country. As we tied the plane down and made arrangements with the local fixed base operator, we found there were others arriving at the same time and also going to the IBM 100% Club, so we could share a cab.

IBM 100% Clubs were massive affairs. More than a thousand qualified Salesmen and System Engineers and other invited guests took over two hotels. SEs stayed at the Beverly Hills Hilton and Marketing Representatives stayed at the Century Plaza. Meetings were conducted in the convention center adjacent to the Century Plaza. Speakers included many IBM Executives talking about the business climate, the company's future prospects and of course congratulating everyone for past accomplishments.

Spreading the Barcode

There was also professional entertainment and outside speakers. There was some time off during the stay and Herb had us all driving down to Long Beach or Huntington Beach to look at the ferro-cement boats. Our other visit was to the headquarters of the International House of Pancakes which Herb felt was a good stock investment at that time.

After the Club, Clay Chapman flew back on a commercial flight and Herb, Will and I reclaimed the Bonanza at Van Nuys and headed for Yosemite. We arrived about sunset but it was dark after tying down the plane and renting a car to drive into the park. We got our campsite about 9pm. It's spectacular to see all the additional stars that normally get blocked by city lights. I remember hearing a jet plane flying overhead but being unable to pick it out because there were so many stars. The next morning we toured the floor of Yosemite Valley. Herb unfortunately sprained his ankle while walking on the more slippery rocks at the base of Yosemite Falls. So, we got back into the Bonanza and flew to Reno. I ended up choosing a direct route after noticing that my original plan to fly to Sacramento and then to Reno had just as unforgiving terrain as flying direct from Merced. The new route took us right over Lake Tahoe, which was a spectacular view.

Herb was a shut-in that night with ice on his ankle. We started out the next morning prepared to fly to Yellowstone. As we crossed Nevada, I checked in with the Flight Service station at Battle Mountain to get an update on the altimeter pressure setting. They came back and reported that "Yellowstone airport had just closed due to a late spring snow so I couldn't land there and what was my plan?" I told them we'd go to Ogden, Utah and re-file our plan. At the Ogden airport we created a new plan: a flyby of the Grand Teton which none of us had seen before, and then go to Mount Rushmore to see the carved faces and if that airport they showed in "North by Northwes." really exists. But it was not to be.

On departure from Ogden the Bonanza's door popped open at about 100 feet off the ground. The 100 mph wind passing over the airplane both sucks the door out and pushes it back in so that it sits open about an inch and makes a terrific noise. I decided to return to the airport to correct the situation, but I was also very tired, programmed for departure, and I neglected to think about lowering the landing gear until the gear horn went off on final approach. I quickly applied power and got the gear down and locked just as we crossed the threshold to the runway -- not 5 feet up as would be normal, but more like 40-50 feet up because I had applied power. Well it was a long runway, there was a lot of noise from the open door, I just decided to put the plane down and get the door closed. So, I pulled the power back, but didn't reset the trim to compensate for the additional drag of the gear. The plane stopped flying just a few feet off the ground but the end of the left wing touched first and the trip was over. One of the fixed base operators was nice enough to take Will and Herb down to the Salt Lake City airport. I left a few days later after making the arrangements for handling the damage with the

Club's maintenance officer. It turned out that after years of an absolutely unblemished record, my incident was the second the club experienced in as many days.

I soon lost interest in piloting an aircraft. It wasn't the accident directly, although everyone in the club knew who I was now. It wasn't the many required sessions of ground school and check rides each Flying Neutrons club member had to attend as a consequence of the two incidents in quick succession. But about a month after the incident the club member who actually carried the insurance for the club's planes asked me to lunch. During lunch he denigrated my instructor which wasn't fair or correct. He and I both had about the same number of hours although he had progressed to twin engine aircraft. I didn't enjoy lunch but I got through it.

Less than 30 days after that lunch he got himself into a minimum visibility situation and crashed the club's twin engine Apache, killing himself and his brother. Although he was never a friend, that was the first time I had personally known someone who killed himself in a private plane. It changed my attitude and I haven't logged five hours since then.

Page 56   Spreading the Barcode

Chapter 4 Living New Relationships

Kroger Kenwood Store Scan Test

1972 was an important marketing time for companies selling checkout equipment to the grocery industry. RCA was getting a lot of positive feed back and support for their omni-directional bulls-eye pattern for the grocery symbol. In July of 1972 Kroger and RCA put their convictions to the test and converted the checkout lanes in the store in Cincinnati's Kenwood Shopping Center on Montgomery Road from standard cash registers to a scanning checkout. The Kroger Industrial Engineers

Sample Bulls-eye Symbol from Kroger Kenwood Store Scanning Test

encouraged me to visit the store. Why not, they sell groceries to everyone there. Kroger's industrial engineers were clear that they wanted to encourage many potential cash register equipment providers to get in the game. They and RCA were in concurrence that there would be no source symbol marking of grocery products unless there were many vendors prepared to sell equipment. And they knew from the experience they were getting at the Kenwood store that the cost of sticking labels on in the store negated the benefit of scanning.

I made several impromptu trips to the store, but soon learned that if I went during the day, I'd quickly have an RCA person approaching me and offering to answer any questions. I became a known face to almost all of them. But if I went in off hours I could just go through the store naturally, stand in the checkout lane and observe the things that happened. It was an impressive installation, featured in Supermarket News, the talk of the industry. I didn't know then but the key Kroger Industrial Engineers, Bob Sloat, Dave Keyser and Dick Blair, along with the Director of Data Processing's management science group, Chuck Stapleton, were soon leaving Kroger to form the consulting company, Sloat, Keyser and Blair.

SuperX Study

At the same time we got started on the SuperX study. Ron Adams put up Bill Magruder to be the SuperX participant and IBM added Harry Molloy, a Systems Engineer, who along with me, was to comprise the three man team.

Page 58   Spreading the Barcode

The three of us started the following week arranging visits to all of SuperX departments in headquarters and also observing activity at the store level. We interviewed SuperX managers at all levels to get information on their operations.

Since there were stores in Cincinnati, we could visit a sample of all parts of SuperX without having to travel. We spent a day in the SuperX store in the shopping center across from Kenwood Plaza documenting how prescriptions were filled, how customer billing information was collected, how merchandising programs got implemented, how orders got created, how merchandise was received, how items were price marked, how shelves got stocked, how the money got to the bank and how the store did its accounting. Here we were in the summer of 1972 investigating store operations in Kroger's drug store company right across Montgomery Road from the Kroger pioneering Food Store that recently started laser checkout scanning with RCA equipment and a bulls-eye symbol.

At SuperX's general offices we spent roughly a half day in each key department. In the Purchasing Department, whose function was to create the list of approved vendors, we documented their procedures and how stores were notified about approved vendors. In the accounting departments we documented all the cash flows, accounts receivable flows, and accounts payable flows. In the merchandising departments we reviewed how programs were developed. We also talked with Real Estate, Personnel, Security, and the line operating staffs. Through this we developed a comprehensive understanding of the information flows, volumes of information, control systems, and a little about the management styles of key personnel. I had two meetings with Ron Adams during the month and was happy to find that he was getting progress reports from Bill Magruder every other day or so. In his low key manner, Ron was keeping tabs on what was happening. From a marketing view, it was important for Ron to be satisfied and from a total success view, it was important that many parts of SuperX be aware of the effort and feel it was a comprehensive study. We wanted broad buy-in when the proposed solution was put on the table.

Bob Costello held an IBM Industry Marketing seminar for Marketing Representatives covering Drug Store accounts about this time. I gave a brief overview of the SuperX organization and indicated that I hoped at a later date to have more to report on a corporate study we were doing.

It took a little over a month to do all the visits. After that Harry and I sat down and conceptualized a system solution. Then we invited Bill Magruder to join us. Bill, who had been with us for all the visits, Harry, and myself spent a day or two at the Education Center in downtown Cincinnati considering what was required and how existing IBM products could benefit SuperX. The SuperX people were looking for a significant proposal and, of course, we were too. We felt that it centered on some computing device in the prescription area. All other store information could be put in through that device. And a SuperX

Chapter 4 Living a New Relationship   Page 59

data center would have to be constructed. The work load looked to require a System 370 Model 145.

Having Bill Magruder with us provided some insight on what could be sold and how to go about it. We spent our time on how to approach SuperX and to some extent Kroger. We were not actually designing software. We were designing for selling software. Then current IBM business practices would require a contract for a fee with the customer to provide a detailed system design to program from. We identified the basic applications and we designed a way to illustrate them to the people at SuperX. We were designing the functions and conceptualizing a user interface to illustrate the systems we proposed be developed when the project was accepted.

Fortunately for us at this time the IMS (a large scale IBM Data Base Management System developed with North American Rockwell) marketing group developed a handy tool, a cardboard mock-up of an IBM 3270 CRT that took 8 ½" by 11" paper in the area where the screen was. All Marketing Representatives received one. So, now we could type up our applications using an orator type ball on a Selectric typewriter and use their container to illustrate in life size how using the proposed systems would look to the user. This resulted in a much more graphic and involving presentation for the audience than just presenting the information on a series of charts.

The same time the data center people had noticed the amount of time we were spending in their conference rooms and seeing an opportunity to help, they offered to code some small demonstration programs. Specifically we had targeted the recently announced IBM 3735 to be the pharmacy machine and general store communications device. From what field people were told at its announcement, the 3735 was basically a Selectric typewriter attached to a control box that included computer logic, a communications interface, and a disk. That appeared to be a small computer to me. The machine had been designed to process forms. The IBM 3735, under program control, assisted the operator with calculations on the form and logic to validate input data. This looked like the device to correctly capture third party scripts, balance the cash registers, input store orders for merchandise and maybe more.

The Data Center obtained a demonstration IBM 3735 unit and agreed to provide some program development support to help illustrate our approach. They assigned Cheryl, a tall, attractive, almost statuesque, female SE to do the work. She made quite an impression on the customers. I thought that was great.

Cheryl did an amazing job. We got samples to her of the store's cash register settlement reports and she created a mock up version that would type out on the 3735. We had some simple Third Party script forms that she recreated in the 3735 at the IBM data center. I think we may also have had

Page 60 Spreading the Barcode

two or three other forms, like a merchandise order form and a merchandise receipt form and some others.

Harry and I designed some IBM 3270 interactive display scenarios and had them typed up by the secretaries in the branch. We could now illustrate using the data center's IBM 3735, how orders originated in the store. After a nightly transmission to the headquarters, they were reviewed by SuperX headquarters staff as illustrated on our cardboard 3270, and then printed as a Purchase Order to the vendor taking advantage of all aggregated volume and other discounts. Later when it was received in the store, the receipt was recorded again as demonstrated using the IBM data center's 3735, and finally paid for by SuperX headquarters accounting as again illustrated on the cardboard 3270.

Sloat, Keyser, Blair

One day during the creation of this, I bumped into Bob Sloat, the ex-Kroger Industrial Engineer walking across Cincinnati's Fifth/Third Bank Plaza. He enjoyed telling me that IBM was now a client of Sloat, Keyser and Blair. But more fun was to tell me, "I'm sure you understand Bill, that although I'd like to tell you about the project we are the prime consultant on, I am prevented from doing so due to our non-disclosure agreement with IBM." He was really enjoying this role reversal with me. We wished each other well, but our paths were never to cross again. More than anyone else, Bob was responsible for exposing me to the methods Kroger followed to design stores and particularly store checkouts, what was important, what to control and how it operated.

Kroger Visit to IBM Development

A short time later I received a call from IBM Marketing headquarters indicating they would like to disclose some aspects of IBM's Point-of-sale activity to Ron Walker, Controller of Kroger. Ron agreed and we arranged an early morning flight to Raleigh to meet with Bill Carey and his staff which included Gordon Vick from the Marketing Division and some of the engineering management.

Although everything was done under an NDA, we never actually saw any hardware. There were some diagrams and lists of functions, but mostly questions centered on how Kroger would analyze purchasing point-of-sale equipment, i.e. What was important and how prioritization of possible options would be done. IBM catered lunch in to everyone inside the IBM meeting room and this was the only time I ever saw IBM able to purchase a meal for Ron Walker.

For people who like to see lights blink and computers operate, this would have been a disappointing trip. But Ron seemed impressed and very upbeat about the experience. Ron was a very smart person and he liked what he was interpreting from the questions he had been asked.

Chapter 4 Living a New Relationship   Page 61

For my part I liked even more the conversation we had sitting on the airport ramp in Piedmont Airline's tiny Fairchild F-227 during its one stop in Charleston, West Virginia on the way back to Cincinnati. Ron commented, "Bill, don't ever worry about the justification for the five to six million dollars of IBM equipment in the Kroger building." I was curious. "Because of that equipment, I know one day earlier how much money has come into the Kroger Company. In a $5 billion annual sales corporation like Kroger, that's more than $20 million a day. I'll use $ 5 million to buy a $20 million dollar asset every time I can," he concluded. That really made an impression on me.

Ron Walker Leaves

The only sad part was Ron was soon to follow a prior Kroger Controller, Bill Martin, and leave Kroger to join American Financial, a hot Cincinnati conglomerate that dabbled in retail dairy markets, insurance companies and movie studios. Down the road they also acquired United Brands.

Other Kroger Coverage

My teammate, Ed Salonus, was doing an amazing job of covering the whole of the rest of Kroger with some help from Paul Grimes, Gary Doyle's replacement. Ed agreed to handle Kroger's Processed Foods and Don Bolce. Ed and Don took a trip together to visit Kroger's chicken raising farms in Hope, AK. It must have been an interesting trip. I remember Ed commenting that you can't know "real fear" until you walk into a brood barn where there are a quarter of a million chickens on the loose.

SuperX Study

Ron Adams was the ultimate SuperX decision maker. He was going to pay the bill for everything. Some of it would hopefully get paid to IBM, some to Kroger, but Ron was the place where all the bills would get paid. Bill Magruder had kept him up to date on what we were doing and told us that Ron was pleased. Additionally I would go see him every week or so to ensure where things stood. As for Kroger's data processing staff, we kept them informed, well sort of. Kroger had an Applications Development Manager and about 4 programmers assigned to SuperX. I made sure he was aware of the scope and magnitude of the project. He was quite supportive of our work. He told me he looked on what I was doing as "employment insurance." Kroger's Data Processing Director was a different challenge. He may have felt challenged by the magnitude of this project. I didn't spend enough time with him to make him comfortable with it and he probably saw it as a bigger risk than a reward.

Page 62   Spreading the Barcode

Delivering an IBM Message

Early one morning in 1972 as I was getting ready for the day, the phone rang. Ed Igler called from Distribution Industry in White Plains. He wanted to confirm that I knew Barry Franz at Procter & Gamble which I did. Years earlier I'd worked across the hall from Barry when I first joined P&G and had given him his first small airplane ride. If I remember, that caused his wife Margie some concern. Ed said IBM needed me to have lunch with Barry and deliver a message.

The U.P.C. Symbol selection committee was formed by the Ad Hoc Committee that defined the Universal Product Code, just the code format, in 1971 and was comprised of representatives from grocery retailers and grocery manufacturers. Barry Franz, an Operations Research/Management Science expert in Industrial Engineering, was P&G's member of the Symbol Selection Committee. But more relevant to that morning's call, IBM felt Barry to be one of the most technically knowledgeable and capable members of the Symbol Selection Committee. When IBM presented its logic for a more easily printed but not omni-directional Barcode Symbol to be used with an omni-directional scanner, Barry might have been the committee member that best understood all the technology presented. I wasn't there, but I know what "My eyes glazed over" looks like and evidently there was some of that by other committee members after IBM's presentation.

Competing concepts included the omni-directional bulls-eye proposed by RCA/Unisys and other circle and half circle type designs. The IBM proposal had included an extensive mathematical proof. Some of the IBM people at the presentation saw indications that Barry appreciated the technological approach but had personal doubts about IBM's commitment to enter this market. It's likely the other proposal presenters would willingly discuss more specifics about products under consideration or under development, while IBM would stoically maintain that they couldn't discuss un-announced products. In any event Barry would not likely support a symbol proposal from a company that wasn't going to be in the market.

My task was to convince Barry that IBM was very serious about their proposal, re-iterate and verify that IBM can not discuss any product before it's announced, and tell him the company appreciated his understanding of the technological issues. As evidence of this I was to tell Barry that Marvin Mann had recently joined Distribution Industry Marketing to work on the project. Marvin's previous position was to introduce the System/3 with its unique small 96 character punch card. Because of that product's success, Marvin was joining Distribution Industry. The corporation was interested enough to dedicate this kind of executive talent to the effort.

I called Barry a few minutes after hanging up with Ed and we arranged for lunch that day or the next. It was great seeing Barry again and catching up on all that was appropriate for him to discuss about P&G. I told him about the call, relayed the information about Marvin and reaffirmed IBM's strict rules about un-announced products. At that time I didn't know very much of the details about products myself, only that Gordon Vick, a prior sales partner had been promoted to Raleigh to work on something that must have been supermarket store related. Barry wasn't under any Non-Disclosure rules relating to the symbol proposals and clearly had been impressed by the IBM presentation. He told me about an IBM mathematician that filled a board with equations to document that the parallel bar barcode would outperform concentric circles. Barry told me the presentation had been moderated by a fellow named Bo Evans. At the end when everyone had questions, Barry had questioned "wouldn't it take a System 360 Model 40 to do all the processing required to keep the check lane productive?" Bo reached into his pocket and held up a single chip while replying, "This is your Model 40." Evidently Bo had the concept of stage presence. Barry had been very impressed. IBM's Distribution Industry Marketing was delighted with the results of the lunch.

Before we parted, and as a friend, I had to ask Barry, "Why is P&G supporting this since it's a net cost to them?" Barry replied that the projections showed that it would cost about 1 percent of sales for manufacturers to include a symbol on a package. But if it really saved 2 percent in cost at the store, they would pay the 1% and help the consumer achieve the 1% net overall benefit. Of course in hind-sight, the benefit has been much higher.

Marvin Mann's Visit to Kroger

Shortly after that Bill Pendl got a call indicating Marvin Mann wanted to come to Cincinnati, review the IBM Kroger Plan and meet some customer executives. Marvin was at a level where you carefully organized his visit. Ed Salonus and I met with him briefly at his hotel the prior night to answer any questions about the visit and get any last minute information requests.

During the next morning we went through the Intensive Planning results in the Branch Office for Marvin. In the afternoon I took him to see Jack Strubbe, Executive VP of Kroger and Kroger's Executive member of the U.P.C. Ad Hoc Council. At that meeting, Jack was reviewing the tremendous projected financial benefits for Food Stores from scanning checkouts. "This will add more than 2% to the bottom line in an industry not making even 1% profit right now!" he pointed out. I had to interrupt, "No, it won't!" Marvin's head did a little jerk like he thought his (soon to be ex-) salesman had lost his mind. I continued, "You won't. I'm not implying any collusion, but this industry has determined on its own that it can operate at 0.68% profit after tax and if some technology suddenly comes in to make that 2.68%, grocers will use that extra profit to gain market share by reducing prices, having more deals, etc. So it's the consumer that gets the 2% improvement to the bottom line." Jack reflected only a second and then said, "Yes, you're right." Marvin suddenly looked more comfortable too.

Marvin and I also met with Bob Cottrell who talked more about their project with RCA without going into any confidential details. Then we headed out for the store. The RCA people had been made well aware that we were coming and welcomed it. Kroger had told them how significant a visit by this IBM executive would be for getting more vendors into the market. I had gone to the store a day earlier and informally answered questions about who Marvin Mann was and what he might be interested in. The RCA people seemed to be as excited about Marvin coming to their store as they would a visit from a top executive from their own company.

The RCA staff could not have been more gracious. This was a real store with customers doing their regular shopping. We were met just inside the door by RCA's project manager who walked us along the front end of the store describing the general systems architecture, the specific equipment at the checkout, and passing along anecdotes about their operational experience.

He took us to a checkstand that was not currently active and pointed out specific characteristics of checkstand design, the human factors of scanning, and a few things about merchandising in the checkout area and then we continued on walking. A few minutes later we found ourselves at the door to the backroom and Marvin asked "What's back there?" He replied, "This is where the computer that controls all the checkouts is located." "We're not going back there!" Marvin firmly commented. I tried to change his mind with, "Marvin it's only going to be a standard Spectra Model 45. "I don't care, I'm not going back there" was the response. IBM was very careful to never look, or even appear to look, at anything that might be confidential to a competitor. Could there have been activity reports, coding books or other possibly proprietary information just lying around? I don't know. Walking around the front of the store was fine, that was a publicly accessible area, but the back room was not. I think the RCA project manager understood and didn't take any offense. Outside, walking to the car, Marvin was interested in whether or not I had ever been in the backroom. I never had, but all I think I would have seen was a Spectra with some lights blinking. For years into the future that RCA Project Manager and I infrequently crossed paths and we were always friendly to each other.

SuperX Project

As soon as Marvin's visit was over, it was time to show SuperX what could be done. We arranged a series of presentations starting with SuperX middle management. In about a two hour talk peppered with illustrations and demonstrations at the IBM data center in downtown Cincinnati, about six blocks from SuperX's offices, Bill Magruder, Harry, Cheryl and I told our story to the heads of merchandising, accounting, security personnel, and real estate. The reaction was amazing. This whole concept of building a centralized integrated system to manage a business was so far from their day to day experience, it took awhile for them to fully get the scope. We asked for feedback and got a hesitant acceptance. We asked if there were problems and were told they didn't see any, but that did prompt some clarification questions. We made one big mistake in these sessions. We didn't have any Kroger data processing people attending.

I'm sure Ron Adams got feedback from his people as soon as they returned and shortly after he wanted Bill Magruder and me to meet with him. He felt it was time to show the presentation to SuperX's President, Mac Shipp, and the two operating Vice Presidents, particularly Glen Evans.

We were able to find a time within a week that everyone was available and they all walked down to the IBM Data Center from their offices up on Central Parkway. The reaction was very enthusiastic. They loved the IBM 3735 as a third party script terminal which appeared to really ease the problems of collecting and formatting the different information required by each third party carrier. They loved the control of information returning from the store each day. They loved the ability to get control over the ordering process and the potentially much greater consolidation of Purchase Orders with standard vendors. Harry and I loved their enthusiasm.

I had scheduled a follow-up visit with Ron a day later and he was in great spirits. Early in our conversation he got serious and asked, "How much of what we saw yesterday is operational?" That surprised me. I thought he knew. I got real serious and replied, "None of it. Nothing is operational. It was only designed to show what can be done."

His response was "I was afraid of that! On the walk back Glen Evans had commented that 'If we can get this system into the stores in the next 3 months we'll move up to number 2.'" Although I could provide him with a pretty firm configuration and requirement for services from IBM, the real key would be programming support from Kroger. We had not achieved a commitment for that and the availability of programming support was a big unknown. He understood.

Kroger Data Processing's concerns for the large scale of the SuperX project were probably not alleviated when in December 1972, Ron Adams walked the two blocks down Central Parkway from SuperX's headquarters to Kroger's offices at Central Parkway and Vine Street and requested they put 40 or 50 IBM 3735's on order, "as a Christmas present" for the work that had been done. I think my manager, Bill Pendl, was the first to let me know that it had happened. I immediately called Ron and thanked him. I let him know that we were going to do everything we could to be worthy of his trust. But we didn't credit any of them for sales quota purposes.

IBM 3735 Surprise

With the order and all the work effort inside IBM we were becoming more visible. I got a call from the IBM 3735 Program Manager who wanted to come and learn exactly what it was that we were doing with his product. This is usually a fun type visit where you get to show the internal people how you are making them successful by selling their product.

Not in this case. He was amazed at what we were doing and then started sharing with me additional information about what was inside the IBM 3735 which had not been highlighted in its announcement letter. He told me it had less than 100 characters (bytes) of random access memory. He clearly told me that the product had been designed for the transportation and freight industry for applications like updating bills of lading. It could do the merchandise ordering but doing the store daily cash register reconciliation was quite a bit beyond what they had originally intended. He was clearly uncomfortable with our including his product in the SuperX corporate system which made me uncomfortable with what I had told SuperX and at the same time awestruck that Cheryl had in fact made a pretty good replica of the sales and cash reconciliation report actually run on the machine. Neither directly nor in conversation with the SE, Harry Molloy, did she ever indicate the IBM 3735 system was not able to handle the job. She just made it happen. Yet here was the IBM 3735 Program Manager clearly trying to talk me out of using the product. I doubt this happened very often in IBM.

The other interesting fact about that IBM 3735 Program Manager was that he had flown up in his own Beechcraft Bonanza, a favorite aircraft of mine. That he was flying at all was pretty amazing after he told me his story from a few years earlier. He had been on final approach to land at an airport when he noticed his peripheral vision was getting replaced by white space. Literally his vision was shutting down. He was all alone in his plane, and five minutes from touchdown on the runway. As he said, "It's not like a car where you can pull off the road. When you are 5 minutes out, you're 5 minutes out and it's going to take you 5 minutes to get to the runway." Only his vision was closing in to an ever smaller circle faster than that. He declared an emergency condition with the tower and fortunately that airport had very precise radar approach control equipment, so they were able to get a person on that radar and talk him down second by second.

When he finally touched down all he could see was about as much as you can looking through the core of a paper towel roll. He could look at a few of his instruments or at just the little part of the runway he was shooting for, one or the other but not both. When he landed, they sent a tug out to pull him off the active runway. They got him out of the plane like they would a blind man and rushed him to a hospital.

It turned out he had a tumor that was pushing against his optic nerves. Duke University Hospital had some expensive experimental surgery that might help him. IBM and the National Science Foundation shared the cost of the surgery which was successful. And here he was flying himself from Raleigh up to Cincinnati to meet with me. Pretty amazing about his health and pretty alarming about his feeling of the IBM 3735's fit in SuperX stores. He was the Product Manager. If he didn't think the IBM 3735 should do it, why would I challenge that? I let my management know about the comments and they began looking around. And my manager, Bill Pendl, got me a Regional Manager's Award for completing the study.

John Akers Executive Visit

Bill Pendl got a call from Distribution Industry Marketing in White Plains to arrange for another review of the Kroger plan. There was a new Distribution Industry Director, John Akers, who had been put into this slot because of all the product development activity in our industry and it was recognized that he was going higher in IBM. (Eventually he became CEO and Chairman, not too bad for an old navy fighter jock.) He was told by his White Plains staff that he needed to see our plan. John came down and was briefed for half a day in the branch office. Per our usual presentation format, Ed Salonus did the introduction and wrap-up and I concentrated on the application plan in the middle. This of course showed our concept of a store system which had been under consideration for at least 1-2 years in Raleigh. I remember John stopped me in the middle of the section on in-store equipment with, "How long ago did you do this design?" "A year ago." we all replied. "I'll be dammed!" he responded. We were never told why he said that, but later I would hear that the internal development software plan had been revised to something closer to what was required to support our plan just a little before his visit. Ed Salonus took him to the Kroger building to meet key executives in the afternoon.

Memorex Competition

The IBM account team did not save the IBM 2701 Telecommunications Control Units. Memorex did install the Memorex 1270s in their place. The Intensive Planning Session resulting from that competitive struggle, elevated the IBM's marketing to Kroger in many ways. But unfortunately we lost the telecommunications equipment in a greater than 3 to 1 pricing disadvantage. And worse, it also gave a competitor a reason to be around the Kroger building.

The Memorex salesman was understandably ambitious. And Memorex was attempting to expand its product line. Kroger's Director of Data Processing liked the way competition felt to him. Ed Salonus carried the load when Memorex pre-announced their MRX40 and MRX50 to Kroger. In return for a commitment to replace all the IBM System 360 Model 20s and IBM 1401s in Kroger Divisional offices, Memorex would provide free hardware for development and assistance at Kroger's headquarters.

Page 68   Spreading the Barcode

This was a very touchy situation. Memorex was already suing IBM about IBM's marketing practices which caused IBM higher management to stay very close to every identified competitive situation. Ed Salonus and Bill Pendl had a required daily call to Ralph Phieffer's office, the President of the Data Processing Division, to report on any actions taken by Memorex or IBM in the past day. IBM's smaller System 370s had not been announced at this time which put the team at a significant competitive disadvantage.

As it turned out the divisional machines were not lost because Memorex's development effort of a unit record like programming language called RPG, simply failed to do the job that the existing IBM equipment was already performing. This ended up being reported in a Wall Street Journal article that outlined Memorex's withdrawal from the computer processor business. Kroger's Data Processing Director later attested to the fairness of the IBM activities during this struggle in an affidavit requested by a law firm retained by IBM. And Ed Salonus did eventually replace the System 360 and 1401 hardware with System 370 Model 125s after they were announced.

Drug Store Industry Marketing Class

The next Drug Store Industry Marketing Class shepherded by Bob Costello took place in the spring of 1973 at the San Jose Education Center and Homestead. In Poughkeepsie and in San Jose IBM had built Homesteads, hotels that you could live in for several days while you attended IBM classes. The rooms were rather spartan with twin beds, a few chairs, a table and a desk. Homesteads had common areas where you could relax with a television, ping pong table, skittles table and lots of magazines. It seemed there were always snacks to eat, but the staff was so unobtrusive I can't imagine how the snacks got there. Homesteads also had tennis courts and a golf course.

I showed the class the results of our study and was clear that although there was strong interest, no orders for a complete S/370 Model 145s had been placed. I summarized the activity on our plan and ended the presentation by taking off my coat and turning around where I had drawn red vertical lines like claw marks on the slightly frayed white shirt I had selected to wear that day. I told the group; even though we hadn't seen a large system order, there had been some personal results. They identified with the symbolic bloody stripes and laughed.

IBM 100% Club

Fortunately again that former Data Entry Specialist from the Branch Office, Will Schwartz, came up with the solution for the inadequacy of the IBM 3735. Will had been with us the prior year returning from the 100% Club and was in the back seat when the Ogden, UT airport incident occurred. It was probably Pendl who contacted him in Rochester, MN about the IBM 3735 dilemma.

Will called me and we talked about the requirements and applications for inside SuperX stores. He knew about an unannounced key to disk product that included some arithmetic logic and considerably more memory. We arranged that on the way back from the 100% Club that year in San Francisco, I would fly a red-eye to Rochester and brief some engineering management on SuperX store level needs.

There would be no repeat of 1972's flying incident. I flew commercial airlines all the way. The club was held in the San Francisco Hilton with the Systems Engineers staying in the St. Francis. Checking into the Hilton put me in an unusual experience with IBM management. In 1973 the clubs had gotten so large they experimented with holding one per region in succession. The Midwest Region was not first. When you arrived you got into a special IBM Club check-in line where they gave you your room assignment (all IBM 100% Club accommodations were double rooms with roommates) your meal tickets, and the agenda times and schedules for the meetings. I was to go to a room on the 38th floor. When I got there I found there was already luggage in the room, one king sized bed, and the telephone message light was flashing. Looking out the window I observed a US Navy Aircraft Carrier crossing the bay towards Alameda. This room had fantastic views. Figuring my roommate had arrived ahead of me; I went over and picked up the message, which was to have my "roommate" call his office in Armonk.

Ahem… Probably shouldn't be my roommate if he was from Corporate Headquarters in Armonk and in my brash youth I looked on him as part of the overhead. He hadn't "earned" his way to this club. So, I left my bags and with his name obtained from his luggage tags in hand, returned to the IBM check-in counter in the lobby where they assured me he should have moved from "my" room to one on the 4th floor in the older section of the hotel. I was reassured that the room where I had left my bags was really mine.

I bumped into a friend from one of the industry classes so it was a few more minutes before I went back up to the room. Opening the door, I found there were two people in the room, one on the bed and the other in the chair. The fellow in the chair immediately jumped up and exclaimed, "Hey Tommy, look your roommate is back."

I stammered out, "yes, there's been some mix-up. They have you in a room on the fourth floor and…"

I was cut off by the fellow on the bed's comment, to himself while reaching for the phone: "Well this changing rooms is a crock of shit!"

At that point the companion in the chair jumped up to intercede with me, apologize and explain that the other person had had a bad couple of days testifying in the trial, but everything was ok now. I did know that the suit had been settled, didn't I?"

"Well, no I didn't," I thought, but I did now understand I was not going to get this room. It turned out that the guy on the bed headed up IBM's Industrial Relations and the fellow in the chair was an old friend of his, Russ Bliese, the Branch Manager from Oakland California, the office that handled Safeway Supermarkets. Today, I can appreciate what a text book example this was of the challenge for IBM middle management to keep everything friendly midst the arrogance of top management and the naivety and a different type of arrogance of IBM's Marketing Representatives. Kudos to Russ Bliese, he kept me occupied with interesting conversation about my industry for 20-30 minutes until the knock on the door. It was the bellman to take me to my new room.

The trip started with the Bellman's apology on the part of the hotel for the mix-up (the hotel never contributed to this mix-up) and he hoped I'd enjoy my new room. I went down from the 38th floor to the 15th floor, but it was a corner suite, three rooms in special Japanese style furniture, and I had it to myself. Everyone should have such problems.

It was a great Club with interesting talks, the "Young Americans" performing Neil Diamond hits, lots of walks along Fisherman's Warf, conversations with branch office friends and lots of cable car rides. After it ended I camped out at Charlie Brown's, a restaurant just south of SFO on the San Francisco Bay, until it was time for my 11 PM red-eye to Rochester, MN.

SuperX Requirements Presented to IBM Rochester MN

I found arriving in Rochester, MN the next morning depressing. Personally I felt like a mess and because the Mayo Clinic is located there, the airport had more ambulances than taxis. I rented a car and then rented a room for 3 hours to get a shower and begin to look like a businessman again.

Will Schwartz met me in the lobby at IBM. I signed the Non Disclosure Agreement all field people signed and re-signed when they met with development people. Will took me to a room where I met with about 4 - 5 people. We discussed the usual background on the size and organization of SuperX and then got into the store level requirements. I may have brought along some visual aids like sample cash reconciliation forms, prescription input forms, etc. I know when it was over, the engineering development manager said the product could do it, and that when announced, it would be called the IBM 3741. That was still a secret until it was announced. All I could say then was that there would be a machine for the store. I was relieved. Back in Cincinnati I updated Ron Adams and the SuperX programming manager in Kroger's MIS department with what I could share.

Chapter 4 Living a New Relationship   Page 71

Background Training for Marketing In-Store Equipment

In the spring of 1973, IBM began intensifying the store level knowledge of its

| Market Basket Store visited | Supermarket checkout circa 1973 |

| Store Manager explains price marking procedures in the Market Basket store | Typical backroom in a grocery store with product waiting to be stocked on shelves |

| Bill Selmeier, Paul Sved and Ed Spiller get an electro-mechanical checkout lesson from a Market Basket checkout clerk | Bill Selmeier and Ed Spiller get familiar with in-store random weight procedures. |

field force. The University of Southern California had a curriculum program focused on supermarket management run by James Stevenson. IBM salesmen on larger supermarket accounts were sent to USC for a special one week tailored training class which he ran. In addition to classroom sessions on retail store accounting, labor management, merchandising, shrink and other management controls, we had lab sessions in real supermarkets where we documented the actual implementation of the course material in real life. My lab was with a group that included my old friend Ed Spiller-the Safeway account manager and Paul Sved who covered Stop & Shop in Boston. We were sent to a Market Basket Store, which coincidentally was Kroger Food's Los Angeles division and was where Ron Walker, the prior Kroger Data Processing Director, had been the divisional controller. The class wrapped up with a several hour skull session with Gene Walsh, CEO of Ralph's Supermarket where he just talked about philosophies of running supermarket stores.

The plane trip back was one of those multi-hop TWA flights and coincidentally Ron Walker, then with American Financial, was also on the plane riding in first class. We recognized one another. Ron actually came back and rode one of the legs with me in coach and then took me forward to introduce me to his travel companion, a new American Financial Vice President, just a little younger than myself. Ron advised me, "My friend here just bought two houses in Beverly Hills for $64,000. You should think about doing that too, Bill." Ron, you were always insightful and a trustworthy friend, but at the time I couldn't imagine coming up with that amount of money.

Raleigh Opportunity

The store products marketing staffs in Raleigh were being expanded and Bill Pendl wanted me to be a part of marketing any new product. I was sent for an interview with Bob Hardcastle, the Manager of the Direct Marketing group, about a position providing direct marketing assistance. While there I saw Larry Goodwin, Ralph Converse and Gordon Vick and met for the first time Larry Questad, Bob Doremus and Jim Lightner. They had just been promoted from from LA, Houston and Corpus Christi respectively. They talked like my coming was a done deal with conversations about how fast property values were rising, so I wanted to get my home purchase done quickly, etc. But again it was not to be.

Bob Hardcastle wanted to offer me a position, but needed concurrence from my branch manager. He tracked down my branch manager in Acapulco, Mexico where he was attending the Golden Circle, a higher recognition forum for people who had achieved many 100% clubs. He actually called my branch manager out of the meetings to ask about me, but my branch manager refused to endorse my going to this new position. I was, at the very least, disappointed.

No one had much to say when I returned to Cincinnati. But Gordon called me from Raleigh and told me not to think it was over. He was going to talk with his manager, Bill Carey, and something would get done. Bill Carey had met me at one of Ed Igler's Headquarters Marketing workshops. Within a couple of weeks I was again on a plane for Raleigh, this time to talk with Bill Carey, Ralph Converse, and Larry Goodwin. Unknown to me, Bill Carey was figuring out how to position the job he could offer me in such a way that the branch manager could not say no. And he succeeded. I was offered a position on the supermarket side of the store product headquarters marketing group reporting to Bill Carey. On the way out, Bill Pendl wished me well and advised me not to return back to that region, if and when I was promoted again – advice that was well founded.

Ed Salonus, my Kroger team mate, wasn't going to let me leave Cincinnati without some memento of my time there. Ed created what he hoped would become a branch office tradition by purchasing and presenting to me a signed John Ruthven print (2020/5000) entitled "Bengal Tiger" in honor of the new focus of Cincinnati, the Cincinnati Bengals football team.

Page 74   Spreading the Barcode

Chapter 5 Raleigh at the Start

I arrived in Raleigh in early July 1973 excited about the unknowns of getting a new product out, but knowing almost none of the details about it. I was entertained on my first night with dinner at the home of Gordon and Gerry Vick. Gordon and I had been, of course, partners on the Kroger team. It was a happy night. Gordon had really wanted me to get the opportunity to come to Raleigh. I really felt good about the chance of changing the future of shopping. Everything ahead was unknown but felt exciting. I felt we were going to be doing something really significant and up to this point, entering stores with electronic point-of-sale was a relatively small and unknown thing inside IBM. We would have the resources of the corporation, but as yet, we weren't under the microscope.

Upon leaving relatively early (I didn't want to be late for my first day on the new job) Gordon mentioned that a house had newly come on the market up the street and I should look at it. So I drove up and turned around in the driveway just past Lindsey Drive on Oak Park Road and noted the "For Sale by Owner" sign before returning to my room at the Plantation Inn on Route 1.

Gordon Vick from internal announcement article

The Plantation Inn hotel helped me realize the adjustment to living in Raleigh. The hallways were lined with pictures from the Civil War. That wasn't so unusual. But up to this time I'd been a northerner, who had only lived in Michigan and Ohio. I'd traveled mostly in northern states. Walking the hall to breakfast, I was quickly aware there were no blue uniforms, only gray, a visible indication that I had crossed over into a different place.

IBM Building 602

The Retail and Supermarket systems were developed in IBM's Building 602, a single story structure on the east side of Raleigh, NC at the intersection of the beltway (US 64 although the route designation has since been changed) and US 1 and Capital Boulevard. The building was 800-1000 feet long and about 250 feet wide. Westinghouse had a plant for making electric meters directly across the beltway (US 64) from Building 602 but you couldn't see it from our building due to the difference in elevation and the number of pine trees present everywhere in that area. Commonly our access was from the Yonkers Road exit eastbound on the beltway or sometimes from Capital Blvd. coming out of downtown Raleigh. This meant we usually had driven past the building and effectively made a U turn to drive back on the service road to Building 602. There were four entrance doors directly from the parking lot along the long side of the building where we could enter using our magnetic stripe entrance cards. The one at the very back of the building had a small over-hang on it that protected you from the rain, if there was no wind, and led directly into the Store Systems Market Support Center where I was going to work. With our own entrance, prospects and customers coming to briefings and meetings would not have to be escorted through the development area that was secured from those outside IBM

IBM Building 602. Most of the building was occupied by engineers and programmers. The Data Processing Distribution Industry group had a separate entrance at the far end.

Most of the building was occupied by programmers, hardware engineers, their labs and a big open space that was to turn into the original manufacturing area for the still unannounced systems. There was one wide hall that ran up the center the length of the building with cross halls about every 20 feet going down to offices or instead there might be a five push-button locked laboratory door. Up near the main entrance on the short front side of the building facing Capital Blvd. were the upper level development manager's offices and the building's cafeteria. At the other end on the left side of the main aisle, occupying $1/10^{th}$ to $1/16^{th}$ of the total building, were the briefing rooms, demonstration labs, and offices for Store Systems Market Support marketing personnel. Our briefing rooms were commonly known as the red room and the blue room. The room used for briefings on the supermarket system had red carpeting on the floor and up the side of the wall closest to the access hall and the retail briefing room had blue carpeting on the floor and up the side the of wall closest to the access hall.

Chapter 5 Raleigh at the Start Page 77

The briefing rooms were fairly large rooms holding up to 40 people in classroom configuration before it got too tight. But normally the large wood tables were arranged in an open U shape with only one or two chairs at each table so that roughly a dozen people would be accommodated. Both rooms had large comfortable Herman Miller leather swivel chairs, whiteboards, electric retractable screens and a podium with enough switches to launch a missile or at least raise and lower screens, open and close drapes, and advance projectors. At the front of each briefing room next to the whiteboards was a door that opened into a hallway or in the red carpeted briefing room into our office area. Presenters would rotate during a briefing. They entered and left through this door at the appropriate time. The back wall was pretty plain except for the built-in projection booth. The fourth wall was covered by a floor to ceiling hanging drape. At the appropriate time the drape could be opened up to half way along the wall revealing a mock store with an IBM Retail or Supermarket Point-of-sale System. These were the only stores I ever knew that had raised floors.

Distribution Industry Marketing entrance

Microphones and speakers interconnected between the briefing room, projection booth, and demonstration laboratory ensured that all aspects of the briefing stayed in sync. If the speaker in the briefing room mentioned a specific type of item, or part of the transaction, the prospective customers looking through the glass into the demonstration lab would no doubt see the model sales clerk handling that type of item or doing that part of the transaction. It was a tightly scripted and well coordinated demonstration. But on this, my first day in Raleigh, using these rooms was all in the future.

But my first day in Raleigh using these rooms was all really in the future. No prospects were coming; the product was yet to be announced. When I got there I was told to pick an office along a particular short inside hallway. It came equipped with a gun metal grey Steelcase desk, a rolling office chair, a three foot by six foot Steelcase table and two naugahyde guest chairs without arms. The only window was the top one and a half feet of the wall to enable lighting to be distributed between all offices. Banks of lights for all the offices along the short halls were controlled by switches out in the clerical area where three clerks sat including the one that I shared. There was a white board on one wall connected to the bottom of the glass area   A four drawer Steelcase filing cabinet completed the standard office furniture.

Page 78   Spreading the Barcode

There was just enough room left in the 80 square foot office to swing the door shut, but it was rare that anyone closed their office door in Raleigh.

First Workday in Raleigh

Bill Carey from internal announcement article

When I asked him what he wanted me to work on, Bill Carey, my new manager, suggested that since I was not yet familiar with the cash register, I should just go into the demonstration lab and get familiar by using the equipment. At this point we had an operating cash register in a checkstand and some mock grocery product display cases along the walls, but the Store Controller which controls all the registers in the system was not ready yet and was being emulated by an IBM 1130 until the real controller's software was completed. An IBM 1130 was a desk size single user computer used mostly for technical work. You could sit in front of it and type commands into the embedded keyboard on its gentle sloping top surface where someone had intelligently put a lip at the close edge so that papers and other things placed there didn't just slide off onto the floor. Above the keyboard, a selectric printer was mounted with a row of toggle switches on the front. Then above that was a panel with the blinking lights to provide information to service people and engineers on what the machine was doing. Down where the drawers on a desk would be there was a thin single platter disk drive behind a panel that could be swung out.

Meeting Joe Woodland

So here I am, a naive store systems person trying to figure out what to do with the first electronic scanning checkstand and register. I wasn't making a lot of progress. Even though I could converse knowledgeably with chain store executives, I didn't really understand in my gut about the details of running a checkout register; where you needed to void an item, or do a no-sale. I didn't know what store reports to get out of the register. I wouldn't have known why some of the entries on them were significant, etc. So I was mostly futzing along when in walked Joe Woodland and Doug Antonelli (Human Factors engineer). Joe Woodland is the man who in 1949 had filed a patent for putting symbols on grocery products and later created a test for scanning them at the checkstand in the back room of a Colonial Supermarket in Atlanta, GA. This is the man whom I had heard was the chief strategist and definer of how IBM should get into the supermarket checkout business, the guy who is only referred to with great reverence and whose words had been quoted to me by Gordon Vick almost as if it was gospel. Joe was a short middle-aged man with salt and pepper hair that was never completely combed, a little of the mad professor about him. He walked with a little bounce and enjoyed even the hint of an ironic situation. He saw the humor in almost everything.

Joe asked if they could use the system for only a minute to check something out. I was only too happy to oblige if I could stay in the room and learn more about what they were interested in. So I stepped around to the side where the customer would usually stand, my hand on the lip of the scanner while Joe and Doug gazed down into scanner pointing out something to each other. Suddenly Joe shouted out, "Oh my eyes! My eyes! You've burned my eyes! Oh my eyes," then covered each eye with one of his fists in pain, whirled around and walked fist first with a loud thud into the door they had just come through to enter the lab.

"Oh My God!" I thought. This is horrible! To call this a terrible accident is not strong enough. I've just blinded the person most central to this product. I've hurt someone badly and de-railed the whole program. And of course I'm through! How could this have happened? And, then I heard Joe laughing, then Doug started laughing, and I timidly asked "are you really OK?"

Joe Woodland, courtesy of IBM Archives

This was Joe's way of introducing me to the fundamentals of the IBM 3666 Checkout Scanner. He showed me the two horizontal electric eyes before and behind the scanning window that opened and closed the beam. I, by putting my hands on the edge rail while observing them, had unknowingly let the laser come up through the scanning window. Of course checkout scanners use very, very low powered lasers. They take advantage of a laser's precise frequency to keep the relevant energy very low. Lasers were chosen for its precision characteristics, not for its power. The IBM laser operated at .0004 watts. As designed it wouldn't cause real physical damage. Now my psyche was another matter. Good thing Joe and I were to become good friends in the next few months. If you had seen us then, Joe was laughing, Doug was laughing, and I was still looking a little shocked.

Joe was the strategist on U.P.C. issues. He had practically invented and patented the automated checkout process at the end of the 1940s.

Page 80 Spreading the Barcode

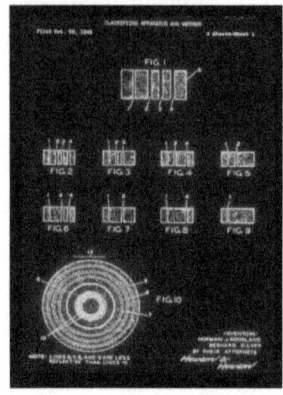	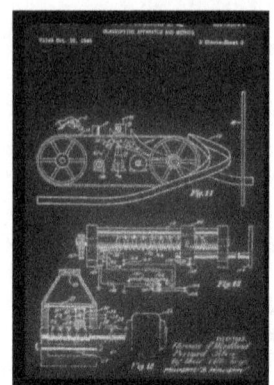
Joe Woodland's patent filed in 1949 for a supermarket product identification code to be used in checkout. This original concentric circle or bulls-eye pattern was used by RCA in their proposal and store test with Kroger.	Patent art depicting automated checkout machinery from Joe Woodland's 1949 patent filing

Equipment used by Woodland in proof of concept test in Atlanta GA Colonial store back room	Scanning a soup can in proof of concept test in the back room at a Colonial store in Atlanta, GA

Early Tasks

In those first few days I had not yet seen the overall plan of how things were organized. We all got assigned tasks in preparation for an announcement at some unknown, but hopefully soon, time in the future. Because I had come from such a recognized supermarket account, I was well known to the others,

Chapter 5 Raleigh at the Start Page 81

but each week new people seemed to pop up and be added to this group that was doing tasks. A lot of what I did was getting familiar with the equipment and then helping with specific tasks associated with getting IBM ready for this announcement.

There were two groups: Bill Carey's product oriented group interfaced with the Systems Development Division which engineered both the Retail and Supermarket products and the Direct Marketing group which interfaced with the field sales people covering Retail and Supermarket accounts. Most field-oriented marketing people wanted to work for in the Direct Marketing group. It was told to me that Bob Hardcastle, the manager of this group, had a great reputation for developing people's careers and this group would keep you visible to field sales managers that might offer you your next job. This was the group I had failed to join several weeks earlier, but you could never tell that from the relationships we all had with each other from the very start.

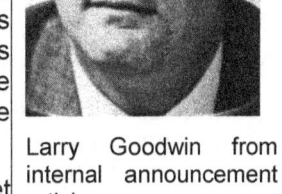
Larry Goodwin from internal announcement article

On the product side of the Store Systems Market Support Center the more experienced marketing support center people, Larry Goodwin and Ralph Converse, took the leadership role in organizing activities. Larry Goodwin wore glasses and was as intelligent as he looked. Reasonably tall and thin, Larry could be very determined and forceful. But Larry always listened before he took a position. Larry took command, but only when he wanted to. He was also very capable of standing at the back and watching what happened from the background. He'd be gathering information prior to making his statement. On the other hand, you never missed Ralph. He had a hard time hiding in the background or being inconspicuous. His higher pitched voice and high pitched energy level made him instantly visible. I don't think I ever saw Ralph walk slowly. Ralph was a high energy individual. All the while Gordon Vick was methodically thinking through the product features.

Ralph Converse from internal announcement article

On the Direct Marketing side Larry Questad was busy finishing up the demonstration lab by stocking it with typical merchandise. Classes were being organized for educating the field force on how the systems worked and how they should be marketed by Jim Lightner and Bob Doremus.

Days were filled with meetings. As a new person I hadn't picked up enough tasks yet to have to participate in many of them, but I sensed the anticipation of everyone was that we were very close to announcement. Ralph and Larry Goodwin were excited about the announcement movie they had made the Sunday prior to my first day for the Supermarket system. North Carolina was a Blue Law State. No commercial retail business was allowed to be open on Sunday. The Colonial Supermarket in Cameron Village Shopping Center was made available to IBM, unsupervised by any Colonial employees, for an "unspecified" purpose. IBM moved out several electro-mechanical register lanes so they could move in the IBM 3660 Supermarket System. Jane Converse and Cloe Goodwin, Ralph and Larry's wives, acted the part of the customers. Liz Questad, Larry Questad's wife acted as the checkout clerk. An eight to ten minute film was shot and then the equipment was loaded back on the truck and the store was put back as they had found it. I'm sure someone in authority at Colonial must have signed a NDA that allowed this to happen, but IBM had the store to itself that day to make the movie.

I'd known Ralph and Larry for some time and they were only too happy to help me "learn the ropes" of working in Raleigh. We talked about different accounts and their trips to visit these accounts. Large grocery accounts had been assigned to one or the other of them for the past two years. Someone told a story about a West Coast account that was calling in for some strategy advice. Ralph had responded, well if you want help, I could be there tomorrow. The ability to jump on a plane and visit an office across the country on your own authority impressed me. I hadn't seen that in too many other jobs. And of course it was only possible if it was used appropriately. We talked architecture, competition, industry events. One side comment I remember from Larry after talking competition was, "buy stock in National Semiconductor."

I also shared a really southern secretary. Actually one of three young ladies that sat in a small open area near the intersection of two halls, Bill Carey's office, the door to the Supermarket demonstration lab, and the presenter's door into the red briefing room. When there was a free moment you could hear them talking about how much they like RC Cola and Moon Pie. (Within six months I had tried both RC Cola and Moon Pie, but I guess it's hard to acquire the taste.) Sylvia Turner a tall slim girl was most responsible for whatever I needed typed. She was also the most southern. She pronounced my name, Bill, with three syllables.

IBM Participation in Symbol Selection Process

The group was very informal. Frequently when we were discussing project and job assignments the conversation also flowed back to activities before I arrived in Raleigh. Bill Carey discussed some of the earliest days. For example Bill told me about going back several years prior when Larry Russell got the assignment as a McKinsey consultant to help the Grocery Industry define and implement a universal code, one of his first calls was to IBM for any suggestions they might have. IBM told him the first thing to do was to establish a solid financial business case for such a code. IBM indicated that if he got supermarket chains to cooperate, the prospective equipment vendors would likely provide the manpower at no charge to measure activities that would define the beneficial impact of such a code.

That was done. From IBM, Gordon Vick, Larry Goodwin, and Ralph Converse with their counterparts from RCA, and other prospective equipment suppliers went out with clip boards and stop watches to assigned stores and measured the work effort required to receive merchandise, stock shelves, price mark product, checkout customers, and do the office accounting activities.

The resulting information was provided to McKinsey & Company who did the data analysis and published the summary in a report that drove the adoption of the program. It showed that a Universal Product Code itself had some benefit, but when combined with a symbol, it had the potential of reducing the annual cost of operation significantly more than $50,000 in a typical store of the day which sold $3 million dollars a year. The largest part, more than half of the total amount of benefits, was the reduction of checkout labor costs due to faster checkout through scanning. IBM and the other participants got back the detailed analysis. Larry Goodwin was turning that into a standard Supermarket System benefits presentation.

About the same time, years earlier, on the technical side a completely independent group of engineers were working to provide a proposal for a symbol. The original group of engineers consisted of George Laurer, Joe Woodland, David Savir a mathematician, Bill Krouse, and Herd Baumiester an optical specialist. But, it was quickly reduced to just George, Joe and David. The initial plan was to support the bulls-eye concept conceived by Joe Woodland and used by RCA in their test at Kroger's store in Cincinnati. The task to draft a document supporting the bulls-eye was given to George Laurer along with the symbol selection committee's guidelines:

- The symbol must encode 10 digits (five vendor identification digits and 5 item identification digits)
- The standard symbol must fit within a 1.5 square inch area and it was not certain that grocery manufacturers would even be willing to give up that much packaging real estate
- The standard symbol must be printable using the standard printing equipment of that day on the standard package substrates of that day which meant lithography, flexography, on different grades of

paper, board and metal surfaces sometimes moving at high speed while being printed.
- The symbol must be readable in six to eight inch depth of field
- The symbol must be successfully read 99.99% of the time on the first pass over the scanner moving at 100 inches per second.
- It must be readable with a wand as well as a fixed head scanner.
- It must be virtually error free, a measure which IBM later interpreted to be an undetected error rate of less than one in twenty thousand.

His boss left on a vacation the next day and as George looked at it he came to believe less and less that the bulls-eye would meet all the guidelines. He didn't believe printing technologies could create a bulls-eye symbol that could encode ten digits within an inch and a half square area. On his own he started development on a different barcode approach, which if the bars were aligned along the direction the material moved in the printing process, would allow ten digits to be reliably encoded within the one and a half square inch area. What a surprise for his boss, Paul McEnroe, when he returned the day before the presentation and had to go with the new approach. Through several iterations and with the additional input from David Savir and Joe Woodland, this barcode proposal evolved into the final IBM proposal, essentially the final U.P.C. It had to compete with other proposals including the bulls-eye proposed by RCA, a half bulls-eye from Litton Industries, Pitney-Bowes, Charecogn, Singer and Scanner Inc. in a fairly open process that saw competing ideas being shared between their proposers, consulting university groups, and other technical consultants.

Announcement Issues

In 1973 two systems were trying to successfully get through the detailed IBM announcement process: the IBM 3650 Retail System with its magnetic pricing tag and the IBM 3660 Supermarket System with its U.P.C. Scanner. Success meant not only that all the steps were completed, but that the product could be built and maintained at the projected cost and would be purchased at the projected price. The Systems Development Division and the Data Processing Division each had its own staff of Industry Representatives and Program Administrators that worried about the marketability, looked for new information in the top 50 prospects every few days that might impact how they would accept and react to an IBM entrance into the market. Mountains of data were cataloged by more than one person on each prospective customer: what store equipment they had, their Information technology capability, network architecture if any, key business objectives, and business challenges. Each of our Program Administrators knew a lot about each customer on their list, and there was another person in SDD who was also tracking the large customers. DPD's Program

Chapter 5 Raleigh at the Start Page 85

Administrators had an advantage in that they could directly call the field sales person and ask a question, although great care was taken to not disclose anything about the un-announced product.

On the IBM 3660 Supermarket System marketing side IBM's Data Processing Division, the marketing company within IBM, was primarily concerned about the price. It was too high. Of course it was much higher than the price of mechanical registers that proceeded electronics, but the detailed benefit studies didn't show us the kind of payback required to get an industry excited. We were to discover later there was more than just price that needed fixing, but prior to announcement, getting the price down consumed our attention. To get the product into a more sellable range, countless meetings went on between business people in the Systems Development Division, and us.

SDD had profit responsibility for products while DPD had revenue responsibility, so there was some natural conflict. The discussions between groups went on for countless days where DPD documented competitive product pricing, customer costs and returns on investments, customer comments about their needs and perceived value of the products while SDD challenged the real impact of this data, asked for confirming documentation, etc. Inside the meetings voices got raised, credibility was questioned, but at the end both groups recognized this was just business. The initial price targets had been set, I supposed, in line with traditional IBM margins. At one point I remember a SDD person declared "You're IBM, you're worth 15% more, to which some astute DPD member replied, "This is NCR's market. They're worth 15% more."

To be fair, SDD had a daunting challenge pricing the product. They had overall profit responsibility and costs came from everywhere: the primary development costs, the sales costs, service costs, even supplies cost if there was an IBM component. Service was going to be challenging. The projected cost for FEs to drive out to all those remote store locations was large. Engineering had responded by making most of the software maintenance possible from the customer's data processing location, a place where IBM presumed the Field Engineers were already working. And somewhere Field Engineering must have had bad experiences with wire matrix printing, because they were providing input that resulted in development slowing down the printer's sweep rate across the register tape. There were an incredible number of trade offs and almost all of them were driven by costs.

Many of the discussions took place in DPD's conference rooms, which were larger and the nicest in the building since they would become the customer briefing rooms. Some of the conversations took place in White Plains, NY at 1133 Westchester which was DPD's headquarter building and some across I-287 at the Harrison, NY office which was the Data Processing Group's headquarters. I wasn't directly involved in these discussions. John Shaw was and he spent a lot of time on the calculator. John was clean-cut and about 6 feet tall, but big. He looked like he could have played fullback in college, and although he loved football and even arranged for our entire group to go see the North Carolina State Wolfpack play his beloved Maryland Terrapins, I don't think he did.

But what I really remember about John was that he was the first person I ever met that had previously worked for the CIA. He shared some stories about the problem he once experienced going to work in Washington, DC. Working at the Pentagon was his cover for where he really worked. One morning when there had been an exceptionally heavy snow fall, John couldn't get his car out of his garage but his neighbor could. Seeing John wrestle with the problem, the neighbor offered John a ride into the Pentagon. John had to accept after going back in his house and notifying his office. His office sent a car down that picked John up at another Pentagon entrance than he'd been dropped at and got him back there that afternoon in time to go home with the neighbor. I'd heard about these things happening, but John was the first (and I guess now the last) person that I knew who had actually done this.

How one negotiated depended on who you were negotiating with. With engineering it was always wise to add a few nice, but not necessary functions, that could be given up if something more important was going to die. Negotiating chips I'd call them. The standard routine between DPD and SDD was that DPD would state and define why the price was too high. A set of functions to be included had been agreed to long before. SDD might reply that the product couldn't reach its profit objectives at that price. DPD might commit to a higher volume of unit sales at the lower price or they might trade a function to see if that reduced costs enough. DPD people had no direct access to detailed cost data but we could figure out much of it. It became a game and we got fairly good at estimating the cost elements.

After weeks and weeks of this, DPD gradually convinced SDD that the price should come down. Reducing the price was itself an incremental process a few thousand dollars at a time. Pricing was done based on a standard 10 register store, ten plain vanilla registers, 10 scanners, a store controller and the communications unit. When I arrived everyone hoped we were only a few weeks from announcement, but the price was about $180,000 for the standard store's IBM equipment.

Standard Store

Unit	IBM Product	Qty in Std Model
Electronic Register	IBM 3663	10
U.P.C. Scanner	IBM 3666	10

| Store Control Unit | IBM 3651 Model 60 | 1 |
| Communications Unit | IBM 3669 | 1 |

Of course supermarkets would also likely be purchasing new checkstands, trenching the floor for cables, and buying an additional register for the office. (Why wasn't this in the standard configuration?) They and we would also learn later to buy a backup power generator. And, possibly they would need adapters on each register for an electronic scale or coin dispenser (sorry no credit card readers in supermarkets in those days.) The size of the total investment required of the chains really concerned DPD, the group responsible for hitting the sales volume.

Every day I'd ask John Shaw, Larry Goodwin, and Ralph Converse what progress had been made. They would usually report that SDD had come down a little, but we'd given up this function or that function. It was clear to us that we could not release a supermarket system that cost much, much more than our competition. We were not the market leaders. We still needed to earn that recognition. This continual attrition of system function for a little lower price was wearing on the negotiators. One day an SDD staffer walked into Larry Goodwin's office and, I believe, informed him that SDD had re-reviewed product costs and would not be able to compromise as much as they had indicated the day before or he might have suggested another function that might be dropped. Larry, totally frustrated with this battle of wills, briefly lost it, probably said something loud, and picked up his standard Western Electric 2500 Set touch-tone telephone and threw it into the cinder block wall on the left side of his office with enough force to split the phone into multiple pieces. When I came in the next day I reviewed the corpse. In those days the telephone sets were provided by the phone company as part of the service and were made one way only - very, very rugged so that there would never require a service call. But this telephone was history. The development staff took Larry even more seriously after that.

House Hunting

I missed that event because I was doing my other job at that time - moving to Raleigh. Within a week of arriving in Raleigh, I started going out up to 4 hours every couple of days with realtors. I don't remember where I met those first people I worked with, but I wasn't finding anything I wanted. I had thought I knew what I wanted from information I'd been absorbing all the way back to my two year earlier visit to Raleigh and the home prices that had been mentioned then. So I told them, I'd like to see $40K homes and they showed them to me. After another week or so Tony Beal, one of the Retail System's Program Administrators, came over and asked me how it was going. When he got a non-committal answer from me, he told me his wife was a realtor and if I'd like, she would be happy to take me around. This was

Page 88   Spreading the Barcode

before I learned that in those Raleigh go-go years almost all IBM wives were realtors.

But I have to admit Teri was good. She knew my group and knew how most of them lived. She knew from a realistic view what I needed to know and would talk directly to me. She asked me about my price range. I told her. She then told me that I was two years out of date, I wanted to look at $60K homes. She told me what I wanted, then she showed me why I should want it. And she was right. She was good! I had a very productive day in which I learned about all the appealing housing locales. At the end of it we drove out to MacGregor Downs in Cary to a cookout at Ralph Converse's house. As she drove down Ralph's street and I saw the typical Carolina golf course fairway running behind the homes with some vines dropping down from the pine trees along its edge, people walking their dogs along the fairway all in the idyllic late afternoon sun, I interrupted her with: "You are really a rascal. Man, do you know how to sell!" To which Teri simply smiled. As it happened I didn't buy my Raleigh home from Teri Beal and I've always felt a little guilty.

Getting the lay of the real estate landscape has traditionally been my task in our family. In the case of IBM moves, I would be at the new location. IBM was generous about visits for the wife to participate, but practically speaking I was on the scene more. And in this instance I was much more alone since my wife had just completed a Masters degree in French and decided to go off for a month to France with a friend of ours from Cincinnati. I was just as happy to stay in Raleigh and get deeper into the future store products.

Marvin Mann from internal announcement article

Re-Organization

So I stayed up with the constant negotiating between SDD and DPD. We'd set dates to have it finished, but as we'd get close, we'd realize the price still wasn't right.

At the start of one morning two or three weeks after I arrived in Raleigh, I was aware of a lot of people in our office halls that I didn't know well. Most of them were pushing their heads into Bill Carey's office. At the time Bill Carey worked for Marvin Mann whose office was at 1133 Westchester in White Plains, NY. Marvin worked for the Director of Distribution Industry, John Akers. We were all quickly told there were to be some announcements and to be in the blue briefing room at 8:30 am for an "all-hands" meeting.

Once there I learned that John Akers had been promoted to Vice President of DPD for the Western United States and was already in Los Angeles. John was going to be replaced by a new Distribution

Chapter 5 Raleigh at the Start Page 89

Industry Director, Paul Palmer. Paul was in the meeting and said that he understood how hard everyone had been working and how disappointed we must feel that the products were still unannounced. So, after he explained how the Market Support Center was going to be reorganized, there would be a day off to play golf and/or tennis. Also there was to be a social gathering for all staff and their spouses at one of the hotels that evening, hosted by Paul's boss, Joe Henson. Everyone could get to know the new team. I went house shopping instead of golfing during the day, but did enjoy talking briefly with Joe Henson that night and getting to know some of the people on the retail system side of our store systems group a little bit better.

The organizational change was pretty significant. No longer was there to be a manager with program administrators handling product marketing for both retail and supermarket products and a separate manager handling customer presentations and sales force interactions for retail and supermarket products. Now there was to be a Retail Manager, Bob Hardcastle, with some staff focused inward on product needs but most focused outward on customers and sales presentations; and a Supermarket Manager with both inward and outward looking staff working for him. Bill Carey would become the Supermarket Manager. And there was to be a third group headed up by M.G. Tomlin or Tommy, a systems assurance group, to validate the configurations that marketing representatives proposed to customers. The genesis of this group came mostly from the efforts of a retail technical analyst, Joe Hawranek, who convinced himself, and many others, that IBM's Retail System could be leading customers blindly into a telecommunications quagmire with inadequate communications facilities that were not properly scalable for all the concurrent applications that would be running on the Retail System. Retail Systems had more demanding on-line and off-premises applications requiring rapid communication response like centralized credit verification and big ticket sales. Joe Hawranek was in his heaven developing communications modeling systems that could simulate large retail chains all the way from small satellite stores to major stores to the Distribution Center then to Headquarters. In the mid to late '70s IBM used to run advertisements with, "Test drive your Network?" as a way to focus on IBM's network expertise. These network modeling tools, I'd guess, evolved out of Joe's efforts.

Tommy Tomlin from internal announcement article

Tomlin's staff included from the Supermarket side: Gordon Vick, Harold Barndt, Willie Ledbetter. Along with Willie Ledbetter, a local Raleigh branch

Page 90   Spreading the Barcode

office SE that had transferred to this headquarters job, and Jim Hartwell, a systems engineer and new face from New Orleans, I was assigned to determine what was required to properly systems assure a supermarket system and then develop the tools needed to do it.

Tommy's management style was different from Bill Carey's. While Bill got to know you by joking around and trading stories, Tommy was more formal and direct. Bill Carey relieved his staff from as much administrative work as possible. Tommy transferred it to the staff. Bill Carey was about collegial relationships, having a laugh while you got your work done and keeping the pace fast. Tommy was about getting things done, feeling good about accomplishments, paying attention to detail and keeping the pace fast. It turned out I could enjoy working with each of them, although each was different. And the unplanned switch from Carey to Tomlin was a bit of a shock.

Early Technical Tasks

Tommy's first task to his group was for each of us to write a description of our background for him. He called it a dissertation and it included our IBM Work Experience, any Prior Performance recognition, any Previous Work Experience, a Description of Our Family, Recent Activities Outside of IBM, and finally Our Personal Objectives at Work. Initially I felt much more detached from this new manager than from Bill, but within a day I delivered the two and a half page dissertation document to him.

Part of Tommy's organizational approach was to document and track everything. He quickly identified 21 activities to track and assigned a task ID, a completion date and one to three of his staff to each activity. My assignments specifically included:

Task ID	Task	Due Date
SS100	Publish Design Guide	
SS300	Control & Operating Procedure Book	11/15/73
SI400	1974 Equipment Scheduling Supermarket Build Schedule	12/01/73
SS100	Supermarket Sys. Design and Assurance Presentation	10/31/73
SS400	Establish Supermarket Room Prep (including the data base)	12/01/73

Being assigned the Supermarket Systems Design and Assurance Presentation task pretty much guaranteed that I would become part of the field training classes.

Tommy had come from the large retail account experience. He had been the Systems Engineering Manager responsible for the Sears account in Chicago. We felt supermarket requirements and our product design were significantly different from that type of retail environment. Supermarket systems essentially operated independently in the store and communicated infrequently sending store information up the company's offices maybe once a day. There was no external on-line telecommunications load except with our backup scheme which had each store controller responsible for their own store and when necessary also concurrently being the backup controller to another store over a dial up 2400 baud line. (No one fully believed we could do it at the time, but it either worked or it didn't.) Unlike the Retail system with its hierarchical leased line communications design, there was no field design tasks to configuring a global communication systems between grocery stores or inside the store. Food chains actually understood the number of checkout lanes they needed better than we did as it was all tied to business volumes. We told Tommy that there was no Systems Assurance role such as in the Retail System. He was new and indicated he would listen to our arguments, but until he said he was convinced, he wanted us to continue on the path he was defining.

The organizational change meant I was going to be even more on the sidelines of what was happening in direct market support. Evidently both Bill Carey and Tommy Tomlin recognized that I might feel out of place on the Systems Engineering or technical side of the business and promised to get me involved in any projects that had more marketing content. To do my job I read the Systems Development Division's forecast assumptions, looked at comparable information from the IBM 3650 Retail system, played with some performance measurement tools written in GPSS and APL, and the results from various studies like one Doug Antonelli had done with Safeway checkers on operating procedures.

I was also helping John Shaw identify the borrowing power of the largest chains based on annual reports and information from First National City Bank of NY. Possibly SDD was arguing that our prospective customers could borrow the money to meet our price objectives. And all this time we still hadn't discovered what our real challenge to market acceptance would be.

Kroger Assessments

I made a quick trip to Chicago where the industry maintained a software development center in Des Plaines, IL. They needed to develop a Distribution Industry position on VTAM, the then IBM promoted communications software package/technology. I went to describe the Kroger environment and help them assess VTAM applicability to Kroger. I also got a visit from Ed Smith from Poughkeepsie who was doing detail analysis on the application of IBM Future System architecture for large accounts. Future System, or FS, was an IBM Mainframe architectural concept to replace all existing mainframe products much like the System 360 had done. (In actuality I think its greatest success was to sell copies of *Computer World* which made a crusade of publishing any trivial data fact they could discover about FS.) Again I was providing input on the Kroger team's behalf. In my Raleigh position I was half inside development and half outside. For as long as I could be seen as "recently from the field" I was credible and it was easy to ask me about Kroger without incurring all the Non Disclosure Agreement administration that IBM required to talk with a field salesman directly. All of these activities were documented to Tommy in a seven page activity report which the following day I got back from him with a comment on each paragraph. Tommy was a hard-working detail-oriented manager.

Otherwise, daily activities pretty much carried on. Neither the retail nor the supermarket system was deemed ready to announce, but both were close. I wasn't close to the issues on the retail side, although I do know that Bill Duncan, a retail program administrator, traveled to California to learn about the BART magnetic card system. The retail system used a magnetic stripe on their sales tickets. A problem of forged magnetic cards had come up at BART and they had evidently resolved it. Bill looked at that solutions applicability to the retail systems sales ticket.

On the supermarket side the issues pretty much centered on the price. Through much discussion, the proposed price had been reduced to around $154,000 from the original $180,000 for a standard ten lane store. But the group felt the price had to get down below $125,000 to have a chance in the market. Even though neither the Retail nor the Supermarket groups were agreeing with all the specific product details, both groups felt that an announcement was real close. We knew we would have to iron out our differences with the development division, ourselves, and the pricing people in Harrison, NY with some compromise. Yet we still didn't realize what would be our largest challenge after we were announced. Price wasn't it.

Creation of Store Systems Offices

About this time a very clever organizational move was made in Store Systems that considerably lowered the system price. In the Data Processing Division, IBM had developed a very sophisticated but expensive administrative system that tied every branch office's administration into centralized business processing applications running on machines in Bethesda, MD. The cost of salesmen, sales support, and supporting this administrative system was reflected in the product price of every product sold in the branch. But if you could separate the cost of the salesmen and systems engineers from the administrative system, you might be able to argue to the pricing managers to including one cost or the other, but not both. And it turned out you could. The separate Store Systems field force was created. Our products carried the cost of Store Systems sales personnel, but not the regular host salesman nor their Advanced Administrative System.

I think Marvin Mann was the originator of this strategy. Essentially we got a lower price for both systems based on creating a separate overlay sales organization, a sales organization that only sold the point-of-sales systems. Since the separate overlay organization was only concerned with electronic registers, each Store Systems salesman or SE could cover more prospects than the regular IBM salesman or SE might have covered which reduced the selling costs in the product pricing equations. Further if the regular IBM sales branch processed the orders for store systems, then the cost for the administrative system was borne in the regular branch office and not in the Store Systems offices. This sounds a little like smoke and mirrors, but it worked wonders in getting the price for both systems into a more competitive range. The allowable 10 lane store system price dropped a lot, but we still were not quite under our self imposed $125,000 target.

Field Training for Store Products

In the meantime product education for the sales force had to start. Marketing and Systems Engineering Managers, lead sales people, and Systems Engineers from the larger grocery accounts were brought in about 20 at a time and taken through a 2-3 day course in the second half of September. They each signed a non-disclosure document that would cost them their job and possibly their first born child if they violated it. They were provided with a three ring binder that documented the system elements, configurations, the checkout functions, benefits, installation activities, and specific information about how competitive systems compared to the IBM 3660. They did not get pricing information on the IBM system since that had not been established yet. Supermarket store systems salesmen and the regular salesmen from each of the larger existing supermarket account teams came for the classes about 15-20 at a time.

My role centered on presentations of the technical services available, not my real interest at the time, but we made the field SEs and sales people comfortable that we could handle technical questions on the product. A configuration tool was proposed, developed, and made available, but really not used much.

Moving

I did get something accomplished though in my other job. My trips out to look at homes were becoming less frequent and at the same time I knew I had to get this task wrapped up. One day John Morissey, one of my several realtors, called me and said he thought he'd found what I wanted. He picked me up and drove me to Oak Park Road near Lindsey Drive. It was a tri-level. We walked in and I saw the prior owner's baby grand piano perfectly framed in the living room's bay window with a view to lush green woods behind the home. I turned to John and told him that I thought he had found it. On the way out I realized this was the same house that Gordon Vick had suggested I take a look at on that first night in Raleigh, but now the property was listed by an agent. My wife flew down a few days later; we bought it, and moved in less than a month later. All the time IBM had been paying for my hotel, meals, travel back to my prior home, and house hunting trips for my wife. Now they paid closing costs at both ends and moving expenses. After everything had been accounted for and all the receipts attached so that everything had been reimbursed, they added another $600 as a miscellaneous amount to cover anything that had been forgotten. How could you complain about getting moved by IBM?

It was to be a great neighborhood. On one side was the Hedgepeth family with whom we were going to spend many Friday nights eating Pizza. On the other side was Al Moreno's family. He ran IBM's Model Shop in Raleigh. Jim Markov lived across from the Hedgepeths. He was significantly involved with developing IBM's SNA architecture. The Handy's lived across from the Moreno's and she was a cousin of Senator Jessie Helms. My boss lived about a dozen houses in one direction and in the other direction was Paul McEnroe, the Manager of Engineering for Supermarket Systems, and just a little farther, George Laurer, the engineer who designed the U.P.C. Barcode.

On Sunday, the first weekend in my new house, Frank Babka, a name I knew as one of the System Development Division's Program Managers for the IBM 3650 Retail System, knocked on my front door. He told me he lived three doors away, had seen the moving van, and asked me for my name. When I said Selmeier, he responded "I married Mary Alice Selmier from Arkansas. Do you have any relatives living there?" I didn't, but my parents were coming to visit in a few weeks as was his father-in-law. When we put the two fathers together, we discovered we were related. She was from the side of the family that had dropped an additional "e" when they immigrated to the United States.

IBM 3650 Retail System Announcement

In September the retail side felt they were at an acceptable mix of function, price and availability to announce. We were going to birth one of our babies. When it happened the engineering group had a large celebratory dinner with speeches by many engineering managers about the accomplishment.

Tommy Tomlin asked me to accompany him to a meeting on October 1st with the retail marketing managers about a week after the retail announcement. The purpose of that trip was to get information face to face from field personnel about how the IBM 3650 Retail System announcement had gone at key accounts. Tommy and I flew to Chicago and met in the IBM Building downtown with four Retail Store Systems Marketing Managers who had flown in from around the country. The group went through the accounts one by one with the Marketing Managers giving the feedback. Sears, ... Montgomery Wards ..... the May company, Federated Department Stores, ... Dillard's,   Bullocks,....Macy's, Bloomingdales, and so on. The reaction was not what we had hoped for. In general, prospective customers were happy to see IBM in this market, but the product did not stand out. The Marketing Managers gave very specific details on the reasons for each customer's response. It added up to a long hard battle to win business for the IBM 3650. Tom left that meeting resolved to get some things changed. No one was smiling.

That weekend back in Raleigh I remember standing out on my driveway talking with my next door neighbor who ran the model shop that builds the mock-ups of everything IBM developed in Raleigh. He was telling me he had been told at the engineering dinner how positive the customer reception had been for the retail system and was a little surprised at my reserved response. Unfortunately history bore out my view. It took a big effort before that system achieved significant acceptance.

Task Assignments for IBM 3660 Supermarket System Support

On the IBM 3660 Supermarket side the battle continued mostly over price. We were still blind to other issues that would arise. Slowly the weight of evidence of competitive pricing, reports on market dynamics, and general overwhelming reformatting of numbers by John Shaw, Larry Goodwin, Ralph Converse, and Bill Carey made the case to the development division for a lower price.

Tommy Tomlin could see that the announcement was coming and wanted the supermarket side of his group to be organized when it happened. He called me and the other two technical support people into a meeting where he acknowledged that in the supermarket architecture the store equipment could be expected to run as independent systems that only called in with the day's results once per night. In the retail system the POS system is intertwined with the companies total information system all the time. But Tommy also didn't want to lose headcount just because he didn't have a comparable technical systems challenge on the supermarket side, so we discussed what role the supermarket technical support might play. If there wasn't a technical assurance role, there might be a technical marketing role? The three of us could see a role providing more technical information in the customer interface and outlined several ideas. Tom asked us what sections of the country we'd like to cover. I decided since my brother was in California I'd like to see California again, so I spoke up first. Jim Hartwell took the Midwest which included his hometown of New Orleans and Willie Ledbetter

Spreading the Barcode

took the east. Among the Direct Marketing people, Larry Questad picked his home town of Los Angeles which paired us up. I really enjoyed my partnership with Larry. Larry was an athlete who still had his athletic build, a bronze medal winner in track and field at the 1968 Mexico City Olympics, and a man to charm you with a thousand stories. He had an ego, but above all he had empathy.

By the start of October we had developed an informal Systems Assurance program that made Field Engineering comfortable. We had questionnaires about store statistics that led sales people to the correct in-store configurations, but for the large part these were unnecessary. We had prepared a document to list the services that Tomlin's group would provide, and it had been included in all class materials.

Chapter 6 IBM Supermarket System Announced

The IBM 3660 Supermarket System was announced on Thursday, October 11, 1973 and by all accounts it was spectacular. I wasn't at the main announcement, which would have been fun, but I now had a regional responsibility to the west. The specific date of the announcement was timed to coincide with the Executive Session meeting of the National Association of Food Chains, NAFC, which was to be held at the Mayflower Hotel in Washington, D.C. I still remember watching Bill Carey, the Supermarket Product Manager, walk back into our area of the 602 building a few mornings later after the end of the NAFC session with a smile from one ear to the other. I asked him how it went and he replied, "couldn't have been better. The top executives

IBM internal "Blue Letter" announcement of IBM 3660 Supermarket System

at the National Association of Food Chains' Executive Session skipped the bar to bring their wives back down to the demonstration area and watch Jimmy Lightner throw a bar of Camay soap the length of the checkstand (as if it were an air hockey puck) over the scanner window and then hear the register ring up the item. Everyone was astounded and asked for repeat performances."

Raising the Source Marking Issue

Bill and I made some small talk about details and then I made the single most significant comment I made all the time I was in Raleigh declaring, "I'd feel a whole lot better about the program, if there were a few more source marked symbols out there to scan." At the time you could walk into a store selling 20,000 to 25,000 different products and maybe 3 or 5 of them would have a U.P.C. barcode symbol as part of its package labeling.

Bill Carey's eyes enlarged slightly and staring at me he said, "Why don't you see what you can do about that!" It was typical of IBM's confidence that it would announce a product into a new market place which depended on tens of thousands of independent decisions to include a U.P.C. symbol on their retail package. What an incredible step. But, IBM was bold. IBM was accustomed to changing the world and accustomed to having to create the infrastructure to make new products function. The difference here was the decision to implement the infrastructure was in the hands of hundreds of

Spreading the Barcode

grocery manufacturers who had no directly related economic connection to IBM.

And that response from Bill Carey defined about a third of my work life for the next 24 to 36 months and moreover I'd just picked up a marketing task. It inserted me right into the middle of what was to become recognized as one of the biggest obstacles to the IBM 3660's initial success. IBM had no install base of point-of-sale non-scanning systems to which grocery chains could be told "Just add scanners" when the symbols appeared. Our product was not targeted to compete against key only supermarket systems. Almost everything about the IBM marketing and product design was dependent on scanning U.P.C. symbols. Of course that required that there be U.P.C. symbols to scan. And there weren't U.P.C. Symbols to scan. This would become a much larger obstacle than the price, but up to that point it had been pretty much ignored, much like that crazy aunt in the basement.

Last Minute Challenges to the Announcement

The hallway conversation happened a few days after the announcement. Actually the October 11th announcement came close to not happening. We wanted the announcement to coincide with the National Association of Food Chain's Executive Session on that date. IBM's formal product announcement release policy requires management approvals and documents to be written and approved in a formalized structured order. A corporate committee with members from each country where IBM had a company had to agree with the announcement. IBM had rigorous policies regarding announcement and information about un-announced products. There were many steps still to complete on the Monday before October 11th and Bill Carey went north to White Plains and Harrison, NY with Larry Goodwin, John Shaw and others to shepherd the process. It was clear we would not have an IBM approval to announce before the truck carrying the equipment to the NAFC session in Washington DC had to start on its way.

The absolute latest time that the privately contracted courier would to leave Raleigh and be able to commit to arrive at the Mayflower Hotel in Washington in time for the equipment exhibit to be set up was about two and a half days before the exhibition time on Thursday. That time was reached without the approval process being completed. A plan was made to load and seal the van, drive it to Washington, and instruct the driver to not let anyone inside until specifically designated IBM people in Washington gave the approval to unload the van. Otherwise it would return to Raleigh still sealed. The truck reached the Mayflower Hotel, and sat there in the unloading area for some time before word came that all approval steps had been successfully completed. There would be an announcement on the following day. The seals could be broken and the exhibit could be set up.

Chapter 6 IBM Supermarket System Announced   Page 99

In the afternoon on Monday October 8th I got a call from John Shaw who was at IBM DPD Group offices in Harrison, NY getting everything processed. He sounded very enthusiastic, even when he told me the price would be more than $170,000 for the standard 10 checkout lane configuration. I was shocked. They had left Raleigh to get everything signed off with an agreed upon price of about $117,000 and now it was over $50,000 higher. I asked, "John, what gives" and he replied, "What? This is a great price!"

I responded, "Come on John, this is Bill here, we've been talking about this for months. How can this happen?"

John only responded, "It's a go. We are out at this price!"

Later I heard from others that the price had been in the $117,000 range until John Opel, then IBM's CFO, changed the number with the statement, "The IBM Company has never accepted this small a margin and it's not going to do it now. So you either agree to my price or you do not announce." That was that!

There was to have been a second exhibitor at the NAFC's Executive Session. Bob Sloat, the former Kroger Industrial Engineer and principal of Sloat, Keyser, Blair, the company that had consulted with IBM a year or so earlier, now headed up a division of Pitney Bowes that was planning to enter the supermarket point-of-sale market with the Spice System product. What Bob was going to exhibit or do in his space is unknown. For some reason when Bob heard that IBM was actually going to use its exhibit space, he canceled the Pitney Bowes' space. Bob may have known IBM well enough to understand what IBM exhibiting meant. If IBM said they were going to exhibit, it meant there had been a product announced and it would be scanning U.P.C. symbols.

At this same time Larry Goodwin was promoted to become the Marketing Manager in Oakland working for Russ Bliese. His people handled the host side of Safeway and Lucky stores among other accounts. John Shaw was promoted to a Marketing Manager position in one of the Los Angeles branches. Both went immediately from the announcement to their new positions. John and I never were able to conclude our discussion on the price of the system.

IBM 3660 Announcement in Western Region

Larry Questad and I left for Los Angeles on Tuesday, October 9th, to help with the announcement in the Western Region. We each went with Store Systems salesmen on two different customer calls. We both kibitzed with the Marketing Representatives and systems people in the Store Systems branch office, answered questions about product details that might have gotten fuzzy since the introduction classes almost all had attended, and we did an announcement review for John Akers - IBM's Western Regional Vice

Page 100 Spreading the Barcode

President and previously Director of Distribution Industry Marketing in White Plains, with his staff. I reminded John that I had presented the applications in the Kroger Intensive Planning Session to him about a year earlier since there didn't appear to be any immediate recognition. Akers really enjoyed this session, passing along comments during the briefing to his staff about where and how certain elements of the system had come to be, battles won and lost. The presentation became totally interactive. The next day Larry then went on to San Francisco to work with the Store System Marketing Representatives handling Safeway and Lucky. I went to Denver to help introduce the system to King Soopers before returning to Raleigh.

Early Customer Executive Briefings

Over the next few weeks, we had many customer briefings. Automating the stores checkout with optical scanning was such a prominent industry initiative, all Store Systems salesman were getting requests for information from grocery chains. Visits to the Raleigh center was managed by a guest services person, Jan Mosser, who was kept busy finding free dates for supermarkets to come to be briefed about the system. Jan was a find. She was short, very vivacious, cute, young, energetic, and organized. If she'd been a juggler, she would have had no trouble keeping four bowling pins in the air continuously. It made her almost perfect for the multitasking job she had. When customers or prospects met her, they immediately liked her. The pace excited her. And she was enthusiastic about opening up this market. She seemed to sense the business objective, not just the task at hand.

From about a week and a half after the October 11th announcement, it became hard to find a single day there was not a company being briefed in our customer briefing center. In good taste we limited visits to one company a day. The IBM corporate Gulfstream jet was put at our disposal and used a lot. Jan Mosser kept track of that. The big guns in marketing, Larry Questad, Jim Lightner, Ralph Converse, and Bob Doremus focused on large chains. These guys were focused on their careers too and I am certain each of them wished that an account they helped with marketing would become the first big order. Everyone was charged up and very excited.

Ralph Converse was super energetic. Ralph's favorite personality was Pete Rose of the Cincinnati Reds, "Mr. Hustle" Pete was called because of his unlimited energy and enthusiasm for baseball. This was before Pete Rose's unfortunate confrontation with Major League Baseball over gambling. At the time Pete was an idol who always put out the extra effort and Ralph completely identified with that. Ralph couldn't keep himself from checking on almost every briefing no matter if the account had been assigned to him or not. He found he could sit in the projection booth between the two briefing rooms and listen to the presentation while watching the body language of the guest executives being briefed. He kept talking about the "Mating Dance." Ralph had this great analogy about the ritual that tarantulas go through prior

Chapter 6 IBM Supermarket System Announced   Page 101

to mating where they circle each other, avoid getting stung, get to know each other better, and eventually mate. Ralph saw the grocery industry and IBM in the "Mating Dance" phase of a relationship.

Early Install Target Accounts

Several accounts had been targeted for early install. The two first installations were expected to be the supermarkets who had agreed to let the IBM's SDD development division test the operational stability of the code in one of their stores. Supermarket's General's Pathmark Division provided a store in Plainfield, NJ and Steinberg's did the same in Duval a suburb of Montreal, Canada, near the airport. As the target install and operational dates came closer, both customers would slip the date a little, but not enough to be a big concern. To help establish market momentum in the real market where salesmen sold and customers paid for their equipment, the Store Systems organization contacted and got an early install commitment from three chains which became known as "Launch Accounts". A Direct Marketing person was assigned to each installation: Bob Doremus to Giant Foods in the Washington DC area, Jim Lightner to Kroger in the Midwest and Larry Questad to Ralph's in the far west. The planned schedule was that by August 1974, less than 6 months after the Pathmark and Steinberg's installation, three more stores would go live with U.P.C. symbol scanning. None of these would make their original schedule. We still had not focused on what would be the really significant obstacles to acceptance of our product, but we were beginning to hear the clues from grocery executives attending our briefings.

Non Supermarket Briefings

We also got requests for briefings from companies outside the supermarket business. Since I was still in the technical side of the organization but acted more like a direct marketing person, I handled those. The first of these was Firestone Tire. They had a tremendous problem of uniquely tracking each tire and had heard that our scanners had great depth of field. They imagined a scanner at the end of their production line that would scan a unique imprinted U.P.C. symbol as the tire rolled off the end. Since this would be an extension to the expected application area of supermarkets, I talked with Joe Woodland about it. The two of us ended up having the humorous conversation with our Firestone visitors centered on the U.P.C. only providing for 10 billion numbers would not be nearly enough for the tire identification application. (The World Product Code or WPC (EAN) which increased the number of codes came later.) Of course our greatest concern was that we saw this application as a complete misuse of the U.P.C. What if someone someday accidentally scanned a tire in a parking lot and it said it was a quart of Borden's Milk?

A second briefing request came from Cities Service. The Direct Marketing people were all occupied with large supermarket chain activities. Bill Carey asked me if I would be willing to help out and do a briefing. I was only too happy to get back to the Direct Marketing activity and readily agreed. The catch was it was my task to talk them out of considering our system. Our initial presumption was Cities Service was interested in a solution for dispensing gasoline (our presumption may have been a little off, since I later learned they did have mini-marts at some of their stations.) They were an important IBM customer so even though they were not in our target audience, we provided a first class briefing.

Source Marking

I was giving some thought to how to increase the amount of source marking. I talked with Bill Carey about it and mentioned that I knew Joe Woodland was handling some remaining issues with the U.P.C. at industry meetings. Bill encouraged me to go to some industry meetings. Neither Bill Carey or Tommy Tomlin were tight fisted, but Bill was much less structured and tended to encourage people to go try things if it looked like it would contribute to the overall goal.

IBM Briefings for Grocery Manufacturers

In Raleigh I soon returned to the track of considering how we could contribute to increasing the presence of source marked product in grocery stores. With all the energy and excitement about supermarket executive briefing visits to Raleigh, I decided that it was time to have a briefing designed for grocery product manufacturers. In early November we initiated a briefing to cover the U.P.C. Symbol background information and expand on how scanners would be used in Grocery Chains. To get attendees we contacted the IBM Grocery Manufacturing Industry Marketing team in White Plains and let them spread the word. Soon we were at capacity in our briefing room with about 35 different companies. In our acknowledgement correspondence to them about attending the briefing, we made it clear that they were going to see a real U.P.C. Symbol checkout scanner and we encouraged them to bring any products of their own that they wanted to test scan. We would demonstrate to them that their product scanned successfully or help them understand what was wrong, if there was a problem.

This proved to be a highlight of their visit. In the fall of 1973 there really were no test beds or U.P.C. scanners in any stores. Grocery manufacturers feared those detailed instructions in the Distribution Number Bank or DNB, (their name was later changed to Distribution Codes Incorporated or DCI when Dunn and Bradstreet decided DNB was too close to their trademarked name) handbook that you got with your assigned U.P.C. vendor code. I wanted to put together a briefing that would educate the industry on the

Chapter 6 IBM Supermarket System Announced   Page 103

technology, reduce or remove the fears, and be an incentive for them to source mark. And separately over the next few months we acquired a lot of additional products for our Grocery Executive demonstrations from manufacturers only too happy to leave their working sample products behind.

Unlike the briefings for supermarket chains, these guests were not traveling altogether in a group. When they signed up we booked individual rooms in their name at the Sheraton Crabtree the night prior. I put together a full page form letter that detailed the day: start times, driving directions, end times, driving time back to the airport, a complete description of what to expect and when to be where. My southern secretary, Sylvia, had an IBM Magtape-Selectric typewriter and this was more or less a form letter, but looked fairly personalized and not much trouble to run out with the name and address list I provided.

The agenda was straight forward. For the first briefing I got several of the key engineering players to present the material, but in later sessions I took over making most of the presentations. For the first one or two I used the real engineers who had invented the U.P.C. and proved its efficacy. Here were some standard briefing elements:

1. An introduction and welcome with an overview of the program status by Bill Carey kicked it off at 8:30 am for about 15 – 30 minutes. Bill usually did the welcome for Supermarket chain visits and could weave in non-privileged items from discussions he had had with executives in major supermarket chains on how important they viewed the U.P.C. initiative.

2. Introduction to the Universal Product Code technology, projections about things to come, and what the Grocery Manufacturers and printers should focus on to make the program as successful as possible. This was initially presented by Joe Woodland, but I took the module over at the third or fourth briefing. I think we embarrassed Joe the first time since unknown to him we introduced him with a short slide show which included the patent application for the bulls-eye product ID symbol he had filed in 1949 and was subsequently used by RCA in their Cincinnati Kroger store test in 1972. Joe apparently had invented the concept of a symbolic identification mark while considering a character code like the Morse code, making representative marks in sand and then pulling them around into a circle. Joe was given 45 minutes to an hour to cover his introduction to the technology.

Page 104 Spreading the Barcode

George Laurer, inventor of the U.P.C. Symbol

3. Overview of the U.P.C. Symbol and how it works by George Laurer. George was the actual inventor of the U.P.C. symbol and discussed details on its self checking features, alternative formats and more. George also got 45 minutes to cover this. With Joe's assistance, I presented this information in the third session. I really enjoyed bringing in people like George. It amazed the grocery manufacturing people in the room that they were meeting the guy who actually invented the U.P.C., but George had other things to do and probably only sort of enjoyed standing in front of a group of printers and grocery manufacturers. The U.P.C. was paramount, but when you went to George's office he had plaques all over the wall for different inventions he had made while working at IBM.

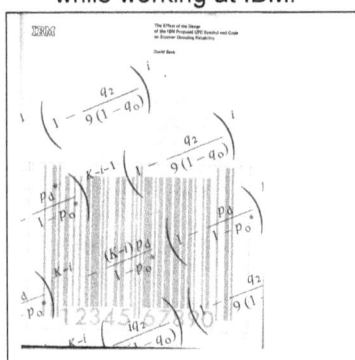

David Sevir's 36 page mathematical proof document

4. A mathematical description of the optics and human factors of a scanning checkout by David Savir, the same person who had presented this to the Symbol Selection Committee a year or more earlier. This material proved to be a little too technical for the packaging and printing people who attended the briefing and we dropped this after the first session. David took 30 minutes for this.

5. I demonstrated the scanning system with our collected grocery products most of which had adhesively attached U.P.C. labels. The curtain between the briefing room and the lab was drawn back and a highly choreographed checkout demonstration performed, e.g. when I mentioned how small products with small symbols were no problem, Jan Mosser, our guest services coordinator, checkout model, and general girl Friday, would be scanning a package of gum or if I mentioned curved

Chapter 6 IBM Supermarket System Announced   Page 105

surfaces, she would be scanning a tomato soup can. The demonstration only took about 10 minutes. This same presentation was done for supermarket executives.

6. This was followed by having everyone come into the lab with any package samples they brought and try the checkout themselves. We did this is in shifts. Normal supermarket chain visits usually were no more than 5-10 people but 30 people was more than the twenty foot by twenty foot demonstration room could handle at one time since it also had checkstands and supermarket style display cases. Each of the guests tried scanning a few of our products and of course any package of their own that they had brought with them. The guests played with our products in a regular checkout mode, but since our IBM 1130 that acted as the store controller was not loaded with their specific products and U.P.C. codes, we'd put the scanner in a diagnostic mode where they would scan their product and see their full U.P.C. code on the checkout display. They really got into this trying to find any angle that worked less well crossing the window, talking and kibitzing with each other about printing challenges and lastly being pretty amazed that everything went as smoothly as it did. We spent 45 minutes to an hour letting them have their way with the equipment.

7. By now it's time for lunch. They were treated just like the supermarket chain executive prospects. We took them out to the Flying Cloud sea food restaurant for a formal lunch except we didn't have limos for transportation but simply car pooled the mile to the restaurant. Over the hour and a half allowed for lunch there was a lot of conversation and congratulations among the attendees about how successfully their packages had performed on a real scanner. Maybe even more important were the war stories that were being exchanged about how each succeeded, only tried, or failed to get their management's commitment and attention to implementing the U.P.C. symbol on packaging. I kept track of some of the more interesting ones and shared them with the direct marketing people talking more frequently with chain store executives.

8. After lunch we presented the supermarket's position. IBM had saved the information worked upon years earlier to determine if a U.P.C. symbol was cost justified. Larry Goodwin had produced a slide presentation detailing the projected benefits of scanning checkout systems. It documented savings of many tens of thousands of dollars a year in a typical $60,000 a week supermarket store. The people in the room had never seen information like this before and we frequently were requested to provide hardcopy of the slides which we were happy to do under NDA. We wanted the grocery manufacturer's management to see the information, but we didn't want it to go outside their company unless we provided it. It's a

Page 106 Spreading the Barcode

   marketing thing! We wanted the recognition that went with doing this work. Certainly we didn't want the information or the recognition to go to a competitor.
9. Lastly, we had a wide open question and answer session. Even though we had encouraged questions all along, there were still more questions which we tried to answer directly or in a rare instance commit to getting back to them with an answer. The only questions we ducked had to do with our sales and installation projections and IBM's costs. IBM does not discuss business volumes outside the company and certainly didn't discuss its cost structure. If interested we'd let them go back into our mock store we called a lab and play with the scanner some more if they had the time. The program generally wrapped up around 3:00 pm, but often they stayed till 4:00 if they went back to play with the scanner.

I still have vivid memories of that first session on November 13, 1973. I could sit at the back of the room and observe since the IBM engineers provided the content that day. In the back of the Red room with me was the Packaging Director from Hunt's. (Actually the following day I would be in New York City attending an American Management Association sponsored seminar on U.P.C. Symbol marking which he was chairing.) He was sitting next to the packaging manager from Delmonte.

Near the start of his part in the briefing Joe Woodland pointed out that one of the things the grocery manufacturers could do "for the good of the industry" would be to standardize the location of the U.P.C. symbol in each category of products. Then checkout clerks would quickly learn the proper face of the package to put toward the scanner making the checkout process even more productive. The Delmonte and Hunt's packaging representatives immediately conferred as to which location on a ketchup bottle would cause the most grief for Heinz. Ya gotta luv human nature! They suggested that to put it adjacent to the front label would simply trash Heinz' keystone label. In the first few months of source marked ketchup distribution, the ketchup from Hunt's and Del Monte did have the U.P.C. symbol on the front label. But in a show of real marketing force, Heinz never followed, put the symbol up on the collar label, and within a year all manufacturers had the U.P.C. symbol on the collar label.

As David Savir was getting deep into the probability distribution of "T_4" errors occurring while collecting bright and dim portions of the light reflected from the scanner, one of the other packaging attendees sitting near the back, swiveled his chair around and just rolled his eyes back into his head. Most likely doctorate level math was not his thing. I made a note to myself to reconsider including this in the briefing since it probably raised more fear in the packaging people and this briefing was about reducing fear.

Joe Woodland came back and assisted me during the final question and answer period. During the Q&A a printer from New Jersey surprised us by

Chapter 6 IBM Supermarket System Announced   Page 107

asking how he could become a member of the Symbol Selection Committee. The symbol had already been selected and the committee had completed its work, but evidently he saw a business opportunity in the U.P.C. He sincerely desired to be recognized as an expert in this new technology. We tried to tell him that the work was complete and although he stopped pushing the point in the session, his body language showed he hadn't dropped his objective.

When the session was over and the guests were headed to the airport, Bill Carey was curious as to how it went. I told him I didn't think it was as spectacular as the product announcement, but all the informal feedback said the attendees felt it was very instructional, productive, and they enjoyed themselves. That turned out to be true since within the week we started getting requests to attend any next session we might hold. But right then I was out the door and on my way to the airport to attend the first one of a series of American Management Association seminars on "Implementing the U.P.C."

Other U.P.C. Meetings

The last day of the AMA session I got an early phone call in my room from the New Jersey printer to say he was having a limo pick me up, if I would come over to his plant at the end of the session. It turned out that he wanted to show off his printing expertise. It was pretty spectacular since he printed Penthouse and had pages from it up on the walls in his production areas. Although I explained it again, I'm still not sure he understood that IBM played no role in the printing of symbols and the format was already determined.

Without realizing it, I was transitioning to a new pattern of life where travel was common. Ten days later I was in Detroit to discuss and answer questions about the IBM 3660 on a call with the local sales team to Allied Stores. I had bought donuts walking home from Junior High School at a Farmer Jack, one of their stores, when I was growing up in the Detroit area. It always interested me how things tie together at different points in time.

From Detroit I went on to Dallas to attend the National American Wholesale Grocers Association's U.P.C. seminar to learn what they presented and how they were addressing this new technology. At this point I was interested in how other groups viewed the U.P.C. Without any scanning equipment in public view anywhere at the time, these discussions appeared theoretical and abstract. I appreciated that when they came to Raleigh, we put them on a real U.P.C. scanner. Scanning a package was less abstract. Even more important, the normality of scanning symbols at check out seemed more imminent.

I ended up flying to Washington with one of the executives of the Distribution Number Bank who had been a speaker on NAWGA's program. I recognized him while waiting in the gate area and introduced myself. We quickly got our seats reassigned so we could ride to Washington together. I was going to

Washington to attend a U.P.C. seminar sponsored by the can manufacturers association the next day with Joe Woodland. Our flight from Dallas was significantly delayed so we had ample opportunity to talk. On business related topics we discussed how many companies were applying for vendor numbers and what types of companies were applying. They were just starting to see some of the less immediately obvious grocery manufacturing companies like greeting cards, kitchen utensils and battery manufacturers, show an interest in getting a U.P.C. vendor number. We hypothesized what types of stores might eventually use U.P.C. scanning, but way under-estimated it.

The flight was so late it was diverted from National Airport on the Potomac River due to late night landing restrictions there to Dulles Airport out in the Virginia countryside. At the time I had no idea where I had been taken or where Dulles was but they put us on limo buses to get us back to National Airport so it didn't matter. I didn't get to the Marriott Crystal City hotel until midnight or later only to learn my room had been given to another. But, they had one of those conference and hospitality suites on the top floor that they would give me, a room used for business and small group meetings. When I saw the price on the notice on the back of the door was about four times the amount I had expected to pay, I checked with the front desk quickly but found I would not be charged that amount. There was no regular bed in the room. Instead it had a Murphy bed that stowed in the wall.

I was exhausted. So, I just got undressed and went to sleep only to wake up about 2:30 am with red lights dancing across the ceiling and there was a bell clanging in the hallway. Running to the window I saw five fire trucks in the street. One had a ladder extended half way up the outside walls. This was my first hotel fire. I knew I should leave, but I wasn't dressed. So I threw on some clothes, picked up my wallet, change, keys, and other personal items I had removed from my pockets (shouldn't I be in a rush?) and opened the hall door. But, the elevator was running across the hall from my room. I could hear it. And up the hall there were some guests walking towards me carrying playing cards and holding money in their hands. It looked like a floating card game to me and I decided if none of them were concerned, I'd go back to bed – not the best decision. The next morning while having breakfast with Joe, we learned there had been a real fire in the elevator shaft which had been extinguished.

Traveling with Joe Woodland

Over breakfast Joe introduced me to the world of legislative reaction. For example, a prominent state's medical director was lobbying to reduce the diameter of the laser beam to get a smaller spot size on the narrowest cross section of the laser. The premise, we supposed, was that there would be less energy. The original supermarket laser was focused through a lens which means the beam has a very, very slight hour glass shape. There will be a

Chapter 6 IBM Supermarket System Announced   Page 109

narrowest point or waist, but in this application you don't want that point to be hardly any smaller than the spot size two or three feet up the beam. This results in a large depth of field. Actually the spot size had been chosen very carefully to allow for handling the smallest symbol (80% of the standard size) to the largest symbol (twice the standard size), a very long focal length, and not be accidentally refocused into something less safe by any other lens we all might carry around, specifically the ones in each of our own eyes. This physician turned politician unknowingly was legislating supermarket scanners into something that would be more dangerous. The spot size would be so small that your eye's lens would magnify the intensity of all of the beam rather than just part of the beam increasing any damaging effect. Joe was busy responding to legislative inquiries so that this ill advised proposal wouldn't get accidentally approved.

I got a lot of additional insight into the technology traveling with Joe, and some humorous anecdotes. When Joe attended the IBM Supermarket System's announcement for the Washington DC area after the NAFC formal national announcement at the Mayflower, he stood next to a prominent supermarket store Consumer Affairs VP. They showed that 16mm film that Goodwin's and Converse's wives were in to introduce the elements of the system and illustrated checking out groceries. In IBM's penchant for making our message less artificial and more human, during the part that talked about the Store Controller, the machine in the store that contained the item database where all the price lookup's occurred, we put in a man to represent the store manager at a desk in front of the machine. At this point the Consumer Affairs VP leaned over and whispered to Joe, "Mr. Woodland, I don't think we can afford your system. I know how much our controller is paid and if we need one of him in each store we'd be bankrupt." Joe was afraid she meant it.

While Joe and I were in Washington, we stopped by the offices of the Distribution Number Bank, the organization originally charged with handing out five digit vendor codes to manufacturers seeking to symbol mark their products. John Hayes, the director, learned that I was going to help promote source marking and made sure I was given my own personal copy of all the manuals and materials supplied to a grocery manufacturer when a number was assigned.

U.P.C. Formats and Structure

Grocery Manufacturers and other vendors with printed packaging that needed a U.P.C. purchased a vendor number from Distribution Number Bank. The amount they paid varied with the number products they would have to apply a symbol on. The largest corporations paid the most and received easily remembered vendor codes such as 10000, 11000, 12000, 36000, and 43000. The last three digits were always 0 in their numbers. Medium size companies paid less and their codes started with 3 or 4 non-

Spreading the Barcode

zero numbers. The smallest companies paid least and got numbers where there were 4 or 5 non-zero numbers.

The U.P.C. code for most grocery products consisted of two parts, a five digit number assigned to each grocery vendor number followed by a 5 digit product number the vendor assigned to identify each of its products. Two to three years earlier, a comprehensive study was made of large and small grocery vendors. It was discovered that almost all manufacturers used a product ID of five digits or less and hardly any of them included any alpha characters in their product IDs. So the U.P.C. came to be ten numerical digits: five digits assigned by the Distribution Number Bank or DNB (soon to become Distribution Codes Incorporated or DCI) and five digits assigned by the grocery manufacturer and presumed to be the product ID the manufacturer was already using to identify the product within its own organization. That combination provided the numbers that needed to be encoded in the barcode. There could be up to 99,999 vendors and each of them could have 99,999 items. That should be enough for the US. Unfortunately we didn't commonly think as globally about markets in those days.

U.P.C. Version A

There were five different symbol design specifications, identified as "A" through "E," for the barcodes symbol formats although 4 of them, "A" through "D" looked the same. The "A" label consisted of two slightly long thin guard bars, then the number 0 to indicate a general grocery item followed by the 5 digits in the manufacturer's assigned vendor code, followed by two more slightly longer thin guard bars in the center of the label, then the 5 digits of the product ID assigned by the vendor, then a single digit modulo 11 checksum and finally two more of the slightly larger thin guard bars. Optionally and also commonly the packager could also include human readable values of the bars below the bars themselves, but it wasn't required. The "B," "C," and "D," symbols would look the same, but the data arrangement was slightly different, and at that time it was not completely defined for all versions.

The Number System is used to classify the type of data. Standard regular grocery items are included in number system 0 and formatted as the 5 digit manufacturer assigned vendor code and that vendor's assigned 5 digit product ID number. Number System 2 is for items weighed in the store and includes a product ID and the price. Number systems 3 was set aside for items that are assigned a National Drug/Health control product ID by the FDA. Number system 5 was established for coupons. Each of them used the "A" version symbol. Additionally, some Number System "0" codes could also be expressed in the abbreviated half sized "E" symbol

Chapter 6 IBM Supermarket System Announced   Page 111

Each number within the symbol is encoded with two light and two dark areas across a field of seven possibilities or modules. For example, **DDLDDLL** (D for dark and L for light) would be one number value, **DLLDDLL** is a different value.

Number System	In 1974 Applied to
0	Regular Grocery Products
1	Undefined
2	Random Weight packaged in store
3	National Drug Code Items
4	Undefined
5	Coupons
6	Undefined
7	Undefined
8	Undefined
9	Undefined

DLDLDLL is nothing at all! It has too many light and dark transitions in the 7 module space. To read the number a laser beam passes across the field and times the transitions from light to dark and dark to light.

It turns out there are exactly 20 different patterns which when put in any order will define two light and two dark areas across a field of 7 modules. Further 10 of them have an odd number (or parity) of dark modules and 10 of them have an even number (or parity) of dark modules. The guard bars at the beginning, middle, and end are slightly different. Instead of being 7 modules wide they are only 4. And, they are two light and two dark modules across a field of 4 modules or specifically always **DLDL** or **LDLD**. So by timing the collection of reflected light that includes two complete transitions (**DLDL**), and then the next two complete transitions occur in 175% of that time (7 modules), you are scanning the U.P.C. and not the Kellogg label or another graphic. Joe Woodland told me once, "4,7,7 that's the secret Bill. Don't ever tell anyone, but that's how we know you've found the U.P.C. symbol on the package."

Detecting the when and where of the dark areas in a scan, identifies the pattern that will match a digit encoding in the U.P.C. Symbol table. The number of dark modules or parity of the number will identify whether the digit is the left or right half of the symbol. By using odd parity on one side and even parity on the other side, the scanner can successfully build up a symbol after scanning each half separately and then put the halves together in its memory. The checksum at the end of the right hand side ensures that the correct right and left halves are being combined rather than possibly two halves from different packages.

Spreading the Barcode

Value	Left Side Odd Parity	Right Side Even Parity
0	LLLDDLD	DDDLLDL
1	LLDDLLD	DDLLDDL
2	LLDLLDD	DDLDDLL
3	LDDDDLD	DLLLLDL
4	LDLLLDD	DLDDDLL
5	LDDLLLD	DLLDDDL
6	LDLDDDD	DLDLLLL
7	LDDDLDD	DLLLDLL
8	LDDLDDD	DLLDLLL
9	LLLDLDD	DDDLDLL

The benefit of scanning the symbol in halves essentially eases orientation requirements. The half symbol is taller than it is wide which assures that patterns that cross at right angles will cross all the bars from one direction or the other. Assuming the scanner's beam is running pretty linear, less forward distance through the symbol compared to its height means a wider range of possible angles where the beam can pass through all the light and dark areas and get a good read. This translates into less orientation required when the package is presented at the checkout. In the "A" version symbol only odd parity barcode representations (odd number of modules that are dark) are used on the left side or vendor side and only even parity barcode representations (even number of modules that are dark) are used on the right side. A scanner could keep several symbol scan candidates and recognize if they were the left or right half of the symbol from their dark bar parity. The check digit at the end determines which left and right halves of a symbol should be together. Certainly in the first IBM scanner and likely in all scanners built into the checkstand, even if the checker moved the item across the scan window very fast, the scanner was so much faster and there would be many half symbol candidates for the system to consider in discovering the product code. Using L for a light module and **D** for a dark modules the 20 possible arrangements are:

The "E" version of the symbol was designed to fit on small packages. Every U.P.C. vendor would have some U.P.C. codes that could be completely represented using the half size E symbol instead of the larger A symbol through a clever zero suppression scheme. The E symbol is half an A symbol and contains 6 numeric values. Note that the E symbol can only be used with items in number system "0" or general grocery U.P.C. codes. If you see a half width label, it must be a general grocery code or Number System 0. You don't have to include the Number System 0 for a general grocery product into the E symbol. It's implied.

Chapter 6 IBM Supermarket System Announced Page 113

Zero suppression works slightly different than most people think. If we list all the numbers from 1 to 1000 people think of 1, 2, 3, 4, ... 999, 1000. But a computer is more likely to think 0001, 0002, 0003, 0004, ... 0999, 1000. The difference is that humans like to suppress the leading zeros, all the zeros up to the first non-zero value.

In the U.P.C. Symbol E the middle five zeros are suppressed. So the ninety-nine largest vendors with lots of items like Procter & Gamble, Kraft Foods, and General Foods received codes with only one or two non-zero numbers at the start, i.e. VV 000. The smallest companies (who pay much less for their number) received codes like VVVVV or with no zeros at the end of their vendor number. With the middle five zeros suppressed this allows the largest companies to use have 9999 items that could be suppressed to an E or half sized symbol, VVIIII while the small company only gets 9 U.P.C. Codes that can use the E symbol, VVVVVI. Well I guess both groups could use Item Code=0, but I doubt if anyone ever did. It just doesn't feel comfortable to have an item "0."

Six numbers were encoded in the "E" symbol: 2 up to 5 vendor-side numbers and 4 down to 1 item code-side number. We don't have to encode the 0 as was done on the regular symbol because that is assumed in the "E" symbol. But, we still have to make sure we scanned the bars correctly. We have to get that check digit back into the detection process.

That was achieved in another clever way. The check digit was always the key to accuracy. And the check digit can be encoded into an E symbol from the parity choice used to represent each number in the barcode. Since every number has a representation in odd and in even parity, it's possible to represent the checksum in the pattern of odd and even parities. No matter what the values in the code are, a checksum can be created using the pattern of the parity of each value. A value was assigned to each of the possible "E" even and "O" odd parity patterns.

Check Digit	Parity Pattern
1	EEOEOO
2	EEOOEO
3	EEOOOE
4	EOEEOO
5	EOOEEO
6	EOOOEE
7	EOEOEO
8	EOEOOE
9	EOOEOE
0	EEEOOO

The scanner considered symbols in blocks of five characters (each character made up of two light and two dark areas within seven modules) with guard

Page 114 Spreading the Barcode

bars at either end. The guard bars had two light and two dark areas over 4 modules. This allowed the scanner to locate a symbol using the ratios of 4 units for two complete transitions, followed by five 7 units for two complete transition. Then if the parity was all odd parity, it's the left half of an A symbol. If the parity is all even, it's the right half. If it's mixed parity, then this is an E symbol and you must use the specific parity pattern to obtain the checksum that validates that you got a good read. These calculations seem daunting to people but the special circuits in the IBM 3660 performed them with ease.

IBM did part of the U.P.C. decode using the circuits inside the scanner and the rest of it in the cash register terminal microcode. Concerns about people easily building OEM scanners and registers drove this design. Engineering felt it would be much more complex for any "would be" OEM scanner manufacturer to connect their scanner to an IBM register if the connection point was in the middle of the decode process.

Joe Woodland and I were running for our airplane at National Airport on the trip back to Raleigh when Joe recognized a former IBMer who had supervised some of the people involved in engineering the U.P.C. Inge Telnaes had left IBM months earlier to pursue a career with Bally Manufacturing, then the world's largest manufacturer of mechanical slot machines. His task at Bally was to initiate the move away from purely mechanical machines to electronics as Director of Bally's Nevada Research Center. This was a time for many different industries to begin incorporating electronics into their business equipment. It was also characteristic that people from IBM stayed friends even if one of them left. Not surprisingly, once you adopted the culture, you preferred to seek out others with that IBM culture to be your close friends. Working in this electronic computer development industry was a common bond.

Tragedies

Two serious human events took place very close to each other. My wife and I had gone to Boston to be with my parents for the Thanksgiving holiday. The following Sunday, I got a call from my mother indicating dad was seriously ill and I should come. By the time we got there a few hours later he had already passed. My brother and I spent a couple of days there helping mom get re-oriented and handling all the paperwork and then my wife and I returned to Raleigh.

Then less than two weeks later it was the last day of deer hunting season in North Carolina. Jim Lightner, an avid deer hunter, just had to go out on the last day. At the end of the day he was a long way from the road and walking back when another hunter made the classic misidentification. Jim was shot through the leg and was very, very fortunate not to have had the bullet be a quarter inch either way. The bullet passed through between two main

Chapter 6 IBM Supermarket System Announced   Page 115

arteries. It took more than an hour to get him out of the field and into an ambulance. He was hospitalized for about 6 months.

Going to see Jim wasn't much fun that first week. He was pretty patched up. But Jim had an indomitable spirit, and by the third week he was kibitzing and strategizing with any of us that stopped by. By the fifth week he was the best gossip source in the group. The doctors had given him Morphine for the pain at the start and Jim argued with them to cut it back. He didn't want to take any chance he might get hooked on it.

Jim Lightner from internal announcement article

He had a lot of friends from prior work lives. Jim had been in the Merchant Marine at one time. When a few of his closer Merchant Marine friends heard about his accident, they came to see him. Not sure what the visitor rules were, they picked up a few doctors' robes before reaching the hospital. So in walk these three would-be doctors with a large vase full of flowers and doctors' bags. When they get to the room the flowers get thrown in the trash to reveal martini's in the vase and Jim's favorite steak sandwiches in the bags. They had a great number of hours reliving old times. When it came time to go, and a flower vase of Martini's later, the three would-be doctors decided to leave Raleigh with something to think about. In the crowded elevators one guy quipped, "Boy, this was a rough day. I cut off the wrong leg." Another responded, "Oh no, what did you do then?" The first guy replied, "What could I do, I cut off the other one." Then the door opened and they walked out of the building without cracking a smile. There must have been some wild dinner table stories in a few Raleigh homes that night.

Jim's accident was a bad thing to happen, but with the holidays coming up the demand for briefings was reducing, so the others could better cover for Jim's absence. The briefing blitz had been very exciting, very enthusiastic, but there had been no big commitment or order for the IBM 3660. We had received some key feedback about system and hardware design that was going to need attention. At the top of that list was the fact that the register terminal had only three department keys: Grocery, Meat and Produce. The system software was designed to handle fifty-four separate departments, but only three of them were reachable using the department keys on the keyboard. Scanned items could be assigned to any of the fifty-four departments, but there simply were not enough symbols to scan. The competition was coming out with nine to fifteen department key options. IBM Engineering could proclaim they had 54 departments, but without symbols to scan that was reduced to just the three. And, the ten key pad followed the

Page 116 Spreading the Barcode

familiar touch-tone telephone arrangement with the 1, 2, and 3 at the top. Unfortunately checkers were more familiar with the standard calculator layout with the 1, 2, and 3 at the bottom of the keypad. This was eventually fixed with a special option to reverse the digits in the keypad.

Additionally, there was still concern whether 2400 baud communication could keep up with checkout activity if the store controller failed. And some chains that wanted to experiment with checkstand design were frustrated that the IBM scanner was so large, 38 inches tall. After that, some had noticed that the IBM printer seemed a little slow. IBM understood the technology; they just were not close to the users that operated the technology in the grocery store.

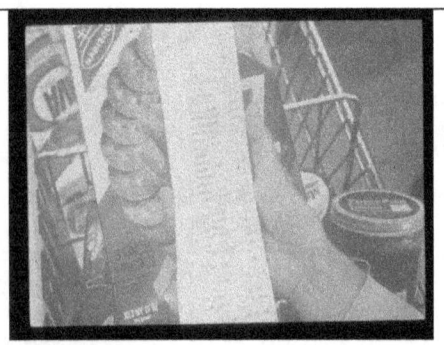

Itemized registered receipt tapes were pioneered at U.P.C. scanning stores.

On the positive side prospects liked the larger 38 print position receipt tape that allowed for a fairly complete item description to be printed. Prior to item descriptions being available during checkout, fifteen or less print positions in a print line was adequate to print the department and price information

IBM originated packaging options where you could get all the electronics, keyboard, display, cash drawer, and printer in a single unit package or you could get them packaged in separate units to distribute around a checkstand. This feature allowed many checkstand manufacturers to become creative. In summary, IBM had come up with a superior systems design that depended on the future when there would be symbols on everything that could be scanned. Until that day, the IBM 3660 system would be a step behind competitive equipment suppliers that had functional key-entry only mode systems with more key oriented capability and store information reporting.

  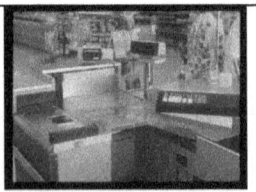

New modular packaging options spark creativity in checkstand designs

Chapter 6 IBM Supermarket System Announced   Page 117

Because there had been some negative feedback on product functionality and there had been no large acceptance, a "troika" of managers was established to meet weekly in the Retail System's customer briefing room. In it, Dave Mackey, the supermarket system hardware development engineering manager, the over-all engineering Director, Paul McEnroe, and Marvin Mann the overall marketing Director, met to identify the problem issues, prioritize them and put an action program in place with individuals and timeframes to get them resolved. The direct marketing personnel in the Market Support Center contacted the store systems sales people covering each of the key prospects every few days. They took that feedback to the Monday morning Troika meeting.

In December it was time to do appraisals. I'd been in Raleigh about 6 months, long enough to be appraised. But first I'd had what was known within IBM as an Executive Interview with Marvin Mann. An Executive Interview is an interview with your manager's manager to provide you more perspective on career opportunities. This one with Marvin didn't make me feel very good as he suggested a career cap at the branch manager level, much below what I would have expected. And now I went for my appraisal from Tommy Tomlin. IBM used a 1, 2, 3, or 4 ranking system in appraisals. To be ranked a "1" meant you were in the top 2% of all IBM employees. The bulk of the people came out a "2." The median was supposed to be between the 2 and the 3, but I strongly suspected human nature pushed the median firmly in the "2" range. To be ranked "3" meant you were below average for sure. If you're ranked a "4," it probably means you're in for some counseling and headed for an "Improvement Plan" which, if not satisfactorily finished, resulted in an exit from IBM. Long story – short story, Tommy rated me a "3" which was the lowest I'd ever been rated. In fact no one had ever suggested that I'd been close to a "3" before. Now Tommy did add a lot more words about how "I was right on the 2-3 border line" and they "were rating some of the more "direct marketing oriented" people up to 1" and they "couldn't be generous to everyone." But, it was still a "3." From my Procter & Gamble days, I believed that this impacted my salary. But I decided I could take it and I'd prove by my future actions how wrong that evaluation was! I was too interested in the work I was doing to stay upset and decided to bury it in the back of my mind. And I decided to definitely become more marketing pro-active. It hurt a lot, but it wasn't going to be the end.

For all of this, tasks were getting done. On the technical side we completed the generic CPM/PERT type project management activity list and network for field people to use when planning for a scanning installation. This is a list of tasks that should be accomplished to successfully install a system together with the sequence in which the tasks need to be done and any dependencies between the tasks, e.g. you must "get out of bed" before you "take a shower" in the morning. And the first issue of the Supermarket MSC newsletter was published to Store Systems sales and systems field personnel talking about issues and, of course, publishing the capabilities of the Supermarket Market

Support group. Tommy had come around to our perspective and recognized Supermarkets were quite different from Retail Department Stores, and we had in fact just about accomplished everything he'd laid out to be done back in July.

By now the Grocery Manufacturers Headquarters Marketing Industry group in White Plains knew it had a hot topic to provide to its client base and decided to use it to enhance their relationship with the industry association itself. We held a special session for them with the grocery manufacturers trade association, the GMA. It wasn't exactly like our other packaging and printer meetings. It started in the afternoon, not early in the morning. It was much more about relationship building than the U.P.C. technology. Although we did the U.P.C. presentations, it was mostly about schmoozing and getting to know each other better. I ended up being more the actor on the stage and not as much part of the group as was the case with the other U.P.C. meetings that had been held. None of the guests had their own packages to scan, although they were all interested in seeing an actual checkout scanner.

I went to dinner with them at what was Raleigh's only recognized French restaurant at the time. But just because it served French food didn't mean there were any real French people involved. For the most part the waiters were students from North Carolina State and were coached to speak with French accents which they did fairly well. But, as they entered the kitchen you could often hear in very plain American, "Hey what's the score now in the State game?" North Carolina State was a national basketball powerhouse under Norm Sloan in those days and frequently the topic of conversation in Raleigh.

1973 ended with a few systems on order, but no IBM 3660 U.P.C. scanning systems operating as the checkout in a store.

Chapter 7 Uncovering the Challenges

Start of 1974 Field Activities

In early January we all sensed that the product was having more than the usual challenges, but otherwise it was the routine for the systems introduction business. I and a few others traveled to Washington, Cincinnati and Los Angeles that month to participate in account reviews for Giant Food, Kroger and Ralph's, the previously identified "Launch Accounts". Bill Carey and Tom Tomlin were there too. In these meetings participation sometimes was a function first of your position in the organization and then your time in grade. As a result, I was more of an observer, and no one expected more than that from me.

Whatever nervousness the Market Support Center people might have felt about the IBM 3660's acceptance was kept behind a professional demeanor intended to portray that things were normal and we would make sure all the necessary steps would be handled for a successful launch. We were there to ensure that there were well thought out installation plans and checkpoints in place so that IBM systems installed as planned. The Industry's Market Support Center in Raleigh was going to do everything it could to help the field sales and systems people make certain that customers at each of these accounts would sign off for delivery at the IBM Production Schedule Confirmation date on schedule.

This didn't actually happen, but if a field person had not done a complete job in planning for anything and everything necessary, someone, most likely the direct marketing or direct support person (someone like myself) from the MSC, would sit down with them and help by adding all the missed items and then what steps were necessary to complete the items – names, phone numbers, whatever would be necessary for that field person to accomplish it. And the MSC person would get queried by his manager after a week or two on how the task list was getting accomplished.

Interspersed with these high visibility meetings were trips on my own to assist with marketing and proposal efforts at Allied Stores, Certified and Scott Lad. By the end of January I had also conducted four Grocery Manufacturing U.P.C. education sessions. Over a hundred grocery manufacturers and package printers would have come to Raleigh to experience scanning their U.P.C. symbols on a checkout scanner for the first time

Grocery Manufacturer Source Marking Briefings

Interest had been growing in holding the next Grocery Manufacturer session. So we scheduled a date and put the word out again through IBM's Grocery Manufacturing Marketing group. This time I got a call at home at 7:15 in the

Page 120   Spreading the Barcode

morning from Marvin Mann who wanted me to know that one of my guests was lost. Marvin was in town and staying at the same hotel, the Sheraton Crabtree, where we lodged our grocery manufacturer guests. At breakfast Marvin overheard one of them indicating he was unsure of how he was to get to IBM for his U.P.C. briefing. I assured Marvin that everyone had received detailed instructions and that I would stop by the hotel on my way in and make certain the man found the meeting. I did and by the time I got to the hotel the man had located his letter and had everything arranged. I told him I'd see him again in a few minutes at IBM. I was going ahead to make sure things were all ready.

Bill Carey kicked the meeting off, Joe Woodland introduced the U.P.C. and told what was significant about it, and I explained how it worked and what was important to consider when printing it on packages. A packaging director from Bird's Eye was in this group. Early in the meeting he expressed concern that in a store his product would likely have rim ice on it when it reached checkout. Scanning a clean, room-temperature package on our scanner wasn't typical of Bird's Eye's real life environment. So we put his sample packages in a refrigerator freezer in the cafeteria and after an hour or so we successfully scanned his rim ice laden package. He was amazed since the staff at Bird's Eye was pretty sure the light icing would stop it from working. This became another "war-story" Bill Carey told to other grocery manufacturers and chain store executives many times in subsequent grocery executive briefings.

And during one of the breaks, I asked Sylvia to show Marvin the copy of the full page letter with detailed instructions that we had sent to the person who he thought was lost that morning. This session went well with all the attendees.

After it was over I stopped by Bill Carey's office and Marvin was sitting there. We all made some small talk about the session. Bill Carey related the Birds-Eye story to Marvin. And then Marvin did something he repeated a couple of times over the years. It always meant interesting work for me. He turned to Bill Carey and said, "I thought we were going to have Selmeier measure how fast U.P.C. marked product is reaching the stores." I suppose it was Marvin's concern for the chain of command, but suddenly it was a two way conversation and I wasn't in it. Bill of course put me right back in the conversation asking me to do the task. Now all three of us could talk about what it would require.

To do the job right was going to be a lot of work. It was going to be a lot more effort than putting on a briefing in Raleigh and it defined a significant part of my work for weeks upon weeks to come. Under Marvin's and Bill's authority I was to contact Store Systems Marketing Managers and as Marvin observed, "since the marketing representatives are not currently busy selling and installing supermarket systems," hand out assignments for their store systems sales persons to meet with grocery manufacturers and get information on where each of that manufacturer's brands were along the path to source marking. If the grocery manufacturer was not already aware of our briefing program, they were invited to attend one of the U.P.C. Education sessions in Raleigh. Since it was now late in the day, I got started the first thing the next morning.

Additional U.P.C. Formats

From time to time I'd bump into Joe Woodland in the halls of Building 602. "What are you working on these days?" I'd asked curiously. At the start of 1974 the answer was the WPC or World Product Code. "What?" That's when I learned that strong interest had arisen for additional codes to be used outside the USA. It was not my main focus, but I was interested. At that point Joe was investigating if and how they could add one or two digits to the U.P.C. to indicate a product from outside the USA. The objective was to not perturb any of the "inside the USA" source marking that had already occurred or been committed to, but at the same time drastically increase the numbers of manufacturers that could get a vendor number. For existing USA vendors they would add some additional leading zeros that would be suppressed so that there was no change for existing participants in the program. But others, outside the USA and not in the original program, would start with a non-zero digit. This meant the USA codes became a subset of the World codes. That's normal, but it struck me strange that the so called "Universal Product Code" would become a subset of the "World Product Code." The universe is a subset of the world? Joe thought it was amusing too. Eventually I believe the WPC evolved to the EAN, the European Article Number.

Joe Woodland was also working on a variable weight code. All that had been specified to date was that it used number system "2" the code started with a 2, but the format after that was undefined. With Cal Gee of Supermarkets General, Joe worked to create a format that looked just like a grocery product "A" symbol except that it started with a "2" not a "0" and the last four digits was the price to be charged. Therefore it could handle prices up to $99.99. The decimal was implied. The product ID was in the digits ahead of the price and could be assigned by the store. This was for use with meat, produce, some deli and similar items that were packaged, priced, and sold by weight inside a store.

The proposal was presented using a process that IBM perfected. Instead of presentation by an IBMer, IBM would work with a different organization, often a customer, who would actually make the proposal in their own name. By consensus Cal Gee was asked to present it as a joint proposal from Supermarkets General to the Variable Weight Committee at its January meeting where it was adopted. It was not uncommon for IBM to take a background role in setting standards as there was much concern about being so prominent that other equipment manufacturers might either procrastinate on the standards setting or drag-on the implementation of the standard. And we were continually aware of how apparent dominance might look to government anti-trust departments.

IBM Distribution Industry Kick Off Meeting

In mid January I was asked to attend an IBM internal Distribution Industry workshop in Stamford, Connecticut to talk about U.P.C. Symbol source marking to the IBM Distribution Industry headquarters group. This meeting allowed the various sub industries within Distribution Industries to understand each others programs and look for synergy. Probably just as important, it allowed Paul Palmer, the Industry Director, to make sure each group was putting programs together that looked credible to a wider range of eyes in the Industry. It was a little unusual for someone with my limited tenure in the Industry group to attend this meeting, but that probably illustrates how unique the whole Source Marking advocacy that I was managing was for IBM. For me personally it provided an additional opportunity.

Taking a Day Off Drive to Boston

My father had passed less than two months earlier and now IBM business had brought me ninety percent of the way to my mother's apartment in Boston. So I declared the next day a personal holiday (something you could do 4 times a year in IBM) and instead of starting back to Raleigh, I boarded the Amtrack for Boston.

Unfortunately I only got to New Haven where something broke with the train and the railroad canceled the remainder of the trip. I quickly located another businessman and a family of three (with a strong British accent) who were traveling to Boston to let their daughter look at colleges and proposed we share in a rental car. It turned out that the family had British accents because they were from Jamaica. As we rode along, I wanted them to know that everyone was getting a price break on the cost of the car because I was an IBM employee and we were receiving the AVIS' IBM Discount. The mother popped up, "Oh, you work for IBM. Our neighbor works for IBM. Do you know him? His name is Vince Learson." I totally froze. Vin Learson was the CEO and Chairman of the Board of IBM. He would retire from the CEO title within weeks, but I didn't know that then. I had just advertised that I was using the IBM discount for a rental car on non-IBM business with neighbors of the Chairman of the Board. I thought about all this while I drove along the interstate towards Boston.

Grocery Manufacturer Source Marking Briefings

The requirement for prospects and customer briefings had unfortunately tapered off, but the demand for briefings for grocery manufacturers was unabated. By now the speakers were down to Bill Carey, myself and Jan Mosser the guest services coordinator who did the demonstration at the checkout. These meetings had a three-fold objective: a) to temper a too high fear that the printing of the bars in the symbol would not have sharp enough edges to scan correctly, b) to alert them to some critical parts of the specification manual that were very often overlooked, and c) to appropriately motivate them to get the symbol on their packages.

There were a lot of good natured exchanges between the participants. The group included grocery manufacturers, printers and packaging people. During this "get acquainted" phase of one session I overheard a grocery manufacturer position himself to his compatriots in the packaging and printing business with a little breakfast story about ham and eggs. He wanted them to know that the chicken was involved in breakfast but the pig was committed! His position was represented by the pig!

I would bring my copy of the Distribution Codes Inc three ring binder into the Red Briefing Room and tell the guests that what we were going to do is help them understand what was behind some of the information in it. I'd tell them how the bars and light spaces were viewed in the scanner's logic. In fact it was really almost impossible to misread a symbol even if there were some imperfections. Because of the cross checking logic embedded in the technology and the POS system, even severely misprinted symbols would only fail to read, not misread to a wrong value. Most of the time the technology was so tolerant even bars missing up to 20% of their width would commonly read correctly.

But there was a relatively small paragraph at the top of a page near the back of the manual that discussed color. It approximately said, "the supermarket scanner is a helium-neon laser which operates in the red frequency range." This means that the laser will see red as white and see any colors with no red in them as if they were black. The notebook recommends that packaging people obtain a Kodak Wratten #26 filter which when placed over the symbol allows a human to see the symbol the same way a laser sees it. IBM believed that if the symbol was visible looking through a Wratten #26 filter, then the checkout system would also see it. One of the first symbols picked up to demonstrate the scanner was a pack of Wrigley's Spearmint Gum which had black bars on a green background. It looks completely dark to the scanner and under a Wratten #26 filter, so it couldn't be read. We also got red bars printed on a nearly white milk carton. Red on white looks all white to the scanner and therefore can not be read. In both these examples the package appears uniformly colored, there is no differentiation for the scanner to interpret as bars and spaces.

In the fourth session this got a lot of attention. As I spoke to this point I heard an unfaltering low-voice come from out from the second row just to the left of me in the group of 30 or so guests, "Coca-Cola's colors are red and white!"

Page 124 Spreading the Barcode

The word Coca-Cola immediately catches one's attention. I quickly responded as politely as I could, "Sir, please understand, this isn't IBM talking or anything political in the industry. This is optical physics!"

"Coca-Cola's colors are red and white!" came back the patient low-keyed response.

Trying again I softly added, "Please understand, this is Mother Nature, not any company or organization!"

And again, very patiently, came the response, "Coca-Cola's colors are red and white!"

Red and White Coco-Cola package with symbol mark solution. The unpainted bars were highly reflective and therefore appeared as a black bar to the scanner.

I think I was beginning to understand! So about 10:45 am during the first demonstration when we let the guests go into the lab and handle the equipment, I got one of the other marketing people to help Jan Mosser with questions and I hustled up the hall in Building 602 to find Joe Woodland. I told him the situation which he grasped immediately. He indicated he'd get back as soon as he could. Joe then went and talked with our optical expert - Lee Dixon, and George Laurer to consider how to resolve the issue. The grocery manufacturer briefing session went ahead on its regular schedule, but about 2:30 pm Joe Woodland came back and asked to make a proposal to the group.

I believe Lee Dixon had come up with a solution. Joe described how the scanner only sees the reflected light. So if the surface is very shiny like a mirror or aluminum can would be and it also is a curved surface, it reflects the whole beam off, still as a coherent beam, in some other direction than towards the Photo Multiplier Tube reading device, the device that collects the light. There would be no diffused light some of which might be picked up by the light collector. This is equivalent to absorbing all the light and would look to the scanner like it was a dark bar. When the beam crosses the shiny part, it puts no light back into the light collector so it looks black to the scanner system. Painted and paper surfaces scatter light in a diffuse pattern some part of which does get back into the scanner's PMT, Photo Multiplier Tube. But, unpainted shinny surfaces on the can reflect all of the laser beam's light away in some direction other than where the light is collected, i.e. it looks like the black bar.

That was the birth of using unprinted shiny areas to represent the bars on the aluminum cans. We had found a way for Coca-Cola to source mark their soda cans and still only print red and white. Their representative at the meeting thought that might be acceptable.

In February, Marvin was in Bill Carey's office again asking how the U.P.C. survey was coming. As we talked, it was clear we needed to have some measurement of each item's unit sales volume to weigh the impact of the date input of specific products in order to obtain a useful general projection. There was a well known market research company that provided an estimate of this, a division of Time, Inc. called SAMI, Selling Areas Marketing Incorporated. SAMI paid supermarket chains to get their warehouse item movement details and then sold the aggregated information to grocery manufacturers. Marvin indicated that he'd see if SAMI could be convinced to help us. A short time afterwards I received a call from IBM DPD headquarters in White Plains with a name and a telephone number of someone at SAMI to go see the next time I was in Chicago.

Outside U.P.C. Talks

In addition to our own seminars IBM was getting requests to provide speakers about the U.P.C. to various packaging industry meetings. I was the one sent to talk. I had reduced the "How the U.P.C. is scanned" and "What to remember when you are adding a U.P.C." pitches to a dozen slide presentation. Over a 6 month period in early 1974, I spoke at six different outside meetings ranging from a few dozen to over 1500 attendees. One of the larger conventions was a Packaging Institute of America meeting at the O'Hare Hyatt Hotel. I was on the program with Al Hildebrand, CTO of Spectra Physics, a company that made the complete scanners it seemed everyone else was attaching to their electronic registers to be in the U.P.C. scanning business. He had a portable laser in a less than a foot long tube that he pointed around the room and gave a talk about bleeding edge laser technology breakthroughs. My talk centered on the U.P.C. scanning issues. After our talks I was running to catch a flight back to Raleigh and jumped in the Hyatt's airport shuttle. I was surprised to find him also jump into the shuttle behind me. He asked me why the IBM scanner moved its beam at over 10,000 feet per second when the others were successful at a much slower speed. That was new information to me and I told him so. When I got back to Raleigh I mention his name and that I had shared a ride to the O'Hare Airport with him and found that he and Larry Questad had known each other in the past, likely at Stanford University.

When I asked the engineers about the beam rate, they indicated it had to do with the particular lissajous sine wave pattern used by IBM. I never tracked it farther than that. I knew enough about the technology to market it. I wasn't going to be engineering it or even evaluating the engineering of it. Not an uncommon attitude for an IBM DPD Program Administrator. It wasn't unusual that IBM marketing people focused their comments on the implications for the customers while other vendors focused on the newness or the impressiveness of the technology. It also wasn't unusual that the IBM marketing people didn't have much depth into the details of the technology.

Marketing Practices Reviews

I should mention that all presentations I gave to people outside of IBM were vetted by the Data Processing Division's Marketing Practices group in White Plains. In my case that was often Anne Compton. Executive Briefing presentations were also reviewed by Marketing Practices to ensure that any competitors were referred to fairly and factually, there was no advocacy of an IBM position based on the size or position of the company in the industry, no IBM proprietary information had inadvertently been included and would become known outside the company, and a plethora of other marketing practices that IBM enforced. Once approved however the marketing people simply talked to the charts, not the exact words that had been approved. My speaking presentations also had a lot of commonality with each other, so that you might think that I could get it approved once and it would be cleared indefinitely. No, evidently the corporation saw each of these talks as independent presentations or there was enough variation that Marketing Practices was not willing to provide a blanket approval such as they did for the executive briefing material. Even after the fourth or fifth time of faxing the visuals and text of the talk up to White Plains, Anne would change something, an adverb or an adjective. For the most part it was just part of the process. I knew the material and simply spoke to the visuals in the presentation, just as you would in a customer briefing.

Additional People

Tomlin's supermarket group added an additional technical person who had been a systems engineer, Jim Rafferty. It fell to me to train him about our group, but his being there permitted me to focus more on marketing activities.

Training on the Store Loop Technology

By the start of 1974 IBM management had their eyes focused on the Store System products. This was a more publicly visible market for IBM and IBM was very sensitive about how the product would be accepted. Our Industry Market Support Group pro-actively conducted branch office training sessions. I remember going to one in Chicago as the technical resource in late February of 1974. I enjoyed marketing the U.P.C. source-marking and scanning at the supermarket checkout more, but I still had technical education responsibilities. The other direct marketing people talked about checkout function and special features, it fell to me to handle objections that

Chapter 7 Uncovering the Challenges   Page 127

prospects had with the system. And there were several. One of the technical concerns was the communications link between the registers and the store controller. The U.P.C. symbol was scanned and decoded to the 11 digit Universal Product Code for each scanned product. The Product Code then had to be transmitted to the store controller to obtain the price, tax status, food stamp status, etc. Prospects had a hard time understanding how a controller and a 2400 baud communications link could keep up with 10-15 registers on a busy day. And to make matters worse, if there was a failure in the store's controller, the backup plan was to manually dial up a "sister-store" which had all the item codes, prices, etc. for both the local store and an assigned backup store. There was a separate communications unit with each controller for handling communications to the headquarters and to the sister store. The controller that was dialed was to handle price lookup for both stores on a 2400 baud communications link.

Data Processing professionals just couldn't understand how it would be fast enough even if it worked. The reason for the disbelief was that people naturally thought in terms of the way communication protocols had run up to that time. You'd expect the controller had to talk to the first active register, then to the second, then to the third and so on with a small delay to let any signals on the line die down before the register at the other end replied that it had successfully received the message. Think of a busy Saturday with all the lanes going, 3-6 people in line, and you can understand the customer's fear. If the controller had to also do this for a remote store, they felt it had to slow their service down.

But it did work, just not the way people thought. First, instead of running separate wires from the controller to each cash register, IBM ran a single loop of wires around the store and attached each register to this one loop. It worked because IBM had changed the protocol so that each time the controller communicated along the loop it communicated with all necessary register terminals in a single pass. There was information for all the registers looking for a response in each outbound message. Every register at the failed store that needed a price look up, requested that price look up on the same input request. Every register that needed the print line back with the item description, price, taxability status, etc, got it at the same time.

It's easiest to think of it like a train. The prior protocol, and the protocol probably used by our competitors, was to make the store controller a sort of round house and send an engine with the freight car of information out track 1 for a register and then return with the receipt acknowledgement, change to the track 2 for register two and send the engine and so on. Getting requests for prices, etc might require sending an empty engine out to the register to see if anything was ready. Each track was handled in turn and all active tracks had to be handled before the first one could operate a second time.

The whole communications protocol and physical configuration was changed in the both the Retail and the Supermarket systems from the common point

Spreading the Barcode

to point or computer to computer technology common at the time. Replacing separate tracks or wires to each register was a double loop, only one of which was commonly used. For our product IBM called this the supermarket loop or sloop. The engine would start down the track pushing a bunch of freight cars of information each destined for a different register terminal. As the train went by the register, it took off its information freight car from in front of the engine and let the other information cars through. If the register had a request or information for the controller, it added that request information car behind the engine. Thus the new IBM protocol serviced all the registers in just slightly more time then the prior protocol would have serviced only one. Many years later one of the development people from that time observed that we were inventing a LAN, but didn't know it.

That was how we presented it to IBM Store Systems field people. My only problem with the presentation was that I had to do it as the last topic on the day's agenda. There had been many questions and discussions. Prior presenters had gone over their allotted time and things were running late. I think it was 5:30 pm, an hour late, when my turn finally came up, but I was determined that these field people were going to understand how to handle the objection of communication speed. At that point no one wanted to know about the choo-choo train, but I was determined they were going to learn anyway. So I covered all the material and then I paid the price. The reward for my over-determination was several months of razing in the Midwest region. You can be sure I didn't repeat the offense when we taught that same class again a week later in Los Angeles.

Estimating U.P.C. Source Marking Time Table

Before leaving Chicago, I went over to the Time, Inc offices overlooking the Chicago River. I was given a 2400 foot reel of magnetic tape with national item movement summary data by manufacturer, by brand, and by size on it along with the data format to be able to pick out the movement information I needed. I think I also had to keep the fact that I had been given the tape a secret for a reasonable time. On the trip back to Raleigh I drafted a short APL program that would sum up all the sizes into brands and brands into manufacturers if I needed that. I wasn't a programmer and probably could no longer have programmed the task in Cobol or PL/1, but I found APL to be mentally stimulating, funky, and fun.

APL is a very unique and special language developed by Ken Iverson. It used a lot of special characters, italicized Greek alphabetical letters each of which represented highly functional commands. We used to joke that you could write a single line just a few inches long in APL and re-create the operating system.

We didn't have any computers in our building that I knew about except the IBM 1130s still being used as store controllers and development machines,

Chapter 7 Uncovering the Challenges Page 129

but we did have IBM 3270 terminals connected to mainframes at Research Triangle Park and to the HONE system. HONE was IBM's continent wide network for field personnel. Someone took the tape and had the data put up on some computer that I could access from a terminal in Building 602. I keyed in my APL program into my own workspace on the same machine.

With this data I had the ranking by unit volume of every product from all major Grocery Manufacturers. Procter & Gamble was the largest in the country with about 2.5% of all item movement out of chain warehouses. I remember calling my brother, Dick, who worked in P&G's Package Soap and Detergent Division's advertising department to find out "How can I get P&G to implement the U.P.C.? "You know" he responded with a little incredulity, "make a business case to the advertising people." Years later I was to learn that my brother had a central role in adding the U.P.C. to P&G products since he was responsible for changing packaging to reflect P&G's reformulations to bio-degradable chemistry going on at the same time.

I identified the top 87 grocery manufacturers and where they were located. Eighty-seven may sound like an strange number of manufacturers to select, but it resulted from picking the manufacturers that had a product among the fastest moving products according to the SAMI information. We had a very good estimate on the movement of all their brands. I called the Supermarket Store Systems Marketing Manager covering each manufacturer's headquarter location and, if they hadn't already, I asked the manager to send someone from his staff to talk with each manufacturer to see if they had a date that they would be adding a source marked U.P.C. to each of their packages and currently where each brand-size was in the implementation process. This required listing out each brand-size for all the products that the manufacturer made.

From the many conversations with the grocery manufacturing people coming to our U.P.C. education briefings, we had already developed a credible time schedule for how long it would take before products appeared in the store by knowing where it was in the sequence of events required to change packaging. We listened to many manufacturers discuss the average wait in the manufacturer's warehouse, the average time for receiving new packaging materials to get into the packing process, the time to get material printed after being approved, the time to get art work done, test printing and management sign-offs, the time to clear out existing inventory, the time in the chain's warehouse, etc. We needed to know the start time for doing artwork. The whole process sequence might take 6 months to complete, but it was generally tied into something else the manufacturer needed to change on the packaging and no manufacturer would just start changing all their packaging at the same time.

Store Systems salesman were not so super busy that they couldn't go talk with packaging people in these companies and identify where each brand-size stood in the process. This worked well even at companies like Procter &

Spreading the Barcode

Gamble who asked, "Which King Size Tide? We have five King Size Tides, one for each water type in the USA and there is a small mark on each box to identify which water type it is. So there are 5 different packages for each brand size with the only difference being a discreet identification of the water characteristics." We collected 5 answers for each brand-size at P&G and other places where that occurred.

Reports came back about some manufacturers that considered this information as too privileged to share. Our possibly incorrect presumption was that they didn't have a good story to tell and therefore decided not to provide information. For those companies we positioned them at the longest lead time which would only make our final summary more conservative than real life. The preliminary results of those responding looked like source marking was running ahead of where the original industry time-table would have put it.

Early U.P.C. scanning tests required much additional labor to put adhesive labels on items so that they could be scanned. Note the number of people.

Source Marking Significance

Getting the U.P.C. symbol to be part of the retail packaging was critical to the success of the program. It was much, much more costly to put on a label in the store. In initial tests, stores spent many labor dollars putting adhesive U.P.C. labels on products to see what happened at the checkout, but it was much more costly than simple price marking:

- the label was physically larger,
- it required larger applicators than price marks,
- it required more discipline to do it without error,
- and when the label was put on, it typically covered up some message on the package that either the customer or the manufacturer did not want covered up.

Added to that was the fact that the location where the label was applied would change from one labeling session to the next which impacted the productivity of learning how to scan them most productively.

Without source marking there could not be a successful conversion to U.P.C. scanning checkouts.

U.P.C. Coupon Code

At this same time Joe Woodland and Bill Carey let me know that my old friend, Barry Franz from Procter & Gamble, was coming to Raleigh and asked me to pick him up the next morning at the airport. Barry was coming to talk with IBM development about support for the coupon symbol. Number system 5 had been reserved for coupons, but the exact implementation of how it would work was as yet undefined.

I met him about 8:30am at RDU, the airport in Raleigh. Barry was upbeat and yet serious about how the manufacturing industry had only supported the U.P.C. project because they wanted help from the checkout systems to make sure that vendor coupons were only accepted when the item had been purchased by the consumer. It was suspected that the manufacturer's coupons redeemed by grocery chains came from many more "unofficial" sources than just customer checkout. I knew that matching coupons to items in the order would not be possible in our system since we didn't keep the item codes separated by register. There was only one item movement file for the whole store. While each order was being rung up, only order subtotals were maintained at the register and at the controller. Nowhere did the system have the list of item IDs identified by customer, which I thought would be needed to police the acceptance of coupons. It would take a complete rewrite of the code to do that. I let Barry know that I thought it would be a difficult thing for us to provide, but left it to the development division to decide how they might accommodate the request. I talked with Joe Woodland afterwards and as I suspected, Barry had left frustrated that afternoon.

Progress on Random Weight Symbols

A standard had been achieved for the variable weight data format. With scanning systems to install at SGC and Steinberg's, IBM was concerned that meat weighing and packaging equipment would not be available to provide readable variable weight symbols at the stores. And possibly there would not be any printer manufacturers making printers for the equipment that packaged meat, and other variable weight items in the store. IBM explored developing a label printer to sell to scale manufacturers. During a discussion in one of our offices we learned that Paul McEnroe, the engineering director for store systems, was an acquaintance of David Allais who was starting a company called Intermec to make portable printers. McEnroe was informally talking with him and indicated he would keep in contact with Intermec. If needed Paul possibly could introduce them to the scale manufacturers. That seemed a better plan than making our own. Additionally we planned that Paul and I should visit the major in-store scale manufacturers, Toledo Scale

Page 132 Spreading the Barcode

and Hobart, to determine their ability to provide U.P.C. symbols at any stores that installed scanning checkouts.

Paul had his staff arrange for the visits. In a late March we made a visit to Toledo Scale in Toledo, Ohio. They were already talking with Intermec. Lou Koewler was the Manager of U.P.C. systems for Toledo Scale and indicated they had the engineering changes to their meat scales well underway. Clearly neither IBM nor Toledo Scale had any authority over what happened in each other's company, but as we both were interested in participating in this market, we were both interested in having the other company think of us as a good associate system whenever we would be installed in the same store.

The second visit was in June to Hobart in Dayton, OH and that included a pleasant surprise. Hobart Scale had started corporate life as part of the Computing-Tabulating-Recording company, the company that Tom Watson Sr. had renamed to International Business Machines in 1924. When we arrived we were welcomed in grand style like close family that had been out of touch for a few decades and were just reunited. The Board Chairman joined us for lunch. Everyone wanted to look cooperative. The result from both these trips was that we were comfortable that there would be meat packages with symbols when scanning systems were installed in stores. But much had happened in between the two trips.

P&G Visit

I received a request to meet from Dick Forberg, Director of the Industrial Engineering Division at Procter & Gamble. He had originally hired me into the Procter & Gamble Company. In April I sat down in a 9 am meeting with him and Adrian Boie, one of the managers working for him who had handled the manufacturing focus within Industrial Engineering when I was employed there. It was great seeing them again! Mr. Forberg was always the statesman. Tall, thin, and wearing thin rimmed glasses he looked like the statesman. After a few minutes of pleasantries Mr. Forberg got right down to business. He wanted to know how successful IBM had been in marketing the scanning systems. He told me he had a weekly scheduled briefing with Ed Artz, then CEO of Procter & Gamble, on the status of U.P.C. scanning stores. They were aware and concerned that acceptance might not be very good. He indicated that P&G was spending considerable resources to implement the U.P.C. and if the industry was not going to accept U.P.C. checkout scanning, they needed to consider the implications. He did not make clear what those considerations might be. Although it was conceivable, I wasn't given the impression that that meant they would stop U.P.C. source marking of P&G brands.

But I was trapped. I really wanted to share with him what I knew, but I also knew full well the IBM policies on not providing sales or internal projection numbers. I had been told second-hand that Paul Palmer had signed up for a $52 million sales projection of store systems in 1974, but like it or not, I saw this as privileged information to be kept inside IBM. And besides it would take an enormous increase in sales acceptance to actually achieve that figure in 1974. So I told them both that I needed to respond carefully to respect my responsibilities to IBM and also to Procter & Gamble. I told him IBM was disappointed that the industry response had not been greater. "But" I told him, "I've seen no reduction in IBM's commitment to make this program a success." As evidence of that I pointed to the commitment we were making to grocery manufacturer education. The company was still adding marketing representatives to field store systems offices. And we had engineering working on changes to the product itself. It probably wasn't the hard numbers he would have liked, but I also believe P&G continued their progress to source mark unabated. At least Mr. Forberg saw that I was still very committed.

Personnel Changes

Maybe it was Jim Lightner's long recovery from his accident, but in April we had another reorganization and I was working directly for Bill Carey again. This re-organization also saw Dean Lyles join the Store Systems Market Support Center to head up the IBM 3650 Retail Store System side. And both Dean and Bill now reported to Tommy Tomlin who reported to Marvin Mann in White Plains who then reported to Paul Palmer, the Industry Director. This was good for me because I again had some direct marketing support responsibility. I was given the Boston and Chicago Regions. Bob Doremus handled from NYC/NJ south which included Supermarkets General's Pathmark store in Plainfield, NJ. I had upstate NY based on how IBM laid out its sales regions. Essentially everything north of the cross Westchester Freeway and the Tappan Zee Bridge was in my area.

It was about this same time that Joe Henson moved on from being the Director responsible for many of IBM's Industry Marking units including Paul Palmer's Distribution Industry Marketing. He was replaced by Dick Tarrant who very quickly came to Raleigh and began interviews with each of the direct marketing support people to get more specifics on what was going on.

Dick was a short bundle of energy that had recently come back to DPD from GSD, the smaller systems division headquartered in Atlanta. His move to this DPD position was not characterized as a promotion but this was not uncommon in IBM. We had a saying that it paid to be nice to everyone who appeared to be in a lateral or descending career in IBM management because you will likely come across them again when they are on their way back up. Some careers sort of yo-yoed.

Page 134   Spreading the Barcode

IBM 3660 Challenges

The IBM 3660 Supermarket system was an excellent technical systems solution to the store level systems requirement, but on the application level it was quite behind the products being offered by NCR, ESIS, Datachecker, and everyone else. IBM system level software and communications software was far more stable then what was offered in competitive products at that time. The physical packaging had innovated in interesting ways, for example IBM was the first prominent cash register manufacturer to separate the scanner, keyboard, printer and display into separate packages. But the IBM development process was still driven by a legacy of internal management that paid the most attention to technology management. In this case the IBM product was failing for lack of function in the area where the customer usually provided it; application software and the user interface. IBM's cash register competitors were accustomed to providing code at the application level and frankly had a more responsive development environment.

Traditionally IBM's application level support had all been with field personnel working more closely with customers. But, in this instance the field personnel were not involved in the development and engineers were off in a cocoon in Raleigh NC. Our department was the link from the field to the development process and frankly we were not adequate. Market Support Center personnel were not present in the day to day operations of the prospect's grocery stores. The communications link for requirements was too long and too linear between the developer and the user.

Prospective customer reaction bubbled up through the store systems sales person and sometimes his manager, to the headquarters marketing person assigned to that area and then generally to the troika, who bubbled it back through engineering managers to the people who actually did the work. And all along the way explicitly or implicitly the reaction was getting prioritized along with all the other activity on the development schedule. It was informative, but too unresponsive. Sometimes the field managers, in addition to the field sales persons, would talk to the direct marketing people. And sometimes the field managers would talk to their headquarters marketing management and to the Market Support Center, but it was still a slow link with few threads and the process tended to dilute the urgency of the message.

Ralph Converse took his different tack to make sense out of the poor response from the market. Ralph kept talking about the "Mating Dance." Ralph repeated his great analogy of the ritual that tarantulas go through prior to mating where they circle each other, avoid getting stung and eventually mate. He saw the lack of interest as a process of IBM and the supermarket industry getting to know each other better. The slow response was only a ritual that had to be completed. It was more than that, but Ralph's enthusiasm did help keep the motivation level up.

The lack of success, or rather the unfortunate lack of firm commitments, was now a significant concern to IBM senior management. Paul Palmer, the Industry Director, had been asked to have a review session each Monday with IBM CEO, Frank Cary, about what had happened in the program the previous week. We were now under the microscope and that's not where you really prefer to be. Bill Carey told me that reports about the grocery manufacturer briefings were a frequent topic at these meetings since it was a part of the program reporting positive results. We conducted 15 to 20 of the grocery manufacturing briefing programs over the course of the year. Over 450 people from manufacturers, the packaging, and the printing industry attended. But the biggest complement I heard for this program was when Bill Carey called me into his office to tell me Kroger had ordered twenty-five IBM 3660 Systems and appended the note, "your systems are deficient in function and capability, but we believe we owe this order to you based on your support and commitment to this industry standardization effort." I'm certain with a caveat like that attached, IBM never considered that those systems were likely to be installed and likely never credited them, but to have written the note was a great complement for our efforts with grocery manufacturers.

IBM Recognition Event

In late March of 1974 I was asked to go to New York City in support of an IBM awards program where they were going to recognize George Laurer for his work in creating the U.P.C. along with other IBMers. It was to be held at the Waldorf Astoria. IBM liked to demonstrate the Supermarket system at these types of events, since it was pretty self-contained, very demonstrable, newsworthy, and interesting for the attendees. I was there to assure it came up normally and that we had a demonstrable set of items to scan, answer questions, etc. I had committed to speak at another packaging meeting in Houston the following day, so I was going to leave the IBM event as soon as the pre-award exhibit time was over and fly out of Kennedy Airport for Houston.

Memorable Flight

God bless my secretary. She noticed that I was leaving after 9 pm and booked me first class. IBM did not approve of flying first class, but in those days the night first class fare, in effect at 9 pm, was the same as the day coach fare. So if you flew at night, you could often go first class without any criticism.

I was in the first row window seat with an empty seat beside me when a very, very large black man with a large Afro hair style got on. I'm not proud of it, but I hoped he wasn't going to sit next to me. He walked back. After several more boarded, the sportscaster Sal Marchiano of WABC-TV boarded with a professional camera crew carrying their cameras in their hands. After takeoff

Page 136 Spreading the Barcode

and the seat belt sign was off, there was a commotion behind me which ended up with a cockpit officer going back and resolving it. Now I was getting curious and flagged down the flight attendant. "What's going on?" I wanted to know.

It turned out George Forman returning from a successful defense of his Heavyweight Championship in Venezuela, was sitting in the last row of first class. The camera crew was from WABC-TV in New York and they wanted an interview that George did not want to provide. He was preoccupied with his mother's poor health. Delta Airlines may have told Sal and his crew that George was flying coach, so that they purchased coach tickets. The flight officer came out of the cockpit to enforce the rule about coach passengers staying out of first class.

After it was settled, George was happy. He was trying to get to Houston to see his mother who had taken ill and was hospitalized. The officials in Venezuela had not allowed him to leave until he paid the taxes on the winnings from the fight and the fight didn't pay him till several days after it was over. So, he couldn't leave Venezuela to get to the hospital. He still had a lot of yellow currency in his wallet which he showed to us in first class.

The plane made an interim stop in New Orleans on the way to Houston. At that point Sal came forward and declared he would keep after George until he got an interview. So, George agreed and they went back to the seats across from the rear galley on the 727. After 4-5 minutes of interview the sports news crew walked off the airplane and up two gates to a flight headed back to New York. When we got to Houston, I was first off since I was in the first row. All the way up the concourse were the camera crews and reporters. What an unfortunate situation for someone trying to get to his mother's hospital bed. But, I think Delta got him off the plane and into ground transportation without his having to go up the concourse.

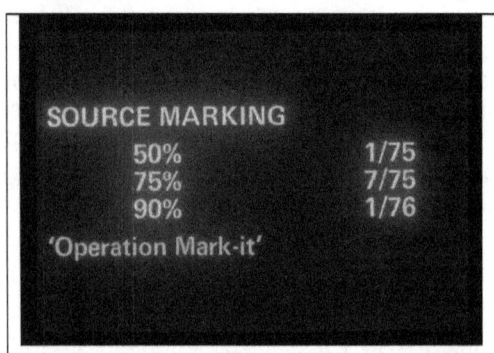

U.P.C. survey results for traditional manufactured grocery products.

Projecting U.P.C. Source Marking

Late in the first quarter of 1974 I was getting quite a few returns back from the visits IBM store systems people had made on the larger grocery manufacturers. As the data came in, I'd put it into a huge matrix that my APL program could analyze. The matrix identified the stage which each brand-size was at among the steps normally required to add a U.P.C. Symbol to the package and the date. We had good averages for the times required to do artwork, get the package printing done, get redesigned package material into the packing cycle, the delay through the

Bill Selmeier presenting the Source Marking Projection Results in the Red Briefing Room

manufacturer's warehouse flow and then the delay through the retail warehouse flow, before it first showed up in the store. The law of large numbers covered up the differences between organizations. We wanted an accurate but generalized result. The fact that Supermarkets General's Pathmark division could turn a grocery warehouse an unheard of 72 times a year was to their credit, but not handled any differently in our calculation. Fortunately almost every brand-size was identified somewhere on the path. There were a few items where the artwork had not been started yet, but some estimate was given for when it would start. All in all it was roughly a 6 month process for each package.

It began to sink in to me what a unique set of data we had built up. I was able to create a graph of projected amount of U.P.C. source marked symbols in the stores on a flip chart. I nicknamed the project "Operation Mark-it" because I liked the double entendre of the "Mark-it" word. Twenty to thirty minutes on this subject was quickly added to the standard list of presentations given to executive supermarket guests. Although the number

Page 138   Spreading the Barcode

of Supermarket Executive Briefings had declined drastically, I was now part of every session to talk about U.P.C. marking.

Consumer Issues

The second quarter of 1974 also saw the rise of consumer concern about removal of the price marks on merchandise in stores with U.P.C. scanners. The original McKinsey studies showed a healthy cost savings for not having to apply individual price stickers on each item. The IBM 3660 was designed with a 38 print position receipt so that a descriptive name for each product could be included for the consumer. Historically mechanical cash registers printed a less than six character department name on narrow paper.

The concern as described in the news of the day didn't make sense to me. It characterized consumers as concerned about how they would know how much they had paid, if there was no price mark on the item when they got home. To my thinking, how would the consumer know the price paid last week when the container with the price mark was thrown out in the trash after the product was consumed? And secondly, wouldn't it be easier to save the cash register receipts which would last for weeks and weeks versus at the best searching through shelves to find an item purchased earlier? Of course some other manufacturer's key entry systems converted to scanning systems had not provided for as wide a print out and couldn't put alpha characters on the receipt.

This issue was coming from some group other than consumers. Consumers were only the vehicle for raising an objection. One possibility might be the retail clerks union. I'd heard that Carol Forman, the head of NOW which was leading the protest, was married to an officer in the Retail Clerks Union. We believed that no checkout clerks would ever lose their job because of scanning. First, except in very desperate business situations, stores generally never had to terminate checkers to reduce staff. The supermarket checkout clerk is a high turnover job. Store management would not need to terminate anyone. They could simply attrite the positions. Simply not replace the clerks who were leaving until the whole force got down to the level they needed. Also the checkout position is mostly a part-time labor force. Management is free to adjust the work hours within a wide range to accommodate any improvements in inherent productivity. I believe what the union saw was going to happen was that the total number of union dues-paying retail clerks was probably going to shrink. That may have prompted unions to promote this issue as a consumer issue.

Larry Questad was delegated the fun of handling this issue and it was decided that IBM would work with Giant Foods who was represented by Esther Peterson, Giant's Vice President of Consumer Affairs. Esther had been the consumer advocate in Lyndon Johnson's administration and was well known in political circles. Larry's assignment meant that Giant had two direct marketing people from the Market Support Center in Raleigh involved in the account. Bob Doremus was not really happy about it, but accepted it. Larry relished the opportunity.

Doremus was slightly older than the other direct marketing people, had salt and pepper hair and liked to discuss the factors that impacted people's careers. He was a great observer of people's careers, which may have indicated he was very focused on his own. Being just a little bit older can present challenges. People talked of getting behind the power curve. You had to hit certain job assignments or positions by certain ages or going to the heights was no longer an option. Bob may have felt that. As a "professional hire" I had a little of that stigma too although Bob would never have said that to my face. Bob would sit and talk for half hour or more about the realistic opportunities for advancement of anyone in the department up to and including Dick Tarrant. He was much more sensitive to career options than I was. Jim Sanderson, Bob's previous Marketing Manager from Houston, joined the Market Support Center and assumed the competitive analysis function. Bob was the first to point out that Jim wasn't going further in his career, if you came to this job from a Marketing Manager's job. But, Bob was easy going. He recognized and articulated issues. Unfortunately he left taking action to get them resolved to others. He was quick to smile, a very likeable guy who eventually went back to Houston to become the Senior Salesman for the Coca-Cola Foods account.

Because of all the press, the Chairman of Giant Foods was called in front of a US Congressional Committee investigating this supposed new threat to America's consumers. At one point a congressman told the Giant Chairman that he was investigating this threat of the U.P.C. program thoroughly because he was responsible to the American people and had to stand for re-election every few years. At that point the Giant executive observed, "Sir I and my company must stand for re-election every day. My customers vote with their feet and at any time they may choose to go elsewhere"

Spring 1974 Road Show

There was a fortuitous chain of commitments for that demonstration unit used at the Waldorf Astoria. The system needed to be in St Louis in April and then in Dallas for the SMI show in May. In between those commitments, we could locate it in cities to help salesmen who had trouble getting everyone in their prospective accounts to Raleigh for a marketing briefing. We conducted a road show in New York where salesmen could bring in more local customer personnel to see the checkout in action using the equipment that had been used at the award event in New York. Then the system went to Chicago where it was displayed for several days in mid-April. Then it was forwarded to St Louis where another road show was held for local grocers.

Exhibiting at 1974 IBM Annual Meeting

IBM holds it's Annual Meetings in April. In 1974 it was held at the Chase Park Plaza Hotel in St Louis, MO. The Supermarket System, because its function was more understandable to the public, was exhibited along with a few other portable systems in a lower exhibit area. Everything went pretty normal for an exhibit. We shared observations talking with shareholders that viewed the exhibits before the meeting. During the meeting we had the exhibit area to ourselves. About the time the meeting concluded on the main floor, I wanted to get something from my room before the exhibits re-opened. I jumped on an empty elevator on the lower level where the exhibit area was. The elevator started up and then stopped at the first floor lobby level and in walked Tom Watson Jr., Arthur K Watson, their sister and Vince Learson. They continued their conversation about something that had gone on in the meeting as if no one else was there. I said nothing, the proverbial fly on the wall, and got off at my floor while they continued up.

The 1974 SMI Show

From the IBM Annual Meeting I was going to my first Supermarket Institute annual convention. The Supermarket Institute or SMI (later called the Food Marketing Institute or FMI), always held its annual trade show in Dallas in early May. Larry Questad coordinated IBM's participation and it was our biggest trade show event of the year. Every competitor would be there as would the hundreds of other exhibitors who sell things to the Supermarket industry. Samples were everywhere. You could eat your way across the exhibit floor! The show was held at the Dallas Convention center which enclosed its covered parking garage and turned it into a two level exhibition space. IBM bought a large booth and planned a demonstration of two store controllers and two checkouts. During the demonstration we would simulate the failure of a store controller and then demonstrate how a failed store could contact the other store's controller and continue checkout after only a small delay, with checkout continuing from the exact point in the order where the store controller failure occurred. Initially my biggest role was to take my U.P.C. Source marking projections from "Operation Mark-it" and print up little cards with the info so that IBM representatives in the booth could provide their prospects with the latest and most accurate projections of source marking penetration over the next 18 to 24 months. It turned out because of all the work by IBM salesmen calling on grocery manufacturers, the projections were almost "dead-on." IBM got a nice positive reaction in the industry since we were the vendor with concrete numbers and making projections that could be verified as time went by.

But we were going to have more fun. With our exhibit professionals, Caribiner, we built a stage, positioned the equipment as if in two separate stores, and practiced a script demonstrating backup over and over. Two phones on the stage simulated the phones in each store. We knew that the telephone numbers of phones we were using had to be kept secret because the telephone switches in those days did not hang up until the calling party hung up. If the first person didn't hang up and the second person picked up his phone to call, the original connection would still be there. We had several practices up till about 5 pm on Saturday afternoon. (SMI shows always started on a Sunday, I suspect because Sunday through Tuesday was the slow end of the week for supermarkets.) We were done for the day and just discussing dinner plans when one of the phones on the store controller rang and none of us had called it. Jan Mosser picked it up and heard a voice, likely a competitor's voice, say, "Hi, I'm taking you into backup!" That was very bad. If someone called one of those numbers during the show and just didn't hang up, our demonstration skit was over. Bill Carey looked at me and asked if I could get it fixed.

I called AT&T. I identified myself as an IBM employee at a trade show where we had two phone lines critical to our exhibit and where the numbers had been discovered by outsiders. "Could I get two new numbers right now?" It was 5:30 on Saturday night and by 6:30 that night we had two new numbers. The program went off from there without a hitch, but we were much more aware of what people looked at in our booth. We also hired security for the night hours and counseled them about not letting anyone near the exhibit.

Then we went out and really did have fun. We'd go to dinner in big groups, tell tales about the day and then often go dancing. This was my first experience as an exhibitor and I found the constant interaction with each other and with prospects very exciting.

The major Electronic Checkout vendors had an understanding amongst themselves that they would stay away from each others' booth during the exhibit hours. But in the hour preceding and following the exhibit hours when attendees were gone and only exhibitors were allowed in the exhibit area, reciprocal tours between vendor's booths could be arranged. When NCR, RCA and ESIS came to the IBM booth we would demonstrate the equipment and provide copies of standard glossy brochures. The competitive spectators only saw the outside of publicly announced equipment – the same as they would see if they walked into a store with the equipment installed. This accommodation had several useful consequences:

It kept competitors from being in booths during the show exhibit hours and possibly overhearing some conversation with your customer that you'd prefer the competitor not overhear,

Since most of the booth staff would participate, the after hours visits provided a wider set of eyes on competitive equipment than possible if only an identified competitive specialist tried to get information. And, It reduced misrepresentation of competitive equipment since it put all vendors on notice that they had been briefed on the equipment and if or when something was misrepresented by a competitor, it was more likely their malicious intent since they had been provided accurate information.

It gave the presenting vendor insight into what his competitor might be spreading around about his equipment since the questions the others asked often were thinly disguised attempts to find weaknesses in the presenting vendor's equipment.

Paul Palmer's boss, Dick Tarrant, whom we called the Super Director since several directors reported to him, also came to the show with Paul and Marvin and more people from DPD Headquarters in White Plains. Dick was not going to be there for the entire show so Larry Questad was picked to give Dick a tour of the show which meant they walked in the aisles by each competitor's booth, From the aisle outside the booth Larry pointed out the significant features, announcements or applications of each system. It went smoothly until they arrived at National Semiconductor's Datachecker Division's booth on the lower level. As Larry Questad told it, because only he (very stocky and muscular, a gold medalist in track at the 1968 Mexico City Olympics) and Dick (short, business like) were there, they were recognized as IBMers before they got to the booth. Fred Bialek, (medium height) the General Manager of Datachecker deciding to challenge them, rushed out of Datachecker's booth and blocked Larry and Dick's way up the aisle. In a loud voice he declared that he wanted them to leave. Larry of course protested that any attendee could walk the aisle, but Fred kept shouting to leave and blocking their path. Larry looked back at Dick pulled back his right arm after making a fist and said, "Do you want me to deck him?" But Dick quickly indicated that they would just leave.

The end of the show saw the first instance of what was to become an annual activity. There were many hundreds of exhibitors at the SMI show. All of them display their products in their booths. At the end of the show, generally in the last hour, it becomes a free give away as booth people are willing to give away the sample display items to avoid shipping them back home. That of course only applied to vendors selling products for resale in grocery stores such as Foster Grant. I picked out a nice pair of silvered lens aviator glasses that I made it a point to replace each subsequent year. All-in-all that SMI show was just about the most exciting event I'd experienced in IBM. I didn't really want it to end, but of course it did.

IBM Industry Education

Two weeks later I found myself going to Ed Igler's Advanced Grocery Workshop in Chicago as a speaker to update the attendees on marketing the U.P.C. Scanning Point-of-sale Equipment business. After being the attendee for so many years while on the Kroger account, this was an interesting juxtaposition.

Product Observations From SMI

At this show it was clear how our competitors focused on key entry automation promising the option of adding a scanner later. IBM management recognized the market could get away from IBM while we waited for the U.P.C. symbol to work its way through the pipeline to the store shelves. IBM came to believe it needed to provide a key entry system with legs that would appeal to grocers, a low end store system or LESS.

Ed Igler from internal announcement article

Call at Wetterau

Late in May there was a hastily scheduled technical call on Wetterau Foods. Dick Malek was alarmed about the IBM 3660 communications technology. He couldn't understand how the system could possibly support 24 check lanes without even considering backup. Bill Carey asked Gordon Vick and me to accompany him on a late afternoon flight to talk with Wetterau. Remember, I was the guy who presented the choo-choo train at the IBM internal kick-off meetings. We were met by the store systems sales and systems engineering people and headed out for an evening call at Wetterau's offices. Dick had a few of his people with him. As soon as we got past saying hello, they got more and more intense about how Wetterau couldn't possibly install anything with as crazy a communications scheme as the IBM 3660. We tried to go into detail about the technology, its architecture, and why we felt it was adequate. They were not buying any of our logic and reacted like we were insulting their intelligence. Voices raised, faces reddened, It was as confrontational a customer meeting as I've ever been in. I'd have to say after an hour and a half, we hadn't made any progress. We finally left feeling that it was a lost cause.

Ralph Converse Promotion

Ralph Converse received a well deserved promotion to Marketing Manager in the Chicago Store Systems office managing the salesmen on grocery accounts. Ralph had been in Raleigh for years before I arrived. As others in that original group also had, he contributed immensely to the products current position and certainly deserved this new job.

Weekend at Nags Head

Bill Carey was a good guy and often invited parts of his staff out to a condominium he owned at Nags Head, NC. When I was first interviewing for a position in Raleigh, Bill mentioned that it was one of his hopes that I could provide an air service from Raleigh to Nags Head. His condo was probably less than three miles from Kitty Hawk, exact site where the Wright Brothers made the first heavier than air flight. He invited me and my wife with Larry Questad and his wife, Liz, for the weekend. The complex Bill's condo was in had a tennis court and many of the IBM staff, including Bill loved the game. There were several spirited games on that court. Following that we went over to Jockey Ridge, a large sand dune that offered Hang Gliding. Well, as a former private pilot, I felt I could do this and it would be an interesting experience. I went to the area where they signed people up. I was the only full sized male adult signing up. Most of the others were in their early 20's or younger and also smaller. We received a 15 minute training course on how to get strapped in and the principles of rogallo winged flight. Then we carried our hang glider to the top of the ridge and with a running start stepped off. Seemed easy enough, but it turned out I was not well matched to the lifting characteristics of my particular Hang Glider. My flight may have been more reminiscent of a torpedo shot than a glider gracing the sky. I ended up not far from the ridge, nose first in the sand and swinging forward and back in the three strap harness that kept you attached to the Hang Glider. The sand was going forward and back about 6 inches below my face. The instructor was quick to arrive and indicated it was often harder for pilots to fly a Hang Glider than non-pilots since the controls are reversed. Push forward to go up in a Hang glider while you push forward to put the nose down in a plane. I didn't want to explain to him that wasn't the whole problem. There was a lot more weight to the problem.

We all had fresh soft shell crab that evening cooked as prescribed by Larry. And the next day was fun. Bill took all of us somewhere where we could rent sailboats. For some reason he had all the women with him on the dock and Larry and I were out in a boat on our own. At some point Larry and I disagreed on how to set the sails for a broad reach. Then it got crazier with the two of us yelling at each other. Our wives and our boss were standing about 45 yards off on the dock. Bill might have told the women, "Leave them alone and they'll work it out." He did and we did even though I still don't agree with Larry about it!

DCI Gets U.P.C. Projections

In early June I was contacted by Distribution Codes Incorporated, the new name for Distribution Number Bank. They had heard about the information IBM had provided on U.P.C. source marking projections and wanted to understand it for themselves. I made a one day trip to their offices in Washington, D.C. They were impressed at the documentation and the effort IBM had gone to facilitate source marking.

Herb Rippe's Last Visit

My old friend, Herb Rippe, a passenger on the second trip across the US to Los Angeles in the Bonanza and the individual who wanted me to invest with him in a ferro-cement sailing boat, attended a class for Retail System Marketing people. As noted earlier Herb was an excellent navigator of ships, a ham radio operator, and an investor in penny stocks. He was sitting in my family room and he was unhappy with the TV reception. Next thing he was saying, "Get me a ladder. I can fix this." In less than five minutes he was up on my roof reorienting my antenna and he did improve the reception. Then he told me about this great sailing trip he had planned, leaving from Ft Lauderdale on a chartered yacht with an SE from the branch office and two people from his account, Federated Department Stores. That was to be the last time I ever saw Herb. It would be a year before I learned that he sailed off from Ft. Lauderdale, a week early, without updating his pre-filed sailing plan, in a fiberglass boat without a radar reflector, he had no radio transmitter, and into one of the busier shipping areas around. It was two weeks after his departure, a week after he became overdue, that anyone even thought to go look for him. He and all aboard had been lost at sea. Months after it happened, people discovered that all those who were with Herb and Herb himself either were divorced or about to become divorced. Strange, and tragic isn't it?

Direct Market Support

My direct marketing support areas did have some activity. In Chicago, Dominick Foods had ordered a system to eventually test scanning at their Morton Grove store. In Rochester, NY, Wegmans had ordered a system for their Fairport store, and Stop & Shop in Boston also ordered a one store test system eventually ending up in a Quincy, MA store. I found it mildly amusing that because of delays in the Launch Account program installations at Giant Foods, Kroger, and Ralph's, the three stores in the two regions I covered could install about the same time as the key accounts, but with only standard branch office support – nothing special. My first action was to call the Store Systems salesmen and ask to come visit them. Of the three salesmen involved, the only one I had previously met was Paul Sved who covered Stop & Shop. In late June I arranged to visit with Paul Sved in Boston to discuss all the sales activity and Stop & Shop specifically.

Paul had a litany of issues where the IBM 3660 didn't meet Stop & Shop's requirements. At this stage I could only document his list of issues and promise to get back to him. The whole Stop & Shop installation project was so seriously delayed, Paul felt there was no point to going to the customer as the store had not yet been selected. Since I was pushing him to visit a customer, he arranged for a call on First National Stores.

An article in Food Processing discussing implementation of the U.P.C. with input from us and some of the participants in our Grocery Manufacturing

Spreading the Barcode

Education briefings in the spring prompted management in White Plains to suggest broadcasting the better than expected news about the progress in U.P.C. source marking in a press release. I met with some of the White Plains industry staff, IBM public relations people and I put the release together in July of 1974.

The first three days of the fourth week of July was spent participating in an IBM 3660 installation workshop in Chicago. Dominick's, Kroger, Fleming, and Loblaws had some U.P.C. scanning equipment on order and additional chains had systems without scanners on order. The installation workshop was designed to keep everyone focused on getting each work item completed. Where necessary we were updating the project management network based on field sales and systems people's experience. I ducked out on the fourth day and went to Poughkeepsie to teach at the Grocery Industry Applications Class.

Early U.P.C. Symbol on Quaker Oats product

Quaker Oats Invitation

The first week in August Bill Carey informed me of a special request from the Grocery Manufacturing Industry Marketing and IBM's Midwest Region. Quaker Oats was a competitive account with Honeywell equipment. IBM had been trying to win it over for some time. Now the IBM marketing team thought they had something that Quaker Oats wanted. U.P.C. Education was something that Quaker Oats wanted to know about. Quaker Oats was asking for someone to speak about the U.P.C. at their National Sales Meeting to be held at Innisbrook near Tarpon Springs, Florida in early October. But first I had to travel to Chicago to meet with Bobby Shehorn, the Supervisor of Sales Training. The Quaker Oats headquarters was located on one or two floors of the Chicago Merchandise Mart. It actually was a very quick meeting and arrangements were made for me to be on a morning agenda focused on the sales channel, namely distribution and grocery retailing. I asked them what they specifically wanted to focus on, and they said they wanted to know most about how the U.P.C. would affect their relationship with grocery store managers.

Direct Market Support

The next day I was off to Toronto to present the IBM 3660 system architecture and backup technology to Dominion Stores as part of their more extensive branch proposal to the account. From there I went on to Montreal to the Steinberg's store to see first-hand how the system was being accepted by customers, checkers, and store managers. All these early installations had to do significant in-store labeling to get the amount of scannable product up to an acceptable level. IBM could not expect mass installations under these conditions. The IBM 3660 system was not as "key" friendly as ESIS, for example. To do it accurately, it took more store labor to put on U.P.C. labels than was required to put on price labels and the U.P.C. labels were more expensive than price labels. Although the projection of the percentage of items source marked fit actual observation, it simply wasn't enough to make widespread implementation of U.P.C. scanning look attractive to grocery retailers at that time.

U.P.C. in-store labelers used when source marking was low. The required number of labelers was so many, and people intensive, most grocers could not afford it and elected to key in the item price.

My first visit to Wegmans in Rochester, NY, a small to medium sized progressive chain of larger than average sized stores was much later than it should have been. Wegman's was experimenting with adding premium boutique sales areas and non-traditional grocery merchandise to their stores, The Store Systems Marketing Representative, Erik Lunkenheimer, was upbeat although he recognized the product had issues. His customer typically pioneered new technology. They had already installed ESIS in several stores and believed they had seen improvements in checkout speed using its unique keyboard. Yet they believed they could do better with U.P.C. scanning and were committed to using it. At their headquarters near the airport, I was introduced to Bob Wegman, the CEO and founder, and his son, Danny. We also met with the people doing the checkstand design and those preparing the message to their shoppers to explain the new system.

Page 148 Spreading the Barcode

The following week I returned to Boston. Stop & Shop had decided to install the system in key entry mode. Paul Sved and I sat down with his systems engineer and discussed all the things that needed to be completed. We went to Stop &Shop's offices on Boston's Wharf and met the checker trainers.

I got to the airport early and had time to kill, so I went to the American Airline's Admirals Club at Logan Airport to wait in a more comfortable environment. I found myself watching the TV with one other man who appeared a little disheveled and stressed out. He commented, "Man, am I beat! In the last week I've been in Omaha, flew to Egypt, then to New York, back to Paris, now I'm on my way to Los Angeles."

"Who do you work for, that wants you to travel like that?" I asked sort of incredulously.

There was a moment's hesitation and he replied. "I work for Sugar"

"You mean Amstar?" I asked.

"No, Sugar," he responded.

"You mean Domino, the Amstar brand?" I persisted. I felt with my U.P.C. work I was at least aware of all the grocery manufacturers.

Then I learned that he worked for a privately owned company that was one of five groups which controlled the distribution of sugar all over planet earth. The five families had divided up the globe geographically. His family's area covered Africa and the Middle East. He insisted that arrangements such as this were in effect for each of the basic agricultural commodities. The more I pressed for a name his only response was that the groups like to keep their anonymity. I never got an answer.

The following week I traveled to Chicago to meet the Dominick's Food sales team and get more up to date on their plans. It was quite a different situation. Where Erik was free wheeling with the highest of expectations for expanding success, the Chicago Dominic team was button down professional. Reserved, they maintained decorum with the customer. Of course Dominick's was a very different customer. This wasn't upstate New York where you just went out and did it. This was cosmopolitan Chicago.

Dominick's was designing their own checkstand. I was shown to an unused cold room that was to be where the new system would be initially installed for test. The salesman and I went out to see the Morton Grove store which is where the system would move to when things were ready. The Morton Grove store was an impressively merchandised, slightly larger than average, grocery. After meeting the store manager, viewing the checkout area, checking on the scale equipment, etc. we headed back to their headquarters and warehouse. Dominick's warehouse and general office was located in facilities they had purchased from Kroger. I didn't make any comment that I had been part of the Kroger National Account team in Cincinnati. I met their project manager, Ron Nuti. Ron was just getting acquainted with what was going to have to happen to make the installation successful. In the lunch room I met and sat next to Marv Hoffan, Dominick's CFO. I remember him commenting that "there are economies in delay. You follow?" I gathered the store wasn't going to be installed on the original schedule. I was most interested in getting as many stores installed and operational as possible to make this transition to a new way of checking out publicly visible. Although the system would ship on schedule and IBM collected its revenue, I wasn't excited about test installations in a warehouse.

First Shipment to Wegmans

It was just a short time until the first system was going to ship to Wegmans. They might be the first normally ordered IBM 3660 system to be installed. Wegmans, that relatively low-key chain in upstate New York, was going to show all the high news image chains how it was done. Or were they? I got a call from Erik Lunkenheimer, the store systems salesman, about a problem the day before the system was supposed to ship from Building 602. The IBM 3663 Checkout Terminal had an optional check franking station which the SE who worked with Erik had evidently thought was a standard option. Eight lanes of registers were configured wrong, without the check franking station, and were just about ready to ship when the issue was caught. My first temptation was to ask Erik where he had been and how he had let this get this far. Didn't his branch do a systems assurance review on this just to make sure such problems didn't occur? He may have responded with something about not killing the messenger just because I didn't like the message.

And he was right. Across the hall from the Market Support Center the manufacturing crew could be boxing up the units as we spoke. They were so excited to be finally building something. Luckily, as I went in, I found the foreman and all the units essentially completed on a roller conveyer waiting to be boxed. I tried to explain to him about the mistake, but initially he wasn't buying it. He was quick to pull the order paperwork from the file cabinet and show me where it was clearly specified to use the covers without the slot for check endorsing. The printers were configured to cross over two stations, the receipt and journal tape stations, not three which added the insert station for franking checks.

His instincts were good. He wanted to treat me the same way I had responded to Erik. But my case finally came down to: OK you can ship these boxes as built, justify it with the paperwork you were given, and get them back in two weeks unopened to modify by adding a check endorsing slot and printer station. Or, you can pull this right now, start the modifications and I'll get you covering paper work as fast as I can and explain why it didn't go out exactly as scheduled to whoever you want.

Sane heads prevailed. He called over some people to take the units off the line and start the rework. My follow-up conversation with Erik was that he better have paperwork in the administrative system within a half hour so the changes came through to manufacturing by the next morning and this accommodating foreman wasn't left "slowly twisting in the wind" for changing the order configuration without paperwork. Getting out a new product is always fun.

Those register units, two store controllers, and the scanners shipped the following week to Rochester, spent a relatively short time in the warehouse site so that Wegmans could validate checkout and store cash procedure manuals, and became the first normal commercial installation of the IBM 3660 to go live scanning at the store in Fairport, NY just outside Rochester, NY. It was the third system to be in a store following the development contracted systems to Pathmark in Plainfield, New Jersey and the Steinberg's installation in Duval near Montreal, Quebec. And, this customer was totally spending his own money to do it. He was real! This was real business! Erik and I would become very good friends! And in all honesty I was very proud that the first IBM commercially sold system was installed in my area of coverage and installed without any special headquarters emphasis that the launch accounts of Giant, Kroger, and Ralph's were to receive when they installed. (The development test beds at Pathmark and Steinberg's were not sold by the sales department and may have been under different contract terms.)

I'm sure the biggest reason for our success in Rochester was Bob Wegman's absolute commitment to make scanning work and thereby be an industry leader. His faith and commitment was the driving force. Supermarket News may report more about Ralph's, Kroger, and Giant, but Bob Wegman was getting it done.

Direct Market Support

In mid-September I was back at Dominick's with Jim Rafferty, the Market Support Center's technical resource for Chicago. By now the proposed checkstand had been constructed and was located in that out-of-commission small cooler. The problem was it barely fit. This was a very wide checkstand and it filled the width of the room to where it felt like only one person could pass along either side of it. It looked huge. I left Jim Rafferty at the warehouse with the field technical person. He had come to Chicago with me to help on the systems work, They were working with Ron Nuti's team. The salesman and I went to the store and probably talked about things over lunch.

When we got back to the warehouse, we discovered everyone had had an exciting time. Unknown to the IBMers at the start of the day, Dominick D'Amato, the CEO, had decided to look at the checkstand and the word went

Chapter 7 Uncovering the Challenges   Page 151

out inside the company. The result was a "command performance" with 20 to 25 managers in attendance. Coincidentally, there were some IBM engineers from Raleigh there applying patches to the controller software. They and Ron Nuti's staff just moved to the back of the room when all the Dominick's executives and managers began to arrive. So there everyone was, waiting for Dominick.

When he came in, his reaction was disgust. It was way too big and looked unworkable. But instead of just leaving, he took to banging on it. Anything that was not closed or fastened, he would hit. The display was simply resting on the top of its support pole. He knocked it completely off with the back of his hand so that it was hanging by its cable when I saw it later. The whole thing was a shocking and emotional experience for the engineers, one that may have made them happy to do most of their work on IBM premises and let sales people visit the customers.

Jim Rafferty was still talking about it as we arrived back at O'Hare for the flight to Raleigh. As soon as the plane lifted off, meal service began. He and I were among the first to be served the typical salad, chicken and rice followed by custard. Somewhere around the end of the salad, the pilot announced they were experiencing something unusual with one of the engines, but instead of turning back to O'Hare, they would proceed to Louisville and see if the problem could be fixed there. Jim and I were able to finish dinner, but after the mechanics checked the engine they said they couldn't fix it that night. Fortunately, there was another plane at Louisville that we could change to and continue on. Because very few passengers ever got the meal they expected, everyone was given a meal ticket to use at any restaurant of our choosing. We had already eaten and decided we would use the meal vouchers to take our wives out to dinner a few days later in Raleigh.

The fourth week of September was my first visit to Wegmans' after they received their equipment. They participated in a "U.P.C. User's Committee" meeting that week. This was also an opportunity to accompany Erik Lunkenheimer to brief Dick Kunze of Flickengers on the U.P.C. source mark and IBM 3660 Supermarket program. Wegmans' equipment was still in the training center, but plans were in place to move it to the Fairport store.

Page 152 Spreading the Barcode

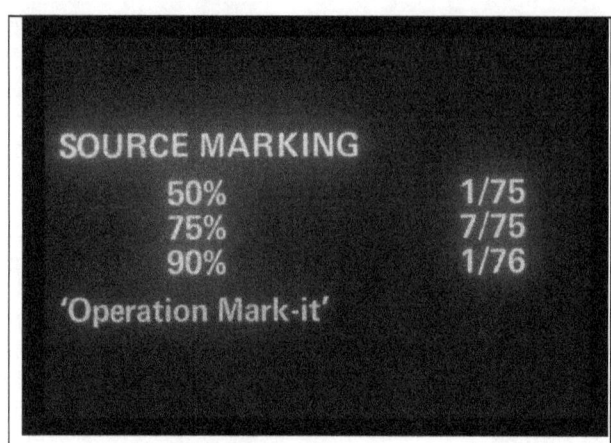

Slide used in Grocery executive presentations after SMI in 1974 and Project Mark-it reported its results.

Source Marking Task Force

I was back in Raleigh a day before departing for White Plains to participate in a Source Marking Task Force. Frankly, I understood the reason. IBM management visiting grocery retail accounts would hear that the industry simply could not install scanning systems unless there was more than roughly 70% of the items source marked. The "Mark-it" projections said that the aggregated amount should be about 50% by near the end of 1974, several months off. That was simply not good enough with the high costs of printing and applying special U.P.C. labels or the cost of checkout in an environment that was half scan and half key. And the keys on IBM systems could only be grocery, meat, or produce. Because of competitive offerings, the industry considered 5 to 9 and maybe up to 15 different departments were required to manage stores. Facing the above information and a weekly review session with Frank Cary, IBM CEO and Board Chairman, it was only natural that management in Distribution Industries felt it had to create a task force to resolve the impasse. Fortunately, carrying the preponderance of data from our surveys and matching it to information gathered from Supermarket's General's Pathmark store since then, the group ended the day sort of understanding that the transformation was in motion, but changing the momentum to make many, many thousands of source marked products appear faster would be near impossible.

Appraisal

Somewhere along this time I had another appraisal. I was back to being evaluated as a "2" performer which was good. In the final part when the manager is to make observations on how the employee could be even more successful, Bill Carey suggested that I lose some weight and get a "rug." Maybe I saw that as a challenge, but I replied, "Bill, this company is run by a short, fat, bald man!" And it was. Frank Cary. I wasn't upset at all by his comment, just struck by the contradiction.

Quaker Oats National Sales Meeting

In early October I was picked up at the Tampa Airport in the Innisbrook Jitney. Quaker Oats had set aside a separate condominium for me. I had contact information for locating Bobby Shehorn. When I reached him I

Condominiums at Innisbrook near Tarpon Springs, Florida

found the formal meetings were over for the day and the salesmen were in a break period where they could be golfing, fishing for Tarpon from charter boats, or I supposed, just relaxing. That night there was to be a western theme cookout outside in one of the large parking lots. I was to eat with the Chairman and CEO of Quaker Oats. Bobby gave me instructions on how to get to the cookout and the time it started. When I arrived I found they also had a western hat and a bandanna for everyone. The Chairman was quite interested in the impact of the U.P.C. We talked for 30-45 minutes over dinner about how the U.P.C. might impact the information base at various levels in the grocery industry, from store to warehouse to merchandising to top management.

The next morning I saw that I followed something on their program called "The Distribution Game." Basically, that was a game invented by Quaker Oats to humorously illustrate the real life challenges of getting product to the customer. On a large screen video portraying a TV game show were two teams with names like Krunchy Krackers and Snappy Snackers competing with each other. Each team had a warehouse manager, traffic manager, sales manager, and financial manager. The TV Host would challenge the teams with a problem, e.g. "Your full rail car for a major customer has been quarantined on a siding in Indianapolis because of a rat infestation. Will you: 1) Expedite a truck shipment from the warehouse for $12,000, 2) locate a pest control house in Indianapolis to handle the problem and the car arrives 2 days late for $6,000, or 3) Return the first rail car to the warehouse, schedule and load a second rail car for delivery 5 days late for $2,000, or 4)..... Each team would pick its answer. When the host revealed the answer, there would of course be other consequences, e.g. "Krunchy Krackers picks 2,

Page 154 Spreading the Barcode

locate a pest control house. (Sound of loud buzzer) OH NO! The pest control house takes an extra day to find the rail car. The shipment won't arrive for another 3 days. You customer's purchasing department is asking for damages because of the delays." It was great fun. And most impressive, when the attendees walked out of the meeting that morning, they each were handed a three foot by three foot physical incarnation of the Distribution Game to take home. Quaker Oats had one for me too.

My 30 minute presentation was not quite as animated as the Distribution Game, but I went into some detail about the information captured in checkout systems, using the IBM systems as a reference but recognizing there would be differences between vendors. I pointed out what would be well documented within a few years, how, since these systems kept item movement in close to real time, there would be a lot more information available about merchandise plan effectiveness and possibly the correlation between different products in the plan. Up to the time of the U.P.C., the grocery manufacturer's sales person often had the information advantage in suggesting ways to improve sales in the store. Grocery Manufacturers simply invested more to get the information by purchasing Nielsen data, SAMI data, collecting it themselves, and other sources. Now for less cost the Grocery Store manager could potentially be equally informed. This is a partnership opportunity for both salesman and store manager to work for the best all round arrangement. (Of course, that was implying significant organizational change and new information flows within the typical Grocery Retailer.)

When the meeting ended the sales people headed off for fishing or golf. The coordinators told me I was free to join either, but I happened to have relatives I hadn't seen in several years living about 12 miles north in New Port Richey, Florida. The Coordinator immediately handed over the keys to a rental car and told me to keep it as long as I needed. So I surprised, well after a phone call, my relatives and they and I had a good afternoon. Late in the afternoon the Jitney took me back to Tampa Airport. But Quaker Oats continued to surprise me. Around Christmas 1974, I was to receive a package from them with a note again thanking me and including some additional items that had been given to the Quaker attendees which I had not previously received. Bill Carey just told me that in my thank you letter back, I had to tell them to stop sending things. I was going to violate the $100.00 rule which was that no IBM employee could receive more than $100.00 from any outside organization per year. IBM was quite serious about their employees not getting lobbied for any purpose. But how could you not like an organization that treats you as well as Quaker Oats did?

Outside Source Marking Talks

The following week I received a call from Ed Igler asking that I present my U.P.C. source marking material to the IOMEC User Group meeting in

Chapter 7 Uncovering the Challenges   Page 155

Montreal. IOMEC was the user group for one of the original companies to build a portable in-store data capture device commonly used to walk around and input products to be ordered. I asked him why should we, as IBM, be talking to what was at some level a competitor's user group meeting? Ed responded that he thought it was important to support the industry. I didn't see this at all, but Ed was pretty strong that this should be done and he did have a lot more time in IBM and IBM Industry Marketing than I did, so I agreed to make the talk. It followed the now very well established procedure of drafting what I'd say, having my secretary type it up, faxing it up to the Marketing Practices group in White Plains, and then going over it about a day later with Anne Compton after she had an opportunity to read it herself.

Having received her blessing that all the "t's" and "i's" were in the right place, I jumped on the plane for Montreal. I was to be the first speaker the following morning. I walked into the room and located the meeting coordinator to introduce myself to learn how the meeting was going to flow. Then I looked out and noticed three or four reel-to-reel tape recorders sitting on the tables in front of attendees. I asked the coordinator about this and he just indicated they were probably press people who were also invited to attend. Oh no, I did not want to be doing a press briefing. When it came to my presentation and I was being introduced, I looked out and each of those tape recorders was moving tape. I stood up, looked down at the text approved by Marketing Practices and read it top to bottom exactly as it was written. It wasn't the most fun speaking experience, but it may have been the most concise.

I was delighted to board a flight connecting to Cincinnati where the Packaging Institute of America was holding a regional meeting, hopefully without tape recorders. I had my standard presentation of what was significant in the U.P.C. and why the industry was so interested in seeing it happen. Also by now we had moved my mother from Boston to Cincinnati where my brother was still with Procter & Gamble. I spent a night with her prior to returning to Raleigh. But, I was back only one day before returning to Chicago to participate in a Flexographical Technical Association meeting.

Spreading the Barcode

Chapter 8 First Steps in the Real World

I wasn't there that first day when Wegmans' Fairport store re-opened with scanning checkouts. That was an oversight I wouldn't let happen in years to

Wegman's Fairport NY store that received the first IBM scanning system to be purchased and installed without special assistance.

come. I later appreciated the importance of a vendor showing the depth of his commitment to events like these. I'm sure it was a gala event and it was mentioned in Supermarket News, but it didn't shake the industry like it deserved. Even by the end of the month the only stores checking out customers with U.P.C. scanning were Wegmans in East Rochester, NY and Ralph's in Los Angeles, CA. I was very aware that one of the two IBM stores installed, the one installed with normal customer support, was in my direct market support area.

The Source Mark task force would report its findings on November 8th. I traveled to White Plains to participate in that. The Task Force suggested re-announcing the Project Mark-it results and committed to creating a flip chart presentation. Even though the number of symbols was growing in stores across America and was pretty much on track for the projections we had made, it still was a long way from seventy percent of the items checked out. It still was a common comment by grocery retailers that the lack of full source marked U.P.C. symbols was an obstacle to installing scanning systems. Not only were U.P.C. adhesive labels expensive to purchase, they were more labor intensive to apply and manual application was not uniform as to location on the package. That led to slower checkout. This issue just kept blocking sales. Our reaction was to ask these chains that used this objection how the source marking implementation program was coming on their private label brands. Some were doing a credible job, but many discovered they were part of the problem.

IBM Share Meeting in Los Angeles

Mid-October Bill Carey got a request for a speaker at the IBM Share Conference, an IBM user group, to take place in early November at Disneyland in California. The talk would be about the state of U.P.C. Source Marking. I was asked to do it. I soon discovered an excellent travel promotion being offered by Eastern Airlines. For cross country round trips, if you originated on Eastern Airlines and returned on Eastern Airlines, you could travel through Mexico City doing the intermediate legs on Western Airlines or Mexicana. And if you chose Mexicana, they didn't appear to care how many times you got on or got off as long as you kept moving towards LA. What a great vacation idea. Although I was getting a lot of travel, my wife had stayed pretty much in Raleigh where she had friends, but that's not the same. So we were able to leave Raleigh on October 26th and travel to Mexico City. We started with a packed couple of day's sight seeing in Mexico City. I'm a Central American Indian culture enthusiast and I learned from my guide that sometime later I really needed to go to the Yucatan Peninsula. We continued on for a day in Guadalajara, and then two more days in Puerto Vallarta. I loved Puerto Vallarta and was very disappointed to learn you were not allowed to purchase ocean front property unless you were a Mexican citizen.

Finally we arrived in Los Angeles on November 3rd. It was a great experience for my wife and good to be able to get away together for a little while. Ray Balsley was the coordinator of the session for Distribution Industry Marketing Headquarters. When I entered the room for the session where I was speaking, the first person I first saw was Dick Malek from Wetterau Foods. Dick may have asked me if I was going to talk about the choo-choo train and I promised I wasn't. Ray introduced me with his stock, "Bill is here from IBM's Headquarters Store Systems Market Support Center where the 'rubber meets the sky'" introduction and it brought the laugh he was looking for.

These Status of Source Marking presentations had evolved from that single chart when they were first introduced into the Raleigh briefing portfolio. Fortunately, it was now becoming apparent to all in the industry that the projections were close to what was happening in real life. That made it easier to accept the projections that eventually extended up to over 75% source marking for scanning stores in 12 months or by the end of '75.

U.P.C. Source Marking Presentations

The middle of November found me back in Cincinnati talking with 80 members of the Cincinnati Art Directors Club. These weren't Art Museum types, these people did package and advertising designs. The following week I was with the Print Services Quality Control Society of America. I had stopped being surprised at how many different organizations included people who prepared packaging.

There was one surprise. I had had all the grocery manufacturer briefings to myself. But in November I was surprised to find that the Chairman of General Foods was in Raleigh and being briefed by Larry Questad. Bill Carey never explained why this one time he did not chose to come to me, but maybe Larry explained it. Larry had recently told me that he had been put on "Executive Resources" a special program intended for employees being groomed for high level IBM executive positions. Larry explained that there were five individuals targeted for each executive position in the company who each had five individuals targeted for their position who each had...and so on. Each of these identified people would be on Executive Resources. This was all planned in advance to make changes in personnel as smooth as possible. I accepted that if Larry was on Executive Resources, this would be an excellent opportunity to add an appropriate executive contact to his vita sheet within the company.

Checkout Productivity Challenges

Almost as soon as stores started scanning at the front checkout in the fall of 1974, a new issue for U.P.C. scanning stores was becoming evident. As much as everyone expected the systems to be productive, somehow they weren't. In the stores that had installed scanning systems, they were not able to remove the amount of checkout labor hours that had been anticipated from the schedule. This was a major issue since justification for the whole program, going back to Larry Russell's studies at McKinsey, had been primarily predicated on reducing front-end checkout labor. It was the major rumor in the halls. Store Systems Marketing Managers were calling Bill Carey and raising this as the issue with the product and the whole program. Tom Wilson who had absorbed Larry Russell activity for McKinsey was reporting he was getting inquiries about it. It was to become a major issue.

Key Entry Systems

But IBM had additional serious issues. One of the large ones was how well competition was succeeding in installing key entry systems with a promise they could be upgraded to U.P.C. scanning at a later date. Every store that

NCR or Datachecker installed in Key entry mode was a store eliminated from a potential IBM system until the store's next remodel many years down the road. IBM recognized they needed a lower cost system and development was working on a lower cost, less capable controller that would use the same register. Thereby allowing IBM a competitive alternative to the NCR 255 system or a National Semiconductor Datachecker key entry only system. Jerry Cogdill was doing the leg work on this with Bill Carey. By the end of November we had reached some consensus with development on the potential forecast. Agreement on the forecast allowed for amortization of the development cost, a very large part of the system cost.

Direct Market Support

I got an unusual, surprising but interesting call from Dave Goliber, a host side IBM salesman in Albany NY. His customer was Golubs, an eastern upstate NY food chain. He promised that if I would come to Albany, he'd meet me and let me drive his new Datsun 240z. I would have come anyway, but what an original approach! I arrived in early evening and he met me at the airport. We went to my hotel and then I went with him to his home where he gave me the keys. I did take the car and tried a few country roads, but then went back to his house and had him take me back to the hotel. What a guy!

In the morning we went to the branch where we discussed an off-site planning session he was arranging with his customer executives in the Laurentians region north of Montreal in Canada. I didn't meet with customers, but did visit some stores to see how they operated. His marketing manager would be participating in the session and the branch manager was not going but would be keeping informed since the branch was footing the bill. This would be analogous to the planning session that I was on with the IBM Kroger team several years earlier except this one included the customer and probably was run with more humane hours.

At the time for the session, I traveled to Montreal and drove up to the Margarette Station chalet which they had reserved. The chain was operated by the Golub family, many of whom had been educated at the University of Michigan as I was. I believe both Neil and Bill Golub went to Michigan and we almost started with a round of "Hail to the Victors!" The Golubs had started moving into larger, more broadly marketed super stores named Price Chopper. They had noticed that other firms making similar store changes had at least talked about experimenting with U.P.C. scanning. I was there to provide first-hand information on experiences that others had had, the effort involved, and some of the results achieved. I was only needed for the first few days, during the environment definition phase of the plan. When it got to their host computer application action items, I traveled on to Rochester to watch checkers at Wegmans' Fairport store scan U.P.C. symbols to check out customers. From there I went to Boston to document an issue Stop & Shop was raising about coupon redemption.

U.P.C. Source Marking Seminar

There was one more trip to make in 1974, a speaking engagement at an AMA-run seminar on "How the U.P.C. is scanned," another in the series that had started in New York City 13 months earlier.

> 1974 ended with five IBM 3660 U.P.C. scanning systems operating as the checkout in a store and three more operating without scanners. There were additional "test" installations in chain offices and warehouses but those are not really visible. We had announced the system fourteen and a half months earlier.

Installed Scanning Stores

By the start of 1975 IBM scanning stores included the initial Supermarkets General Pathmark store where DPD, the marketing division of IBM, would assume contact responsibility at the end of the development division's test. The development division conducted these tests to ensure that the IBM 3660 operated in a real life environment the way it was expected to operate. If that wasn't necessarily the way the customer expected the IBM 3660 to operate, getting that changed was more the responsibility of the IBM marketing division in negotiations with the development division. The development division now known as SCD, or Systems Communications Division, was broken up into business units one of which was store systems. Bo Evans, the Vice President who led the IBM presentation to the U.P.C. Symbol Selection Committee and had actually earlier been the IBM Vice President of Development that sold Tom Watson Jr. on doing the IBM System 360 development, was the Business Unit

Dominick's Morton Grove Store at dusk

Manager. Scanning with the IBM 3660 system was live at four accounts: two of the three launch accounts, Giant Foods and Ralph's, (Kroger had not installed in a store) and in Dominick's Morton Grove store and Wegmans' Fairport store, the last two accounts were my responsibility for direct market support. Additionally, Stop & Shop did install in a store, but without scanners. I relished that half the operating scanning systems were in my area and they got there without the "launch" designation.

Midwestern Kickoff Meeting

The year started with a quick trip to Chicago to attend the Midwestern Store Systems Branch Kick-off meeting. Joe Powell, the Store Systems Branch Manager who previously had been the account manager on Kroger in the mid to late '60's, hosted it. Joe quipped as he looked out the meeting room window at the smog, "I won't breathe any air I can't see!" He made a heroic effort to keep the situation upbeat. Ralph Converse was there as a Marketing Manager. Ralph doesn't let any challenge get him down: Charlie hustle. This was also the point at which I started getting interested in documenting what these stores looked like so others outside their local area could see scanning checkouts in operation. I had recently purchased a Canon A-1 camera for myself and began carrying it on all trips where I'd be near an IBM equipped scanning store. I shot some scenes inside Dominick's Morton Grove store while in Chicago.

Checkout stands for electro mechanicals at Dominick

Direct Market Support

Travel was getting crazy. The next week I took my "Operation Mark-it" flip charts to Chicago for local presentations to customers on Source Marking on Monday through Wednesday. Wednesday afternoon I went on to New York to discuss Operation Mark-it with the staff in White Plains and then traveled to Cincinnati to handle the U.P.C. variable weight questions in a meeting between Kroger and Hobart Scales before returning to Raleigh on Friday. The following week found me in a similar meeting, this time with Steinberg's and Toledo Scales in Montreal. Traveling back through Boston I joined the Store Systems staff in a briefing for Purity Supreme, a regional chain. The last week of January I participated in IBM's internal Supermarket Workshop in Chicago.

Some time in January the group started its focus on processing the information from scanning systems. That was the Grocery Information Planning System or GRIPS.

U.P.C. Source Marking

Procter & Gamble invited me to come to a dinner in early March. I received a call from Dick Hurst, a fellow University of Michigan alumni, who was employed in P&G's Advertising department where he got sample packaging and promotion materials for market tests prepared. He indicated that P&G was asking more than twenty of their print and package vendors to come to a dinner meeting at a hotel in Northern Kentucky between downtown Cincinnati and the airport to learn and discuss their U.P.C. strategy under the sponsorship of the local chapter of the Lithography Association. Would I come and put on my U.P.C. tutorial? Deciding this did not take long. P&G is two and a half percent of all item movement in the U.S.? Sure I'll come! Although I was quick to agree, as luck would have it, I almost missed it. Actually, I should put part of the blame for almost missing it back on P&G since, as their employee, they first trained me to leave for the airport at the last possible minute in order to get more accomplished at the office.

It's wasn't real simple to get from Raleigh to Cincinnati by air. P&G's schedule was to have a social hour at 6 pm followed by dinner and the educational session starting at 7 pm. The only reasonable arrangements I could find was to fly from Raleigh to Washington National on Eastern Airlines and then catch a Piedmont flight to Cincinnati after a two hour layover. I would arrive at the Cincinnati airport (which is in Kentucky) about 6 or 6:15 pm so I should be able to get to the hotel in time for my tutorial. I started for the airport at my usual last moment, but then decided to stop at a photographic materials supplier for a Wratten #26 filter to show the people that evening. The clerk was busy with a previous customer and consequently the timing got unbelievably tight. I got to the airport, left the car in the lot, ran through the terminal and down the open breezeway concourse to Gate 1, where my Eastern 727 still sat facing the gate area. But there was a not so gentlemanly person in front of me almost screaming at the agent and demanding to be boarded. The steps were away from the plane, the aircraft door was closed, and it looked like the Eastern agent would be happy if this passenger facing him never flew Eastern again. It went on for a few more minutes until the other person stormed off in a rage. By now the 727 was rolling off the ramp area and down to the end of the runway.

The gate agent turned to me and asked what he could do. "Well" I calmly replied, "that plane was supposed to take me to Washington National, where I was supposed to catch a Piedmont flight to Cincinnati, where I'm supposed to give a talk tonight." He reacted instantly taking me to the front ticket counter and looking through his airline version of the Official Airline Guide. He found an Eastern flight in thirty minutes that went to Atlanta with a 13 minute connection to a Delta flight that takes me back to Cincinnati. He overrode all the systems to get me booked. I mentioned that Eastern and Delta were at opposite ends of the airport and I knew there were carts that went up the concourses. With all that I was carrying, a large case for flip charts, hanging garment bags, brief cases with slide carousels, I asked if one of those carts could meet the flight and help with carrying all the materials. He called back to Atlanta and indicated it wasn't a commitment, but they would try. Then he told me that whatever flight I was on, I should let the crew personnel know about my challenge so they could help in any way. Wow, did it work. As I climbed into the first Eastern flight to Atlanta I put my head in the cockpit and asked if we'd be on schedule. Sure replied the captain, why did I want to know? He offered a brief exclamation when I told him I had a 13 minute connection to Delta. The cabin crew had me sit in the front row with all my baggage cinched down on the seats with seatbelts. I was told when we got to Atlanta, not to wait for the seatbelt light to go off, but as the plane entered the ramp area, grab my bags and walk to the front so that I exited first. On the approach into Atlanta the Captain came on and explained that while they had arrived in the area 4 minutes ahead of schedule, Atlanta approach control was putting them into a 10 minute holding pattern which turned out to be 12. I was down to a 5 minute connection. When I got to the door, the steps were down and a man in an Eastern parka was running up them and opened the door.

"Where's the passenger for Delta?" he exclaimed.

"I'm right here!" I said.

"Get in the van." he shouted. I wasn't even going to go into the terminal. We started racing around the outside of the terminal and under it in some shortcut he knew. All the while he's getting directions on where to take me over his walkie-talkie radio. The Delta plane was parked in some overflow area where they brought passengers out from the terminal gate in trams.

We arrived ahead of the Delta tram and the Delta agent out there wanted my driver to take me back to the gate at the terminal because their tram hadn't arrived as yet. But while they were arguing it out the Delta tram arrived, so the Delta agent simply took my ticket and I boarded the flight. I ended up arriving in Cincinnati about 45 minutes earlier than my original Piedmont flight. I was able to enjoy the social hour with P&G advertising people and their vendors. Getting there was much more eventful than the presentation which went off as usual.

The day after returning I was off to Green Bay, Wisconsin. There was still snow on the ground as I drove to Neenah to see Kimberly Clark, the manufacturers of Kleenex. This visit had been requested by the local branch office. We talked in a meeting with nine or so Kimberly Clark managers about the U.P.C. opportunities for Grocery Manufacturers. But what was most memorable about that trip was the snow. It was still everywhere and there were snowmobile tracks all over the fields beside the road.

Direct Market Support

In the third week of March, Boston called again for a review of installations of key entry only systems at Stop & Shop and Fernandes, a Rhode Island based chain. The following week I participated in a California State Fullerton seminar on "New Technologies in Retailing – Fixed Head Scanners"

Checkout Productivity Issue

The introduction still faced many challenges and the number was growing. Chains continued to point to insufficient source symbol marking. But a new concern was being increasingly expressed. Even in stores with higher U.P.C. symbol levels, the expected level of checkout productivity was not being reached. Wegmans, Giant Foods, SGC's Pathmark store, Shop Rite in Fort Worth, Steinberg's and others all were reporting they had not been able to reduce the checkout schedule to the degree they had expected. IBM's initial reaction was to work with Giant Foods to video tape checkout in a scanning and a Mechanical Cash register store for analysis.

Mid-April found me at Wegmans getting more personally familiar with the scanning productivity issues they were concerned about. Erik Lunkenheimer had raised the flag for this being a significant problem and some response was required. En route I stopped by in Albany where Dave Goliber and I discussed strategies on getting Price Chopper to move forward.

Erik met me at the curb outside baggage claim at the airport in Rochester, NY. We drove around to the headquarters of Wegmans located adjacent to the airport and met briefly with Bob Wegman. He expressed his concern about the lack of checkout productivity, but also his understanding that these changes in procedures sometimes have to iron out the kinks. After Erik picked me up the next morning we spent our time in the store seeing if we could find anything obvious.

The only thing I observed was something that had been painfully obvious since before the first system shipped. The printer had a significant delay in time between when the item was scanned and when it started printing. Even after it was printing, it wasn't very fast. It might take three quarters to well over a second between the time the scanner beeped that it had a good read before the printer started printing the item description and price at the receipt print station and then another second or more to complete the print line. It appeared that checkers mentally waited for the printer to complete printing. That little delay put a kind of stutter step into the rhythm of scanning and bagging groceries. Maybe that choo-choo train protocol wasn't fast enough at 2400 baud on the supermarket loop? If not, we'd have to document that. While we were out we walked through and observed an ESIS store and a NCR class 5 register store. Then we returned to Wegmans' headquarters and shared our observations.

The Wegmans people agreed with us and had made similar observations on their own. I discussed what I knew about the work we were to do with Giant foods and video taping checkout in the store. Bob Wegman wanted to hear what we learned from Giant when the results were obtained and also expressed willingness to have us return, and if it would help, to do similar video recording in Wegmans' stores.

Slow printing had been first identified as an issue in the early days of the Troika, early in 1974. The response at that time was that printing had to be that slow because Field Engineering would not sign off on the product, if the printer ran faster. They argued that at a faster speed, the life of the print wires would wear much faster and that raised their costs, so they would raise the price for service. The Data Processing marketing division was still concerned about the high cost, so increasing the print rate was deemed a bad trade-off. Now, it appeared the slow printing could sink the customer's productivity benefit. Field Engineering might end up making a fine margin, but on no business.

I flew on to Chicago on Thursday to speak at the Packaging Institute of America meeting and then to stop by Dominick's Morton Grove store to see if I could reconfirm our suspicions from the visit to Wegmans' Fairport store. Although Dominick's had not been raising the issue as aggressively, it appeared their checkers were doing that stutter scan waiting to hear the printer print, just as at Wegmans. Tom Wilson who had taken overall Supermarket work for McKinsey was reporting he was getting inquiries about it. This was becoming another top industry concern.

Key Entry System

And, of course, a key challenge for IBM for some time was the way prospective store installations were limited by our almost total focus on installing scanning systems, while our competition sold key entry systems in large numbers, at much lower cost, lower system capability, but with better store application capability, and only the promise of scanning in the future. Once a Datachecker or NCR 255 system was installed in key entry mode, that store was no longer a candidate for a U.P.C. scanning system from IBM for many years. It was clear that stores that installed electronic registers were not likely to change equipment for 7 or more years. It generally took a major store wide remodel for a chain to change the front checkout equipment.

For over a year SCD, the development division, had been working on a lower cost, lower capacity controller that could work with the standard supermarket system registers but not support scanning size databases, etc. That system was planned to be announced at the end of April, in time to take it to the annual SMI show.

Chapter 8 First Steps in the Real World   Page 167

I traveled with Bill Carey to the Chicago Branch on May 1st to help announce the IBM 3661 Key Entry System to the Store Systems Branch Office before the FMI Show. It was an emotional trip. He was seated next to the window and in small ways it appeared things were bothering him. It took me a few moments to figure it out. Bill never said a word that gave any hint of it, but I sensed he had just felt his IBM career capped. We arrived in Chicago where I learned that Joe Powell, the Store Systems Branch Manager had been reassigned. In his place was Bill Carr, most recently administrative assistant to John Akers. Akers was now President of the Data Processing Division, DPD, the sales division for large computers and store systems in the U.S. He would end up being IBM's Chairman and CEO for eight years beginning in 1985. There had been talk that this Branch Manager's job had been offered to Carey back when the scanning system was announced a year and a half earlier. At that time Carey turned it down indicating he wanted to stay in Raleigh and ensure the product successfully got into the market. Now he had to watch as another was given the reins he would now wish to pickup.

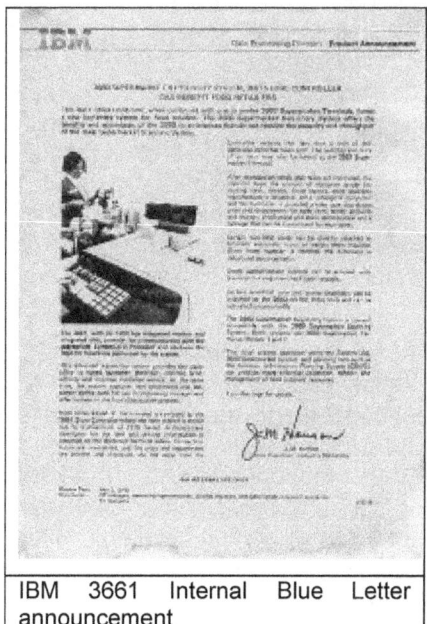

IBM 3661 Internal Blue Letter announcement

Actually I should not have been the one to go with him and present except for the fact that I was responsible for the local sales area. I had spent most of my time with U.P.C. symbols and U.P.C. scanning and I frankly was not aware of much of the detail about the Key Entry system. I was using someone else's flip charts that I had seen once before and was struggling to figure out what the point on one of them actually referred to when I heard Carey exclaim and jump up, "Oh for God's sake, let me present this!" I was somewhat relieved to not have to figure out the charts, but much more I was happy to see him have something better to do than watch a career's worth of his effort dry up sitting in the back of the room. After that, the trip home was better than the trip up had been. We discussed target accounts and kept ourselves occupied. The sales force seemed excited to have something to sell that they didn't perceive to be all hung up in industry issues.

The following week at the 1975 SMI show in Dallas we showed IBM's new Low End Store System (internally it had been known as LESS) to the world, the IBM 3661. It was sort of compatible with its big brother the IBM 3660 system. It had equivalent reports, worked with the same register hardware, but couldn't handle anywhere near the same number of price lookups. It was in a smaller cabinet, about the size of a two drawer file cabinet that replaced both the larger 4' x 4' by 3' IBM 3651 required for a scanning system and its 3669 communications unit. The key entry system did not use the sister store concept for backup. Instead each cash register kept the key subtotals during an order. If the controller failed, it kept additional rolling totals until the controller was repaired and it automatically updated the controller (unless it had lost power, which wasn't good.) The 3661 controller used an 8" floppy drive instead of the much larger single platter hard drive in the 3651 scanning system controller. Externally in the check lanes and its interface to its users it looked the same, but internally in software it was very different.

There were also major differences in how the two systems' software were maintained and upgraded. At the time of the IBM 3660 Scanning System announcement, the development division had been very concerned about IBM people seeing customer proprietary information like store sales figures. For that reason, software in the IBM 3651 controller was maintained by going to the customer's data processing department and with the customer establishing communications with the store controller then sending any patches or full re-loads of software. But a year and a half of real life experience told the developers that when there is a problem, the customer is less concerned about his store sales figures and most concerned about starting to sell again. All the driving to the customer's DP shop, etc. just added time. So with the IBM 3661 controller, when a problem came up, the call was routed to Raleigh and a specially configured 3661 would attempt to reach the machine with a problem. If successful, information on the problem would flow directly into engineering. Patch fixes would be loaded on the Raleigh system and communicated directly back to the store with a problem.

Further, the Raleigh system interrogated each customer controller as to its current patch level and automatically applied all patches that had been created since the last update that the customer's controller had seen. One can imagine how much faster this was then the planning and deliberation that took place between field engineers and the customer's data processing systems people in IBM 3660 scanning system customers.

1975 SMI Show

SMI was an exciting show again. On the second day of the show, Jim Sanderson, the market support person responsible for tracking competition, rushed up and jumped into our car as we were leaving the show. He began, "You'll never believe this. I was walking out and saw the NCR folks all leaving together. (NCR exhibitors all wore similar khaki colored suits.) So, I caught up with them and introduced myself as from IBM in Raleigh. One of them just looked at me and asked, 'Why did you let us up?' I didn't know what they meant so I asked him what he was talking about? And he said, 'you had us dead, flat on our backs two years ago. Why didn't you guys kill us off?'" "You're kidding?" we all responded incredulously. But Jim stuck to the story. None of us had seen that to be the situation two years prior. The truth was if anyone in a position of responsibility within IBM had seen such an opportunity, they never would have acted on it. IBM didn't want anyone to go out of the business. There was too much fear of being considered a monopoly in the eyes of the U.S. Government. But it was also true that we didn't want anyone else to get a lot of business.

The SMI show was an exciting experience. I didn't want it to end, but I had previously committed to speak at a packaging meeting in New York City the last day of the SMI exhibits. I had a red-eye scheduled from Dallas to New York, and I told Bill Carey I'd come back and help tear down the booth. He just looked at me like I was wacko. "You're not coming all the way back here. Go give your talk and go back to Raleigh!" he said. So I went to New York and after getting a room so that I could get a shower and clean up, gave the talk in the Hotel Roosevelt's ballroom. After the session I walked around New York a little bit and then went back to Raleigh on Wednesday afternoon.

U.P.C. Coupon

Thursday I was on my way to New York, to meet with Tom Wilson about coupon validation strategies. Grocery manufacturers believed they redeemed more coupons from grocery chains than customers had actually presented. They believed even more strongly that chains were not enforcing the terms of the coupons, e.g. only one coupon per customer. Since grocery manufacturers used coupons as a technique to get product trials to people not already using the product, they felt cheated when an existing user bought multiple numbers of products they were going to purchase anyway at the discounted price on the coupon.

Direct Market Support

Following the meeting at McKinsey I caught a cab over to one of IBM's midtown offices to meet the young, vibrant, and attractive Marketing Representative handling Nabisco. For some reason, never fully made clear to me, presenting IBM's expertise with the U.P.C. had become a significant part of her marketing strategy with the account. She was looking for my assistance in an executive briefing for Nabisco a few weeks later. We briefly outlined the information I would provide. This was to be a slightly different Executive Briefing. First, it was being done for a single executive only, the Director of MIS. She indicated she wanted to put him in a knowledgeable position within Nabisco. Second, it was to be done on the customer's premises, not IBM's. In fact, we were going to meet him in his office. I agreed to return in about 10 days for the briefing.

I left then for Boston where we worked on challenges at the Fernandes installation in Providence, RI before returning to Raleigh.

Spreading the Barcode

I returned to the IBM office in New York City on Monday, the third week in May, for the Executive Briefing. She popped the two of us into a cab to return to Nabisco's headquarters office in a midtown skyscraper. She appeared to anticipate that this was going to be a significant part of her year's activity with this account. Sitting in his office half way up that skyscraper it felt a little too formal. He indicated the standard presentation was what he wanted, so I started through a series of slides and flip charts which he sat back and observed dispassionately. I wasn't comfortable and I could tell the Marketing Representative was becoming uneasy. He was uninvolved. She and I tried all the standard 'get the listener involved' techniques of asking our own questions, drawing analogies to what we knew about his company, and leaking appropriate behind the scenes information. Nothing piqued his interest level. We got to the end of the content and he thanked us for the information. We thanked him for his time, packed up and left. Not all presentations go well. The marketing representative suggested she introduce me to the Palms Restaurant on Third Avenue. While she sipped her Dewar's and water and I sipped my tonic with a lime twist, we debriefed each other on what had gone wrong. After a dinner, which she graciously paid for, we were no closer to understanding why things had gone the way they had than when we left Nabisco's offices. Eventually I had to go to LaGuardia Airport and continue on to Albany.

In Albany the issue of checkout productivity was being investigated by Larry Friedman of Golub's Price Chopper markets. I went with Dave Goliber to review what we knew with him. From there I was on to Boston where Paul Sved took me to see Stop & Shop and Fernandes.

Shortly thereafter Erik called from Rochester to remind me the performance issue had not resolved itself. I talked with Bill Carey and we decided we should probably do more on-site research. Earlier research had not resulted in any improvements, just documentation. Somehow nothing was progressing on this issue at Giant Food. I hadn't heard about any video taping.

We decided I should revisit Wegmans in Rochester in late June but after arranging the trip we decided it would be better to come up the following week and video tape just before the busy July 4th weekend. So I returned to Albany, continuing the planning process with Golub, and from there to the IBM Store System's office in Cranston, NJ. IBM had a program to build applications based on Store System information called MAEP, Major Application Extension Program. Henry Steele was assigned to help design these. The IBM supermarket system delivered a plethora of data. Of course there were the standard sales and cash reports that broke out cash flows by checker and summarized for the store. There were reports to show the number and value of transactions by store department. And, of course, there was a rolling item movement value by item. And then there was the log file. Every checkout exception, e.g. a coupon accepted, a refund, a voided entry, a price override adjustment, anything and everything that was not item ring-up or cash tendered was recorded in the log file and tagged with a timestamp, checker ID, check lane and any other associated data. The problem was there were so many entries and no one was making enough sense out of them.

More projects: What could we tell about the yield of the butchers using the front-end variable weight information? How could we use item movement information to do a better job of merchandising meat? How about more closely assigning checkers to the time periods that shoppers were finishing up shopping and ready to checkout. There was almost no end to the things that could be envisioned.

Checkout Productivity Issue

When we returned on July 2nd to Wegmans to document store productivity, we video taped live checkout. Wegmans gave approval to install a camera over a regular checkout lane, lane 4, on a Friday, a very busy shopping day each week. Erik and I went into the store after closing on Thursday night. Using a ladder we pulled a ceiling tile back far enough to put the camera in over lane 4 looking down at about a 60 degree angle. It also included sound. We needed to hear the printer run and hear the scanner beep as well as see the scanning process. The camera cable was strung in the ceiling above the ceiling tiles about 65 feet to the locked room where the store controller was located. There it was connected to a cassette recorder with a small monitor. I had about 8 blank cassettes.

The next morning we returned about mid morning. We only wanted to record the activity in high demand times, so there was no point to being around before the store started to get busy. Wegmans' management had briefed the store manager and he could not have been more cooperative. Erik left a short time later since doing this was essentially a one man job. In a conversation with the manager and the head checker, they agreed to have their best checkers and some average checkers put on checkout lane 4.

We wanted the fact that we were recording to be as far out of the checker's mind as possible to get the truest representation of normal checkout. Of course the checkers knew we were there. Three or four times a day I'd go back to the break area in the back of the store to get some coffee from a vending machine. The checkers would recognize me as the unfamiliar face hanging around the store office and ask me what I was doing. I told them I was from IBM and we were measuring the equipment. I never saw the slightest hint of disbelief, distrust, or other response that would indicate they were uncomfortable about what was going on. They accepted it.

During the day 5-6 checkers were recorded working on the lane for a total of 10 to 12 hours. When head checker or manager would assign a checker to lane 4 I'd start watching on the monitor. About half the time the checker would give some initial indication that they knew this was the lane with the camera because they would be unusually stiff in their interactions with customers or they might stand a little more rigid than usual. Once, right after she'd been assigned to Lane 4, I caught a checker's eye glance up to the ceiling tiles to check where the camera was located. But we didn't start recording until well after these mannerisms had stopped. In all cases, customers started coming up, those cryptic short conversations that are normal between checkers and customers happened, and in 15 to 20 minutes the checker had pretty much put the camera out of conscious thought. That's when recording started. There was no evidence of a customer ever being aware the checkout was being recorded. When a checker starts adjusting something that bothers her with her undergarments or shares a slightly off-color remark with a shopper, it signaled that she'd forgotten about me for now. We'd get a record of the sales on that register at the start and end of recording each checker to measure what was accomplished in the tape.

Back in Raleigh the next week with my boxes of tapes we found some unused offices near my own and set up a cassette tape player, monitor and a repeating timer. The tapes were analyzed using a technique called "work sampling." Forms were created that identified the various work elements of checkout. As the observer, although I received plenty of offers to help after people, I would mark what activity the checker was doing each time the timer beeped every 10 seconds. That resulted in more than 2000 data points. From those you could with a level of statistical significance, determine the time spent on each work element.

But after the analysis was completed we decided it wasn't enough. These initial results confirmed that our scanning checkout productivity was not much different, if at all different, from what we thought could be done with old mechanical cash registers. We wanted more data and on more different types of checkouts, so we arranged to return to Wegmans at the end of the following week.

Direct Market Support

Also that following week I had been scheduled to help with what Lloyd Ellis, the Store Systems Branch Office Manager in the West, was calling a "Blitz." Lloyd was a very large man, nicknamed "the bear." I went out on Sunday to participate in a session that included a visit to a Ralph's IBM scanning store. While standing at the front of the store as inconspicuously as anyone could in a dark blue suit, white shirt with rep tie, and Florsheim Imperial shoes, I was approached by a man who looked very agitated. "Do you know what this is?" He asked. "This is from Satan, the work of the underworld. Take my word for it and look up Revelation 13! The Beast's work! This is the Devil's work!" I was taken aback to say the least. I thought I had been brought up in a

Chapter 8 First Steps in the Real World

reasonably religious environment, but I had no memories that came even close to whatever this person was talking about.

That evening, using the handy Gideon Reference Bible found in every hotel room I'd ever stayed in, I looked up the referenced chapter in Revelation in the King James Version and was amazed and then shocked. Chapter 13 of the Book of Revelations includes (the bold type is my emphasis):

> **11 And I beheld another beast coming up out of the earth**; and he had two horns like a lamb, and he **spake as a dragon.**
>
> 12 And he exerciseth all the power of the first beast before him, and causeth the earth and them which dwell therein to worship the first beast, whose deadly wound was healed.
>
> 13 And he doeth great wonders, so that he maketh fire come down from heaven on the earth in the sight of men,
>
> 14 **And deceiveth them that dwell on the earth** by the means of those miracles which he had power to do in the sight of the beast; saying to them that dwell on the earth, that they should make an image to the beast, which had the wound by a sword, and did live.
>
> 15 And he had power to give life unto the image of the beast, that the image of the beast should both speak, and cause that as many as would not worship the image of the beast should be killed.
>
> 16 **And he causeth all, both small and great, rich and poor, free and bond, to receive a mark in their right hand, or in their foreheads:**
>
> 17 **And that no man might buy or sell, save he that had the mark, or the name of the beast, or the number of his name.**
>
> 18 Here is wisdom. Let him that hath understanding count the number of the beast: for it is the number of a man; and **his number is Six hundred threescore and six**.

IBM's U.P.C. scanner was named the IBM 3666. Looking just at the bold text above and knowing that the IBM Supermarket Scanner was called the IBM 3666, I was suddenly struck by the incredible coincidence. I knew IBM. I liked and trusted IBM, but for just an instant, I had to ask myself if I'd been duped into becoming the devils handyman.   But, no we didn't deceive people. We weren't the tool of Satan! I just couldn't accept that what I'd been doing at IBM was a tool of the Devil! But how had IBM been so naive, unlucky, or unsophisticated as to label our machine, the machine that scanned the U.P.C., something that included six hundred threescore and six? Fortunately I did not meet too many others like that shopper at Ralph's.

Checkout Productivity Issue

On Wednesday I returned to Rochester. With Erik I purchased a dozen video tapes and Wednesday night we re-installed the camera in the Fairport store. The recording was pretty much the same as the first time. We got 16 to 18 hours over the two days, and I was on the way home on Friday. I remember some interesting conversations with Erik the little time he was in the store. He crewed on a Swan 50 sailboat that raced on Lake Ontario. I had crewed on smaller boats on Lake Huron years earlier. But in heavy wind and without enough reef in the main sail, the owner had managed to knock it down while Erik was on it. Reef refers to taking in a sail in high wind, shortening it a bit while still keeping it taut to reduce the surface exposed to the wind. Knocking down refers to rolling the boat over in the water and coming back up on the other side. Erik had been on a 50 foot sail boat that turned over. That's a thrill I hadn't had the opportunity to experience.

The following week I was back in my "alternate" office doing the work sampling on the additional tapes. It took about three days to analyze the two days of tapes. The results showed the same lack of productivity. The information was provided to Erik and he passed it along to Wegmans. Wegmans expressed appreciation for the analysis and offered to let us conduct a similar study in other stores, e.g. an ESIS key entry system store and a regular NCR Class 5 store. We accepted since we needed to develop some base line productivity information. I would return to Rochester to complete this in late August.

Somewhere about this time I saw an announcement about a new local communications system developed by Datapoint called Arcnet. Traffic flowed around a ring similar to the IBM 3660's store loop, but unlike the IBM 3660 store loop all the devices were peers. In the IBM system the Store Controller was in charge and when it failed, communication stopped until a backup controller was connected by dialing a phone from the IBM 3669 communications unit. Using something like Arcnet it might be possible to operate in a degraded state with the registers using other resources to stay operational at least in a keyed mode. But there was no more traction on this idea beyond idle curiosity. Gordon Vick and I talked about it. It certainly seemed to offer more architecture flexibility, but we would have to give up the choo-choo train.

Working Vacation

In mid August it occurred to me that there needed to be a more complete library of photos of stores with IBM 3660 systems installed. To accomplish this and to give my wife another trip out of town, I planned what would best be characterized as a working vacation. We would drive up the Atlantic coast and take pictures of supermarkets with IBM systems and see other sights along the way. The first stop was the Giant Food Supermarket in Landover, MD. Since it was a vacation and on advice from Larry Questad, I

Chapter 8 First Steps in the Real World   Page 175

had learned about this very nice hotel on the harbor at Annapolis. We stayed there. What a picturesque view our room had of sail boats at their moorings, excellent seafood breakfast. It was an idyllic setting.

But I was focused on supermarkets. After a few outside the store pictures and inside pictures of the IBM checkout system at the Landover Giant Food Store, we were off for New Jersey. We found the Pathmark store in Plainfield, NJ. No one knew we were coming so I just casually took some pictures of the exterior and then a few shots of the IBM checkout registers. No one seemed to mind and no one knew who I was.

From there the shortest path to Boston was through New York. I wanted to show my wife the IBM DPD building I was traveling to for meetings, and the Hutchinson Parkway I normally raced down to make return flights to Raleigh. I wanted her to see my environment working in store systems in those days. The way to do that was to cross over the Hudson River using the Verrazano Narrows Bridge and connect north on the Brooklyn Queens Expressway. It might have been a slightly crazier than normal day on the Brooklyn Queens, but that traffic totally shocked my wife. I think I may have been still paying the price for that drive years later. She developed a great fear of traffic in NYC. We did make it, crossing back to the Bronx from Long Island onto the mainland via the Whitestone Bridge. That put us up the Hutchinson Parkway which was the same route I usually took from LaGuardia Airport to IBM's DPD Headquarters. Unfortunately I thought she would be interested in experiencing things I experienced, but instead it made her fearful.

In Boston, I spent a work day with Paul Sved and we drove out to the Stop & Shop store and to their offices down on the wharf talking mostly about productivity. Then we started for Rochester and Wegmans. I thought about stopping at Golubs' Price Chopper, but since it hadn't been arranged in advance, I deferred and just walked through a store near Albany with my wife. That evening we arrived in Rochester and had dinner with Erik Lunkenheimer and his wife and probably the store systems SE that worked with Erik. The next day we visited Wegmans IBM 3660 scanning stores and captured them on film. I also went into more detail about our findings from our earlier video recordings. After the presentation, Wegmans was even more willing to continue the analysis in their other stores with ESIS and NCR Class 5 registers.

The trip back to Raleigh started the middle of the next day with a strong recommendation from Erik and the SE that we stop in Skaneateles, NY at the Krebs restaurant for some family style dining. It was terrific. The vacation was on again. We stayed near there overnight and the next day we drove down to Gettysburg. For me this was my third trip to Gettysburg but the first for my wife. I knew that President Eisenhower had had a farm near Gettysburg and was fascinated by the history of the whole area.

By now I had a little over 2 years of living in North Carolina. What struck me most this visit was how one sided all the monuments are. Flat in the ground or standing up, but no larger than the average personal tombstone, were markers stating "Here stood the Army of Northern Virginia," while some distance away stood multiple 20 foot tall statues to various platoons from Wisconsin and New Hampshire. It doesn't pay to lose a war. I guess I was becoming a southerner. After a day of walking the fields, looking at talking replica models, and going to the top of a tower to see it all better, we continued on back to Raleigh and home.

Appraisal

In the early fall it was time for the annual appraisal. Bill Carey had me come in early one morning and for the first time I was appraised as a "1" performer. Obviously I felt very good. This is an exceptional rating, targeted for only the top 2% of all IBM employees. I felt some of the stigma of that initial "3" rating was being erased. Bill also allowed me to violate one of the rules about appraisals, and I made a copy of his evaluation. For my part I expressed my appreciation, and we discussed my longer term objectives, one of which was to be seen as more the "Marketing" and less the "Technical" resource.

Checkout Productivity Issue

In the last few days of August I made the next trip to Rochester, NY to record a similar amount of video in each of the ESIS and NCR Class 5 stores and then brought it back to Raleigh for analysis. The results showed that the ESIS store had the most productive checkout. This was a major setback! I summarized the results for Wegmans and then, putting the best face on it, I summarized a more generalized presentation to be given to everyone else. It wasn't long before we had a trial for this second presentation when, in the second week of September, I included it in a briefing to Food Fair Supermarkets in Philadelphia, PA.

Direct Market Support

In the second half of September, the Washington, D.C. salesman, John Flynn, asked me to visit an army commissary with him. He met me at National Airport and he had his Systems Engineer along. He appeared really excited about the opportunity to sell to the commissaries as he drove us to the Cameron Army Commissary. I was impressed! I had never seen any retail stores quite like this commissary.

First, it wasn't one large room. It was an unknown number of rooms with doors sometimes the width of a single car garage door and sometimes the width of a double car garage door between them. For all the time I was there, I was only in four of the rooms. Merchandise was stacked in shipping cases with the sides cut out. Shoppers were pulling multiple shopping carts along with them and filling them. When I asked John about this he replied, "Oh yes, military retirees are allowed to shop here and the prices are so good sometimes they come from great distances, but only every other week or once a month." There were more check lanes than could fit in a single room. If I saw them all, they stretched across two rooms and every one was currently manned by a checkout clerk. It was late Friday morning and there were 3 to 5 shoppers in line at every checkout, and the clerks were really ringing the items fast. Every station had baggers that just barely kept up. When John asked me for an opinion of how much our scanning system might improve productivity, I almost laughed.

I probably was too close to the productivity challenges we were facing at currently installed accounts. Anyway, I told John we probably couldn't help Cameron Army Commissary right now. In fact our system might actually bring them to their knees, which would be horrible press in the industry. Since John Flynn also handled Giant Food, he understood. I returned to Raleigh impressed with commissaries and trying to figure out a way we could make it work. Outside of installing several systems which would be a kluge, nothing came to mind.

Checkout Productivity Issue

Interest was growing in IBM's analysis of checkout productivity. Tom Wilson had been talking with Bill Carey and getting summaries of what we were finding. He requested that I come up and brief McKinsey on what we had discovered. So at the end of the fourth week in September I stopped by the McKinsey offices in New York City on my way to present our analysis to Wegmans in Rochester. We showed Tom the Wegmans presentation. We knew that the lag in the printing sound contributed to the lower productivity. But, we also knew that the system operated faster than the checkers were doing in our videos. The net was there was no simple solution from us at this time.

In Rochester it was a command performance. After it was over, the Wegmans' management indicated they appreciated the quantification of what they were intuitively feeling in their own stores. We both agreed we would continue to work on improving performance in our own spheres and to provide the video tape recordings to Wegmans. A package with those tapes was sent from Raleigh the next week. I left Rochester to help the Store Systems staff in Boston put together a presentation for Stop & Shop.

While we were all letting the results settle in and considering what options IBM might have, I got a call from Erik Lunkenheimer in Rochester. He told me Wegmans was "throwing IBM out." "What does that mean?" I implored. "They want us to stay out of their stores for about six weeks and then we'll see what is next," he replied. This sounded terrible, but realistic. Erik added, "They said we can't fix the problem and it's time for them to try." While this

Spreading the Barcode

was quite challenging to my "either IBM or I can help anything" ego, think as I might, I had no better alternative than to honor their request.

Chapter 9 Launching the IBM 3661 - a Baby Brother

IBM held a Grocery Customer Executive Workshop in Poughkeepsie the first week in October. I was asked to present the IBM Supermarket System family. By now we were not just discussing the IBM 3660 U.P.C. Scanning system, but also the IBM 3661 Key Entry System announced at that spring's SMI show, although it still had not had its first customer shipment. It was getting closer to its first customer ship date. Fred Altomare, the workshop's manager, made arrangements for me to stay at the IBM Homestead the night before my presentation. My overview covered the functions and architecture of both systems, the state of U.P.C. source marking and an outline of the benefits. The question and answer period gave me the opportunity to talk about consumer activists and checkout productivity with the grocery executives.

There were many questions. I was rescued by Fred. When I got outside the room Fred told me, "Your boss is calling for you and wants you to call him back." On the way back to Fred's office to make that call we passed a table with 25 - 30 booklets on them that immediately caught my eye. "Fred, these are IBM song books. Can I take one?" Fred emphatically denied my request, but he would let me make a copy of several pages from one on the nearby IBM copier. That was as close as I had ever been to one of the fabled IBM Song Books from the days of Tom Watson Sr. and 100% Clubs held on the grounds of IBM's Endicott Plant. Salesmen there sang songs to the glory of company executives. I wanted one as an artifact, but at least I had a copy of a few pages.

IBM 3661 Field Test

When I reached Bill Carey on the phone his opening line was: "Where are you? What are you doing up there?" I replied, "Well, I'm talking with customer executives. I thought we agreed that I needed more time in a pure marketing role?" Bill knew exactly where I was. He had signed the travel request. This was just Bill's style. Bill rejoined, "Well get back here! I want you to run a field test of the 3661 at A&P." That stopped me and I countered with "Oh, is that a good idea? I thought you indicated I needed to be seen more as a marketer and less as a technician. Running a field test sounds pretty technically oriented to me." His response was to come back and we would talk about it.

I left Fred's office just before lunch and went straight to the airport. When I got to Raleigh I went straight to Bill Carey's office arriving there mid afternoon. As we discussed it Bill simply indicated that he thought running the field test was the kind of thing I'd do a good job at. And he thought it would be high visibility activity. If I really didn't want to do it, he would find someone else, but I should go talk to Tommy first since both of them thought I was the person to do it. Tommy Tomlin covered the same ground, and indicated that it wasn't something I had to do if I didn't want to. I went back to my office and sat there thinking about it for about 10 minutes before I realized that both these guys had a good track record for reading me and my skills. They probably knew what was best for me better than I did. I walked over and stuck my head in Bill Carey's office and said, "If you think I should do this, I'll do it." That was one of the better career decisions I've made.

Very soon Len Saltman, the IBM Store Systems Marketing Representative for A&P, and several other northern New Jersey Food Retailers turned up. Before Carey had called me, A&P and IBM had already agreed upon a store in the Colony Shopping Center near IBM Building 602 and several of the Cranford, NJ technical people were in town to get introduced including one who probably felt slighted for not running the test himself. In a gathering my wife and I had for IBM's A&P team at our home, this systems engineer attempted to intimidate me about being able to handle the responsibility of working with a customer's business. And he was a guest in my own home?

Bill Moran headed up the hardware and software engineering team that had created the IBM 3661 controller and the code it loaded into the IBM 3663 Terminal register. The first of several great parts of the A&P Field Test of the IBM 3661 was when Bill Moran asked me to stop by his office. Privately he told me to bring any requirements I saw during store test operation directly to him. He was totally committed to making this project a success and if there was anything that needed to be improved, changed or added, he wanted to be the first to know because, as he told me, he could make sure it got done. No more troikas and endless meetings. No more long communication lines to get things into development. This forged a relationship that was to have profound significance on the future of IBM's supermarket store level products. Little brother, the IBM 3661, was going to show big brother the way out of the doldrums and into a more widespread acceptance.

Bill had already made some important modifications. For one, we had a new keyboard with 9 department keys instead of just the old Grocery, Meat, and Produce.

Within a very few weeks I was totally immersed in the test. A&P sent MIS directors down to introduce us to their in-store headquarters checkout training team led by Karolyn Galyua. They were all there to learn about the IBM 3661 as well as to make sure we didn't cut any corners on A&P mandated procedures for checkout. But, we did get into the middle of conflicts between headquarter mandated rules and local rules.

One conflict concerned the No-Sale key. This key, available on many cash registers, would simply open the cash drawer when it is depressed, e.g. when someone asks a checker for change but is not purchasing anything,

Chapter 9 Launching the IBM 3661   Page 181

the checker hits the no-sale key, the drawer opens, and the checker makes change. However if you have a dishonest checker who through any of many different dishonest methods ends up with more money in the cash drawer than was actually rung on the register, a no-sale at a private moment is one way the checker removes the extra money from the register to keep for himself. Another book could probably be written on the ways that checkers can accomplish this. It's truly an amazing tale.

On IBM systems the occurrence of a no-sale key depression was always documented in the log file with a time stamped entry, but that didn't make much of an impression on the headquarters staff. Corporate policy was that "No-Sale" was not allowed and the headquarters people insisted that function be removed and the key be modified so that it would not depress. No one disagreed, so since this was a test, the code was removed and a shim was created to lock the key in its regular up position.

About a week later after the corporate people had left for the day the local district manager asked "how does a checker get the cash drawer open fast when there is a robbery." The assumption in the grocery business is that eventually you get robbed. He didn't want them to get killed too.

We had to tell him that we had been advised to remove the fastest way to accomplish this which was the "No-Sale" function. He let us know that our store would not go live without his people having a quick way to open the register if they were under a personal threat. During the previous 6 months, A&P store open hours had changed from regular retail hours to staying open 24 hours a day 7 days a week. The test store was a small to medium size store and probably had some more exposure to robbery because of its smaller size under the new additional hours. The next day the different viewpoints were resolved in a discussion between the corporate staff and the local operational management. The result was we removed the physical block we had installed and made the "No-Sale" code operational again.

A&P also sent down one of their store facilities engineering managers. He wanted to meet with IBM hardware engineers about the electrical and mechanical requirements. Before Len Saltman or I realized why he wanted to talk to engineering instead of field engineering, we had arranged for his visit. He was an old salt electrician. I don't exactly know why, but he took a tack of trying to embarrass the IBM engineers because he knew more about "Green Wire Ground" and the difference between 4 gage and 10 gage wire. IBM field engineers could have handled his comments with ease, but IBM hardware development engineers were more concerned about the traces on circuit boards in the internals of the machine. Both Len and I tried to redirect him, but he cut us off, too. In the long run the visit had no impact and the hardware fit well within the stores physical and electrical configurations.

It quickly got to where I spent seventy percent of my time at the A&P store with Harvey Mitchell, the store manager, Dave Verckler, the person from

Spreading the Barcode

A&P Montvale that was there to audit what went on, and initially three headquarters training people as well as Harland Berland, the Market Support Center's training coordinator. Harland took the functional description document and, coordinating with the A&P trainers, wrote the in-store training course for checkout persons.

The entire building staff and especially the Key Entry engineering group were excited that finally they would see one of their products in live operation near where we all worked. I also believe that Bill Carey and Tommy Tomlin were working behind the scenes to ensure any resources that might be needed were available. Two or three field engineers just showed up ready to be trained in the Key Entry environment. We were offering conference rooms for planning meetings, but most of the planning took place in the store, or around the corner at the Lock, Stock and Barrel restaurant. Jerry Ziegler, who had done a lot of the work fitting the IBM reports to the Pathmark store's accounting requirements, came down from the Cranston, NJ office to help fit the IBM store reports into the A&P system. I had become as much an A&P employee as an IBM employee and was up to 12-13 hours in the store or with A&P people each day.

Key Engineers, Marketing and Field Engineers at installation of IBM 3661 field test in A&P's Colony Shopping Center store on Six Forks Road in Raleigh, NC. Left to Right, field engineer, Harland Berland, Stan Brothers, Field Engineer, John Provetero, Ken Macior, Bill Selmeier, Alec Jablonover, development engineer, Bill Moran, development engineer.

Chapter 9 Launching the IBM 3661   Page 183

And then one week, early in the week when business was lighter, we moved the IBM 3661 equipment into the store. First just a few lanes so that their checkers could be scheduled into those lanes for training while the store still operated on mechanical cash registers in the other lanes. There was one checker, a kid, who started asking me a lot of questions about keys that A&P wouldn't normally use. I asked him why he wanted to know and he indicated he had been hitting each of the keys just to see what would happen. After I had answered his questions I caught up with Harvey, the store manager, and asked him what he knew about the kid. Harvey told me he was an engineering student at North Carolina State University and was just earning school money. I suggested that Harvey and I wanted to make him a friend, because if anyone was going to beat us, I'd bet on him. Training went very smoothly. We were ready to go live with three shifts on a Thursday.

In about a month we had gone from nothing to an operating store using IBM equipment and meeting the operational requirements of one of the more established grocery retailers in the country. And the store was seeing a minor sales boom from the IBM families coming in to buy a loaf of bread or a quart of milk.

After the store went live, my work day started a little before 8 am when I arrived at the A&P store and ended about 10 pm at night. I'd go over to my office once or twice a day just to pick up messages and say hello. At the store I was virtually an A&P employee, directing customers to the right aisle when I knew where the item they were looking for was, following the office employee or manager to the bank to make the cash deposit once or more a day, or telling the checker's how to handle a specific exception. Generally at some point in each week, I was in that store on each of the three daily shifts.

The District Manager used to come by and check on how well things were operating. I can't remember any operational failures that early in the test so these visits were opportunities for us to talk about benefits of the system and how it compared to alternatives in his eyes. One day while we were standing there talking, an older shopper walked up to us and wagging a finger began to exclaim, "Do you know what this is? The work of the Devil. See Revelations 13. This is the work of the Devil!" and he walked out. The District Manager just looked at me in disbelief and asked if I knew what he was talking about. I fessed up and told him about the "Mark of the Beast." It was North Carolina, and he understood.

One night when I was there after midnight talking with the third shift supervisor, I started to wonder about how a robbery would be handled. The store used a two compartment safe where the upper safe kept the change funds and could be opened by the office staff. It had a one-way drop, through a door, to a lower compartment that hardly anyone could open. If this store had had armored car service, it's likely only the armored car personnel would have been able to open the lower safe. As it was whenever

Page 184 Spreading the Barcode

office monies went above a reasonable amount, the extra was packaged up and dropped into the lower safe to be taken to the bank on the next day.

So I had to ask the third shift night supervisor what he would do if the store was robbed. All the money is in the section of the safe where he has no access, and A&P policy is that personnel should not sacrifice themselves for the money. His reply was that he would plead with the robber to understand that he can not open the safe, but if the robber would back up his car to the front of the store, he would do his level best to help the robber put the safe in the vehicle.

Checkout Productivity Issue

As I stopped by my office the first week in December, I had a message from Erik Lunkenheimer. I returned it to find it was the good call from Erik that I had been waiting for. Wegmans was inviting us back to re-measure their stores. They had quietly gone off by themselves and worked on the scanning productivity challenge for about 8 weeks. They reported that it appeared the productivity had increased. Bill Carey told Tom Wilson of McKinsey about the call and Tom asked if one of his staff could accompany us when we re-measured the stores. That would be great since, if we documented good news, it would have more of an industry affect if McKinsey and Company had participated.

IBM 3661 Applications

Before returning to Rochester, I had an idea for a financial application based on data transmitted from a store system. Thinking back to the comments Ron Walker had made years earlier about the advantage of knowing about Kroger's money a day earlier, I extended that into store systems. There was no reason that store systems could not report the deposit of funds into each store's local bank allowing the headquarters to consolidate that money a day earlier. Based on this I asked Len Saltman to arrange a call on the controller or financial officer of A&P and flew up to New Jersey the first week in December. It was an interesting call. I learned that A&P already had arrangements with banks to draw out fixed amounts of money daily based on projected deposits. They didn't need the information in the store's controller. Based on the volume of dollars a supermarket does and the predictability of its deposits, most if not all banks would allow A&P corporate finance to consolidate the expected deposits from each store every night, i.e. A&P got the money whether it was deposited or not. A grocery store's business was so significant, banks simply covered the occasional over draft.

Checkout Productivity Issue

It was a good time to get out of town. Karolyn Galyua, the A&P headquarter trainer, was telling me I needed more sleep. Although they said the test was

Chapter 9 Launching the IBM 3661 Page 185

depending on me, I knew it was depending on the work of those engineers, both the field service engineers and in Bill Moran's key entry group, and things were going along just fine. So, I left.

I met the young McKinsey staff person in the evening in Rochester the second week in December 1975. We had dinner and then went around to the store to re-install the camera over Lane 4 with the other recording equipment. My casual observation that evening with only one lane operating before the store closed, suggested there was a new focus on checkout. It looked like Wegmans had broken their checkers habit of waiting for the printer to print. The checkers moved ahead to the next item based on hearing the beep when the scanner registered a good symbol scan.

The next day the McKinsey consultant and I arrived at the store again after it had started to get busy and went to the controller room. After talking with the manager, we tried to stay out-of-sight to the checkout staff. This time the store manager took more interest while we were taping, often standing with us in the cramped controller room where we had located the video tape recorder and the monitor. The room happened to be next to the locked area where checkers turned in their cash drawers when returning from the checkout lanes.

Once when the manager was with us, for some reason the door was not closed tight. The head checker was turning in her cash drawer after working a lane and caught sight of the monitor. "Oh, is that..." she exclaimed, but she was cut off by the manager who interrupted with, "Yes, how could she be working more productively?" The checker responded with some hasty suggestions, none of which really mattered. What mattered was that the checker's sense of management's priorities had been reinforced on how important productivity was to her store manager. I realized I had just observed another of the ways that Wegmans had addressed the productivity challenge.

The manager was true to his word and kept the pressure up on the lane where we were recording. Checker's seemed just as talkative with the customers, but the conversation seemed to take place at the start and during the tendering portion of checkout. When they were ringing up items, they stuck to business.

It appeared during the recording that productivity had improved. When we got back to Raleigh and did the "work sampling" on the videos, we found Wegmans had in fact brought scanning up to where we thought it would be all along. The McKinsey consultant was with us in Raleigh for about two days; long enough to see where it would come out. After my return to Raleigh, I started my days by dropping by the A&P test store, but since things seemed smooth and they had somehow lasted without me the prior week, I'd go over IBM Bldg 602 and start the work sampling on the tapes.

Spreading the Barcode

As we considered the results we had to give high marks to Wegman's managers. They had changed the checker's perspective on what was the right work rate. They had broken the interdependency on hearing the printer run before scanning the next item or rather replaced the printer's sound with the beep the scanner provided after a good read. It provided perspective to IBM marketing and development management that the equipment didn't determine the productivity, checker's attitude did. And more specifically how those attitudes were influenced by their managers. The scanner could be as fast as the fastest electronics, but it was the checker who paced the operation.

It was a good Christmas present for 1975. Someone had shown you could lick the productivity bugaboo. Wegmans was happy with the results, IBM was happy with the results and McKinsey was happy with the results. There was a success story to tell.

> 1975 ended with twelve IBM 3660 U.P.C. scanning systems operating as the checkout in a store and more operating without scanners. There were additional "test" installations in chain offices and warehouses, but those are not really visible to the world. We had announced the system twenty-six and a half months earlier.

1976 started with the continued focus on A&P. A&P opened a new store in Raleigh with an NCR 255 system just off the beltline on Wycliff Road. No one could explain why NCR Key Entry had been chosen for that store. But more interesting was that they had heard about our performance measurements at Wegmans and offered to let us measure the performance of their NCR system. That was too good to turn down. We installed cameras the first Monday in 1976 and returned on Wednesday, Thursday and Friday to record the checkout operation. We expected to record checkout in the IBM 3661 store to determine if we could document any performance difference.

Direct Market Support

The middle of January, I attended the Eastern Region Store Systems Branch Kickoff meeting in New York and called on A&P management on the same trip. I returned the following week to help the local representatives do their own productivity measurement at Shoprite Fooderama. Otherwise, I was spending a lot of time in the IBM 3661 A&P test store observing the many different store activities that occurred. We were ready and video recorded checkout at the IBM 3661 store at the end of the first week in February. As much as we would have liked, we did not identify any significant difference in the results at the IBM 3661 store on Six Forks and the A&P store on Wycliff Road equipped with an NCR 255 system.

Chapter 9 Launching the IBM 3661 Page 187

Starting in February it was back to the same direct marketing support rigor. The following week I went to Syracuse to discuss productivity with P&C. The last week in February I was in Boston to discuss security with Stop & Shop and then participate in a planning session after a day in Rochester at P&C to discuss what was necessary to have a productive checkout in their store. I then talked with Star Markets in Rochester about enhancements they required. That Friday we held an Executive Briefing for Harris Teeter in Raleigh.

The month of March saw me less and less at the Six Forks Road A&P test store. Even though there had been no specific recognition of an end to the test, in my head I thought the store had transitioned to normal operation and I started behaving like that was so. The activity had transitioned from initial concern that the system would stay operational, keep doing checkout, and correctly report sales to understanding what additional information they wanted. I transitioned more to gathering product requirements, mostly requirements for changes to software.

I now worked with the IBM A&P team in NJ to develop a bid package for installing IBM systems in future A&P store remodels, presented productivity results to the Eastern Region Branch meetings, reviewed and helped interpret the productivity analysis done at Fooderama in Philadelphia, listened to product enhancement requirements from Winn-Dixie in Jacksonville as well as requirements from Grand Union and A&P in New Jersey.

IBM 3661 Product Enhancements

Many of these requirements centered on providing equivalent accounting and security controls to our competition. IBM designed an excellent information system that ensured that any exceptions would be documented. But, it was short on what would sell in two regards: 1) it didn't sufficiently take into account that in this industry some of the customer's employees would be dishonest and would manipulate the system to steal, and 2) the industry had developed an historical approach to controlling theft by checkers which, although not as detailed as the IBM approach, was very widespread. Every grocery chain understood it, and the IBM systems didn't conform to it.

The detail information in IBM's accounting system, in fact, went considerably beyond the competitive accounting systems which controlled the checkout using transaction summary totals, X, Y, and Z totals. Historically registers had to balance to X, Y, and Z totals.or there had to have been some unaccounted for exceptions. Then the manager or auditor had to start thinking through all the ways the summary totals could come up out of balance and investigate. In the IBM system every exception was logged on the disk, but there were hundreds of these records. Many in the industry had become accustomed to the three summary total cross-footing technique and just didn't trust any system without them.

Of course the IBM approach would only be acceptable if all the information got to and was saved on the disk. If there was some way to keep information from getting to the disk, possibly a dishonest employee could keep sales from getting combined in the store totals. As it turned out, there was such a way tied to the IBM 3661 systems backup scheme.

Organizational Changes

IBM moved some of our management about this time. Paul Palmer came to Raleigh with Marvin Mann and announced that Marvin would be leaving DPD marketing to assume responsibility for Store Systems within the SCD development division. Marvin accepted our congratulations and then left for his new office at the front of our building. After he was out of the room, Paul got that sly smile on his face and said, "Don't worry about Marvin. I collected some chits before he left."

IBM 3661 Product Changes

By early April, IBM had received a Request for Proposal from Acme in Philadelphia. The salesman, Brendon Murray, and I spent some time discussing store accounting and how it had applied to A&P's existing policies. We drove to Cranford and met with Len Saltman and the A&P sales team. Two days later I had a similar discussion with the Jewel Tea Store Systems sales team and some of the Jewel Tea trainers. More input on accounting requirements was offered.

The following week was the presentation to Acme Markets in Philadelphia. Marvin Mann and I were going to participate in the briefing, and we were both scheduled on the same flight. I was late as usual going to the airport and when I arrived at RDU's gate 4, I saw my DC9 on the tarmac with those built-in stairways sticking out horizontal ready to retract into the airplane. I just told the gate agent that that was my plane and he started running for the ramp agent. They succeeded in getting the stairway re-extended and the door opened. I climbed on and looked up the aisle and did not see Marvin, in fact I didn't see a seat. I just started down the aisle looking for a seat that had to be there. And in the back row, there was the seat, next to Marvin, who already had his head down and was reviewing his correspondence. I probably don't want to know what he thought of my late appearance.

IBM 3661 Field Test

I was busy collecting input about accounting requirements from the north, south, along the east coast and from Jewel Tea in Chicago. I had not even entered the Raleigh Six Forks A&P field test store building for roughly two months, when I walked in on Good Friday in 1976 and asked Harvey, the store manager, "How have things been going?"

He replied "Fantastic, today's sales are over $80,000."

That snapped my head back. That was more than this store often did in an entire week. "What's going on?" I had to know as I chased him up an aisle.

Harvey slowed down, walked back to me, and confessed that they had not been able to get the system to do the end-of-the-day accounting closing for the past 4 days.

"Why didn't you call me?" I questioned and he replied "We didn't want to get you into trouble." I quickly responded that calling doesn't get me into trouble. If anything, not calling gets me into trouble. I immediately committed that we would get the problem fixed and we would do our best to keep the store up and running through it all.

It turned out that was more challenging than I first thought. We were in North Carolina and Easter in North Carolina is a special holiday. Both Good Friday and the Monday after Easter are considered part of the holidays. Businesses are closed. I immediately drove home and called Bill Moran, the Engineering Manager, at his home but I couldn't reach him. So I called his boss. Paul McEnroe, who was my neighbor about ten doors away. Paul realized the problem and contacted some of Bill Moran's direct reporting managers to find engineers that could work on the problem. But, it was Good Friday. Easter became the challenge. The next regular work day was four days in the future and evidently given a 4 day weekend, no self respecting software engineer stays in town. All were evidently soaking up the surf and whatever else at the coast and couldn't be reached to be called in.

Dennis Kekas, one of the managers reporting to Bill Moran, called me about 90 minutes later to tell me he couldn't find anyone, but that he would personally come in and see if he could fix it. I arranged to meet him at the store in 15 to 20 minutes.

The store was packed and almost every lane had a line behind it when Dennis joined me in the raised office overlooking the check lanes. He took the controller off-line for a minute leaving the check lane registers to keep their own totals until the controller came back. Whatever diagnostics that he tried to run, didn't tell him enough and he told me we'd have to take the controller's internal 8 inch floppy disk to the lab in Building 602 to look at the problem further.

I took a deep breath, because when we take the controller off-line, which we'd had to do, any power hiccup at a register would cause it to lose its accounting figures. (This is one of your opportunities to steal the money.) Normally the totals in each register terminal are recorded on the floppy disk in the IBM 3661 controller at the end of each customer checked out. The IBM 3663 register equipment was strictly semiconductor transistor and lost

Spreading the Barcode

everything if the power glitched. Any power interruption caused the non-volatile boot code in the register to ask for a reload from the IBM 3661 controller. So, if we did lose a register from a power glitch, the register wasn't coming back until we restored the controller.

I printed a complete set of accounting figures on the office terminal. Then Dennis took the controller off-line making all the registers act in stand-alone mode, pulled out the floppy disk, and left for building 602. I told him I'd be there shortly. I invited Harvey around the corner to the Lock-Stock and Barrel restaurant for a quick lunch and reviewed with him what had happened. We did not know yet what the problem was, but we'd stay with it for as long as it took. Harvey didn't look too worried. I worried for the both of us as I left for Building 602.

I walked down the main hall and banged on the door to the key entry system lab. Dennis opened it for me from the inside. All laboratories had those 5 push button key locks with combinations that only engineers and custodians are allowed to know. Dennis didn't look like he'd figured anything out yet. He was hunched over staring at a terminal connected to a machine that I suspect had A&P's disk in it. "Oh, here I see the store sales figures," he commented. "What would you like them to be?"

I did another head snap, "Don't even joke about that!" But when I looked at him, he was smiling.

Getting more serious he looked down into the terminal and worried me when he said, "I'm going to remember how these things are coded." He poked around in the code for about two hours and then indicated he didn't think he'd fixed anything, but we should try it in the store. I took the disk and beat him back to the store, less than 5 miles away, by a good 4-5 minutes.

At the store I inserted the disk and enjoyed the drive's' klacking sound as it updated its information with the off-line totals coming in from the check lane registers collected while its floppy disk was at Building 602. It was getting late in the afternoon. We soon would have a number of checkers ending their shift and turning in their money. Dennis suggested we start again fresh in the morning so he could use the intervening time to study up a little on the store accounting closing code and maybe try again to reach someone on his staff. We arranged to meet at Building 602 around 9 am and I was to have the disk.

I got to the store early on Saturday and checked the systems accounting against where cash actually was in the store. All seemed normal. The system appeared to be correctly tracking money in each register's till, moving it to the office figures when checker's ended their shift, showing deposits to the bank correctly. It appeared to be normal except that it couldn't seem to turn today into yesterday as it was supposed to do every night. So, store sales figures just kept climbing, not starting over each day.

Dennis Kekas was already there when I got to Building 602. I knocked on the lab door again and he let me in and then commented with a smile, "Hey, you aren't allowed in here!" I looked down at that hexadecimal babble he was sifting through and told him his secrets were safe with me. He hadn't reached any of his people, but he had studied the code and supporting documentation. After a little over an hour we started what became a small ritual. He pokes around on the A&P disk and declares it's time to try it. I take the disk, drive like mad to the store and get the check lanes back into a system mode with all the totals updated. About then Dennis arrives and we try the daily closing only to find it's still broken. We run a set of current reports and Dennis takes the disk back to Building 602 and I follow.

We repeated the ritual about 4 times until something unusual happened. It was getting darker, likely around 5 pm when as I sped up Six Forks Road, I saw the dreaded blue light in the rear view mirror. I pulled over. I'd been busted by the North Carolina State Police. The officer walked up to the car and commented that I must have something very important to have to drive that fast.

I looked over at the floppy disk on the passenger side seat and replied, "Yes, this disk runs the checkouts at an A&P Grocery store just ahead. And, if I don't get this disk back to the store before they have any sort of a power glitch, the store will probably lose all its sales accounting."

His face registered my concern and he responded with, "Well drive carefully. There are a lot of crazy people out here."

Kekas was waiting for me at the store, having driven past while I was talking with the officer. And the second unusual thing about that trip was that Dennis had fixed the problem. When we tried to do the store accounting period closing procedure, the system obediently rolled its totals into the prior day's number fields and started us out with a fresh set of zeroed-out daily totals. We were all happy to be going home. I returned to the store on Monday and updated Harvey, the store manager, on what had happened.

System Applications

Later at the end of the April, Gordon Vick and I returned to Wegmans to discuss work Gordon had been doing to build a store labor scheduling program. Gordon's plan went beyond just scheduling checkout labor. He attempted to use all the data automatically collected by the system and then extend it into other areas of the store such as receiving, bakery, deli, meat and produce departments, restocking, and more.

1976 SMI Show

The SMI Show was May 2-4, 1976. The IBM exhibit focused on the IBM 3661 which was now shipping to customers. This was the last time that Larry

Questad, Bob Doremus, Jim Lightner, and I would be together for a show. It was a good team and we had fun.

When I was back I saw what was becoming a pattern. Direct Market Support personnel are promoted right after the SMI show. This time it was Larry Questad who was being promoted to a Marketing Manager position in San Antonio, TX. I called my wife first, but really didn't want to leave much room for family negotiation. I wanted to do it. I quickly offered to host his promotion party at our house. I wanted it to be a special recognition. I had really enjoyed knowing Larry.

The name of an artist who could create a painting that looked like the cover of Time Magazine's Man of the Year issue was passed along to me. We had the picture of Larry, taken for a recognition award, that the artist needed and outlined his experience with the consumer activists and other memorable Market Support Center activities. As Ed Salonus had done earlier in Cincinnati, I too hoped that creating these paintings would become the traditional gift for people promoted from their jobs in Raleigh. We scheduled a date in June for the party.

About this time, Bill Carey told me he'd gotten me a slot in the IBM President's Class. Jim Lightner was the only other person I knew who had attended a President's Class. Three to four times a year, IBM conducted a two week long Harvard Business School case study class for 40-50 selected IBM employees in an auditorium at 1133 Westchester, DPD's Headquarters, in White Plains. The class sessions went all day. On half of the days we had special IBM instructors focused on business topics, and the other half of the days Harvard Business School Professors and one Columbia Business School professor taught.

IBM 3661 Product Changes

At the end of the week of SMI, I was back in New York answering questions about productivity at an A&P store in New Jersey. This time I was accompanied by Marion Getz, one of the key software engineers who wrote the microcode that the IBM 3661 controller loaded into the IBM 3663 register terminals when they started up. It's very helpful for the engineers that do the actual work to see their products in their operational environment. Years later it became much more commonplace for engineers to go directly into the application's environment, but in the more structured organizations of the '70s it was not so common. Marion showed a lot of interest in what he saw. In addition to observing, we collected a full set of operator reports that provided some measure of key rates, etc. We put in a full day in NJ and scheduled ourselves on the last flight back.

On the way back to Newark airport I stopped off at another A&P that had an IBM 3661 to get some comparative reports to the set we had obtained earlier. I waited to use the customer service terminal to run the reports.

Chapter 9 Launching the IBM 3661   Page 193

Soon the clerk had answered and processed everyone in the line in front of her. I started running the reports. The IBM register printer was terribly slow as usual. Key entry systems printed at the same slow rate as scanning systems again because of the same Field Engineering concern about the life span and cost of servicing the printer. Marion noticed the line of customers grow and grow while the printer continued to print the reports I had requested. He made some notes.

About two weeks later as I was walking up the main aisle to the cafeteria for lunch, he came out from the cross aisle which led to his office and asked me to join him in the lab. At a register he asked me to key in a price as fast as I could. I used two hands to key-in "5 Grocery, 5 Grocery..." as fast as I could. By the time I'd keyed in 10 to 12 entries, it hadn't printed half of them and I wondered why I was here. He moved me aside with his elbow and a comment that he had to enable some new microcode. I repeated the test and this time after a dozen entries, the printer was less than one item behind. I just looked at him and asked what about the field engineering rules. Marion responded that it all depended on how you interpret them.

When I asked about the regression test, I learned that it was completed. A regression test is when you test new software against all existing software configurations to discover any incompatibilities. Based on how I'd just seen it demonstrated to me, I said, Great, let's pick a good test store and check it out." He replied, "OK. But the six stores that already have it running haven't complained of any problems." My momentary concern about exposing customers to untested code went away when the fact that no one had yet complained sunk in. The IBM 3661 maintenance policy of applying all unapplied software patches every time a live system called for updates, was an amazing tool to fix functionality.

Later that week I traveled to Philadelphia to be available for questions about the IBM 3660 Supermarket Systems at a Northeastern Weights and Measures conference. The middle of the following week I was with A&P to help with configuration of the new IBM 3661 System going into the A&P Passaic Store.

Larry Questad's Promotion Party

On a Saturday evening in June we celebrated Larry Questad's promotion and said good-by. I had wanted it to be a special evening and since most of my family's entertaining to this date had been simple dinner parties, we were sadly light on items for entertainment. I thought a pool table would be appropriate, but to put a full size pool table in our family room, the only close to appropriate place in our house, would have pushed out the couch, the TV and probably two bookshelves. I settled for a bumper pool table. The table arrived with an installer Thursday afternoon. He leveled the table with a firm warning that to move it would make it unplayable until it was leveled again.

Spreading the Barcode

Saturday night was great. The house was full of people. As soon as Larry and Liz arrived and before most of the other's had arrived, I was offering Larry all the good advice I could. I should have realized it was not really needed, but I took him up to our master bedroom and showed him how there were separate closets and a sink in my closet that allowed us to both get ready at the same time. Larry told me he'd already purchased his home in San Antonio and that he and Liz had separate closets connected to separate dressing rooms with sinks and then connected to a common bath. Years later I saw the closets on a visit to San Antonio.

We were all packed into our family room and up one level in the living room. The pool table was a big hit. Larry liked the painting and other thoughts people remembered about him. Later in the evening, one of the wives unexpectedly hopped up on the pool table and just sat there interrupting everything. I looked at her husband but he just stood there. I walked over and asked her to stand up, but she teasingly refused. I think she was having too good a time. I noticed Bill Carey had now noticed it and probably was wondering about my management style in this case. I looked at her husband, but he made no effort to assist. I asked her again and she simply replied, "Nope!" So I just put my arms under her, lifted her up, and turning around set her on her feet. No comment, she just stood there. I declared the pool table ready for play again and it was over. We had a great time. I met a lot of spouses I had never known before, had great conversations, and ended up the night listening to my boss accompany the hi-fi in a chorus of "50 Ways to Leave Your Lover."

Larry was gone but the issues carried on: Non-resettable accounting totals in accounting, productivity, the 38 inches of height in the scanner that limited it in some checkstands, all remained as challenges.

IBM President's Class

And Sunday evening I was on the way to White Plains for the two week IBM President's Class that started on Monday. The days were full and started with a highly interactive lecture followed by case studies on financing, personnel development, cost management, venture funding, legal awareness, managing research, and a wealth of other subjects covered in MBA programs. We were commonly broken up into groups to respond. Our responses would be picked up the following day and we might get feedback. In one of them someone was trying to start a computer company and applying for a loan from a bank in Boston. Later the staff confirmed that the case study had been created from some of Ken Olson's experience starting Digital Equipment. I learned great stories about Con Edison, about factoring receivables, and other subjects not covered in my engineering curriculum. But most of all I remember the way of looking at businesses from a top down view. What was the return on the equity that had been put up?

IBM 3661 Product Changes

Our experience in that class was somewhat unique. For me in particular, since I actually left the class for a day on the middle Sunday to travel to Jacksonville, FL for a previously committed meeting with management at Winn-Dixie about implementing the X, Y, and Z non-volatile accounting total functional requirement. Winn-Dixie insisted upon it in our store accounting system. The salesman for Winn Dixie was Bill Hamilton, who previously had worked as an Industry Administrator in Distribution Industries. Give him credit, because of his background, he knew exactly where to call to get action.

Ray Hodge, a business manager in the development division, joined me in a call on Harry Wade at Winn-Dixie. Harry was adamant that IBM registers had to maintain non-volatile totals in them similar to NCR. Our architecture probably required that we do it slightly differently, but Winn-Dixie was a very significant prospect and we wanted a way to meet their need. Ray and I spent up to four hours listening to Harry and other Winn Dixie managers talk about their requirement by retelling war stories of cheating store managers, office personnel, and checkout clerks. We asked questions for clarification and probed the limits of what they would accept to be sure to completely understand the parameters we had to meet. After it was over Ray flew back to Raleigh to write the specific definition and I returned to White Plains and the President's Class.

IBM Presidents Class

The last day the President's Class is always addressed by a corporate CEO. The Presidents of Texaco, PepsiCo, and other local NY firms had participated, but the CEO scheduled to address our class was IBM's own Frank Cary. Thus, when about 15 of us decided to take in a Broadway Show on Thursday night, it really got the attention of our class managers. They may have been contemplating the impact on their career, if Frank Cary walked in the next morning and ten or so class members were wearing sun glasses to hide the darkness in their eyes. They verbalized their concern, asking us if we had considered the wisdom of our plans. But we went anyway. We had a great meal and a show and got back to our rooms as early as we could. We were each there early the next morning. I don't think Frank Cary noticed anything out of the ordinary because, after all, he was our CEO too, and we wanted to look good just as much as the class managers did!

IBM 3661 Product Changes

The functional changes we'd been getting pushed to deliver by our customers needed to be precisely defined. I was invited to spend a lot of time with development business people defining exactly what each new function would do, how it was calculated and what the benefit to the customer would be. Ultimately this exercise resulted in how many more systems would DPD, the sales division, add to the forecast. The rather easy way the business of being successful was abstracted in this process made me uncomfortable. The development people, with the exception of the engineers in the Key Entry area, saw the forecast as their reality. If IBM didn't sell many of the systems, that was the sales division's reality. But the Key Entry people going back to that first conversation I had with Bill Moran, stayed focused on delivering requirements the customers wanted.

The Fourth of July celebration that year was very special, the two hundredth, or Bicentennial, anniversary of the signing of the Declaration of Independence. But the very next day I was en route to Maine for a planning session with the IBM sales team to create programs to get interest at Star Markets in Massachusetts, Hannaford Brothers, and Finest.

Organizational Changes

Sometime about then Paul McEnroe was promoted to New York to become, as he described it, the Chief Technology Officer for IBM. It felt like the end of an era having Paul go. Paul was active in Oak Park activities. My wife had been to ladies club activities at their home. It was going to be different.

Direct Market Support

On the fourth weekend of the month, A&P opened the Passaic, N.J. store. This was my first superstore opening with the IBM 3661. A&P did it up right. Of course there were many A&P executives, but there also were vendor executives. Frank Perdue of Perdue Farms, one of the largest chicken growers in the east, was there. Frank appeared in most of Perdue's advertisements, and those who saw those ads may agree that Frank was appropriate for his product.

IBM 3661 Product Changes

In the other weeks, when I wasn't traveling, I spent time with engineers, or more likely development business people like Ray Hodge, defining and justifying enhancements that should be made and how our customers would use them, e.g. what does the report look like, what is on the display, how was the value calculated, what were acceptable limits or did the acceptable limits need to be set by the customers for their own environment. There were many, many things to be defined.

IBM Marketing Promotion

One of IBM's corporate advertising staff members and I had lunch in August. He was looking for information and support in developing a series of TV and print ads about the IBM store system products. Frankly, I didn't see that our lack of adequate sales was from a lack of awareness on our prospect's part. Our sales people had reached out to almost all chains. I couldn't certify that the CEO of each prospect had been called on personally by an IBM Marketing Representative, but IBMers weren't known to be shy in calling at the top. I'm afraid I didn't concur that advertising would fix our sales problem, and much of the remainder of the conversation centered on how unusual it was that corporate IBM wanted to do product-oriented advertising while the sales division favored image-oriented advertising.

Appraisal

I was appraised again and very happy to be evaluated as a "1" performer again. It's relatively easy to get or give a "1" performer appraisal. There is so little disagreement. I did wonder how long this could go on though. But it helped me to start forgetting that low mark three years earlier.

IBM 3661 Product Changes

By mid September we had a good plan on how functionality of the IBM 3661 was going to expand. I stopped by the original test store and took the store manager to lunch to discuss it with him. He was helpful in describing how he might use the changes in reports to better manage the store. Some of this was shared the following day at an education review in Poughkeepsie. Then a desk check review with the A&P team and a few A&P trainers to recheck that we completely understood the impact of proposed changes.

Direct Market Support

At the end of the September, Milo Moran, another MSC marketing person, and I had the opportunity to give our wives a mini-vacation when we went to Disney World to handle an exhibit of the IBM 3660 U.P.C. Scanning system at the Florida Retailers annual convention. Bill Hamilton came over from Jacksonville to help out, so each of us got a few hours to visit the park with our wives. I remember wondering where Disney hired such a perpetually friendly staff. Every last one of them had such a pleasant disposition.

IBM 3661 Product Changes

In early October I made a quick trip to discuss scanning productivity with Safeway's Washington, DC division and then went back to developing the presentation of the functional enhancements on the IBM 3661. We decided it would be called "Function Rich." When the IBM 3661 was released, except for the additional department keys, the system's user function operated fairly similar to its big brother scanning system without the scanners. But a lot of thought had gone into the upgrade and maintenance architectures to make it

Page 198 Spreading the Barcode

superior to the more cumbersome approaches used in the IBM 3660 scanning system.

By the end of the month the announcement materials were being finalized, we had articles for the Store Systems Newsletter for sales persons, and I went to New York to get this all approved by marketing practices. Before the November roll-out of Function Rich, I made a quick trip to help the Executive Briefing for Hannaford Brothers in Portland, ME. A day after returning I left with others from the Market Support Center for LA, the first stop on a cross country education roll out of the new function prior to making it public.

A 16 chart presentation on the new functions e.g. week to date department sales figures in addition to the original current day and prior day, departmental customer counts by hour to help with labor scheduling, inclusion of time away from the lane in the checker's figures in the system, warning limits on keyed prices, a listing of checks accepted by lane to help with cash pickups, a monitor mode so that a manager in one lane can see the rings of a checker in another lane, non-volatile totals in each lane, signals to the office when a lane's cash drawer exceeds the policy limit and more was created. A total of about 40 improvements were exceptionally well received by the field salespeople. Sales people were called into each branch: LA on November 4, Chicago on November 5. We did the New York branch education the following Monday.

The "Function Rich" announcement changed perspectives throughout the field sales teams calling on supermarket accounts. It was the biggest upgrade of new customer functions and report changes since either system had been announced. Baby brother, the IBM 3661, was showing big brother, the IBM 3660, the way to customer excitement. To the sales people it appeared that the things their customers had been asking for, the missing things that made the IBM sales teams feel functionally inferior to our competition, even though we were the scanning champs, might actually be made available. Within just a few weeks time the sales focus shifted from talking about scanning systems to a new strategy of installing IBM systems as key entry systems and scanning later. This was the same expansion strategy being used by our competition at NCR, Datachecker, and a new company, Data Terminal Systems.

The evening of the New York branch meeting and prior to its public announcement, I returned with Ray Hodge to Jacksonville, FL to review our solution with Harry Wade at Winn Dixie. We had a fairly complete discussion on all the outcomes for various situations that might occur at a checkout station. Harry expressed confidence that we had developed a non-volatile total solution that would provide protections for all the scenarios he had laid out. We went through each one in detail, with Ray noting any comments from Harry. At the conclusion, in a private exchange, Harry told me that IBM was demonstrating its unique capabilities. I took that to mean I had finally been able to match the NCR marketing prowess in explaining in-store controls.

The "Function Rich" enhancement announcement was out and I was anxious to get back into the U.P.C. side of the business. All the Function Rich additions did nothing for the large system. The large system controller still downloaded the equivalent of its original terminal microcode. IBM still needed something to increase its appeal. One of the areas that appealed to me was to create a complete system with a closed information loop for meat within the store. Giant Foods was also interested in doing this and I was anxious to work with them on it. In hindsight this was an incorrect pursuit. It is always exciting to push out the frontier of applications, but what IBM needed was to integrate the two systems, not differentiate them more. It would be another year before that would happen.

Direct Market Support

Before I could start anything, regular direct marketing support rose in priority. I participated in a customer briefing for Food Lion in Charlotte, NC, an education and communications program in White Plains, NY, sales assistance in Boston, discussions with P&G in Cincinnati on U.P.C. Source Marking, and a briefing on the 3661 functional enhancements with Wegmans, and Star Markets in Rochester, NY, then Safeway in Washington, DC. This announcement meant that I would be spending even more time on the road delivering the message of this upgrade function with the IBM Store Systems salesman to their customers.

Organizational Changes

And an era ended at the same time. Bill Carey, who had led the small Data Processing Division staff investigating getting into the cash register market starting in 1971 was leaving the Store Systems Market Support Center to take the Account Executive position on the J C Penny account in New York City. He was the man responsible for my being in Raleigh, he was the man who said to me "see what you can do about that" that opened up the whole source marking activity in 1973 at the time of the announcement of the IBM 3660 Supermarket Scanning System, and he was the guy that got me into the IBM 3661 functional leadership position.

I now worked directly for Tommy Tomlin until Bill's management slot could be filled. Tommy moved into Bill's old office. I believe our building, Building 602, had been intended to be a warehouse by the original builder. It had few windows, but Bill had managed to have one of them. Tommy moved into the office and put up a full wall mural in wallpaper showing the woods in fall with the colors changing. With the light coming in from the window it was quite striking.

Store System Applications

Fred Altomare, one of the instructors in the Distribution Industry Education Center in Poughkeepsie, was also focusing on applications. Fred passionately felt that host applications, using store information to make better food chain decisions, would demonstrate the value of IBM systems. In hindsight, Fred was right, just too early. Over the years, the value of the information collected in the store greatly exceeded the simpler in-store measurements that excited grocers in the mid '70s. In early December Fred conducted a five day session for host and Store System sales people at the Dunfey Inn in Dallas, TX. I was an attendee except for one of the days when I went to make a U.P.C. presentation to a North American Wholesale Grocers Association meeting in Memphis. But I was there the night the entire group went to dinner at England 1500, a medieval dinner show that operated in the Dunfey Inn. We shared the restaurant with a group from Ford Motors on a corporate outing. Everyone was having a good time. I remember becoming a little concerned that some of our staff was becoming too familiar with the female Ford employees, but disaster was averted.

Direct Market Support

At the end of the year I drove to Florida and spent a short time with Bill Hamilton considering market programs for Winn Dixie, but the biggest benefit was that my family was able to spend Christmas with my mother, newly relocated to just north of Tampa in Florida.

Chapter 10 Revitalizing the Market

My first trip to Boston in early January, 1977 wasn't productive. I arrived at RDU, the Raleigh airport, for my early morning Eastern Airlines flight that had an intermediate stop at National Airport in Washington, DC. On the way to the airport, the radio news talked about a huge snow storm that was affecting the whole northeast down through Virginia. Although everything looked normal in Raleigh, National Airport in Washington DC was close to being shut down by the snow when we arrived. The runway had been cleared but there was only the narrowest of paths up the taxi way and no snow removal on the ramp itself. I remember hearing the wheels lock up while the plane was still moving and about 50 feet out from the gate. I imagined how exciting this looked from the cockpit with the terminal building approaching, but the plane stopped perfectly lined up with the jetway.

We did the normal gate time turnaround and left for Boston. The pilot announced that Logan Airport in Boston was closed, but was supposed to be open by the time we got there. It was, but inside the airport it was just confusion personified. I managed to get a rental car, and left for the IBM branch office. It was a slippery trip! Most roads in Boston had not yet been plowed, and it probably took 25% longer than normal to get out to the branch office in Waltham, MA. When I got there, it was deserted. I was there to meet Paul Sved to help develop a special presentation for Star Markets. He wasn't there, but his store systems SE arrived about the same time as I did and let me in. He told me the Branch Office had decided to close for the day because of the snow. I called my office to see if I'd gotten any messages, but of course I hadn't. So, I returned to the airport and flew back to Raleigh a little unhappy for all the effort I'd made.

IBM 3661 Product Changes

I needed some time to talk with Dick Lynch, the IBM lawyer in Raleigh. A special bid package being developed for A&P and a few other accounts needed the legal staff to concur that what it provided A&P and those other accounts was consistent with other special bids. The additional functionality of the "Function Rich" release was opening new markets as it provided core capabilities many chains had as "must haves," but it didn't include everything that some of our larger prospects were demanding. This Special Bid package was designed to handle that. The microcode portions of "Function Rich" were available to every IBM 3661 store, but the items in the special bid would require additional development and would not be available to everyone. We were not certain all customers required them. We needed to develop ways that were legally defendable and equally fair to every customer.

Direct Market Support

At the end of January several of us from Raleigh, including Dennis Kekas and Lee Dixon, the laser specialist, and I provided a highly tailored briefing to Supermarkets General in New Jersey. Afterwards I went on to IBM DPD's 1133 Westchester office to discuss plans for mounting a trade advertising campaign centered on the extended capabilities of the IBM 3661. The "Function Rich" presentation had become the message that Store Systems people wanted to present to prospects and customers. So I combined the original store function presentation with the "Function Rich" presentation which removed the "just announced" references from it. And we created an additional presentation to provide the background on both of the supermarket system's reliability features, availability features, and serviceability features. RAS was a buzzword in those days, and it would become a focal point for IBM's exhibit at the coming FMI Show in Dallas.

Organizational Changes

The Executive Presentation for Star Markets in Boston, postponed by that extreme snowfall the first week in January, actually occurred the first of February. And I had a new manager again. Paul White had been brought in by Tommy to fill the slot Bill Carey had occupied. My relationship with Paul was quite different than my relationship had been with Bill Carey. Bill had been the original manager on site. He had started it all from the perspective of most of us. Even his manager, Tommy Tomlin, could match him, but seldom exceed Bill's understanding of the market, accounts, etc. Most of the time, they were on a par with each other. But Paul White was new to the Market Support Center, and consequently he was viewed as more of a caretaker than a fundamental strategist. I found I continued to get most of my direction directly from Tommy.

IBM 3661 Product Changes

A Jewel Tea Vice President from Chicago visited us in Raleigh in February with two Jewel Tea checker trainers. Jewel Tea was the company that had defined the ESIS system with Nuclear Data, the small company in Rolling Meadows, IL. In 1971 and 1972 ESIS looked like a rocket in the POS marketplace with creative keyboard design, more in-store department information, and reporting good productivity gains. But over the years it was tough to keep investing the additional development money to meet the additional tweaks requested by customers. And then, of course, U.P.C. barcode scanning happened. ESIS never had it. Subsequently, ESIS had been purchased by Pitney Bowes who was going to make a U.P.C. barcode scanning system, but somehow that too never made it to the shipping dock. And now here was Jewel coming to see IBM since we had just announced major functional enhancements for a non-scanning system.

Chapter 10 Revitalizing the Market   Page   203

Jewel Tea received well deserved recognition for the functionality of ESIS. It was the result of years of continual improvements. But Nuclear Data was out, and Pitney Bowes may have had reservations about more development. Jewel Tea had come to expect all vendors to be responsive to their requirements. So when Tommy and I sat down with the three of them in a conference room, the checker trainers just began by listing all the things IBM would have to change or add in order to meet Jewel's minimum requirements. It was a pretty respectable list, and when the trainer finished, she stopped, waiting for our reply.

Tommy took a moment and then told them that IBM would be willing to consider their requirements. But first we would want to study them in more detail and we would have to estimate the resources we would need to provide them. After that, we would only begin development work, if Jewel Tea provided either the development funds on a schedule to be defined, or committed to a delivery schedule of sufficient systems to fund the special development effort from additional sales.

I saw a small amount of shock register on the trainer's face and no one said anything for a moment. Then the Jewel Vice president said quietly, "You know, we've been thinking that we might need to find a vendor that would be tough enough for us." The Vice President understood, but the trainers still looked mildly surprised. We took their prepared list of functional adjustments and put them with the others that were still coming in. Many of them did get done, but Jewel never offered to fund the development or to commit to sufficient systems to fund any special development. The functions that did get done were required by many customers in addition to Jewel. Tommy's proposition to Jewel Tea was very similar to the way things operated between development and marketing divisions within IBM when formal lists of new functions were involved. If DPD wanted some list of functions to be included in the system, then DPD had to increase the commitment for the number of systems that would be sold by an amount needed to fund the development.

About March the key entry engineers first showed up with their creative new idea. Although there already were a few wire matrix printers in the world, it was still a pretty new technology. Not too many people had yet realized just how different sweeping a row of dots or wires stacked on top of each other over a paper opened up the possibilities. This wasn't typing with bouncing balls or fixed cast characters. This was more like sweeping an artist's brush across a canvas. The key entry engineers had realized this, and they were proposing that IBM deliver a shelf label printer for only $600.00 using the wire-matrix register printer.

Spreading the Barcode

My 1977 FMI show badge with the sample shelf label attached.

I didn't get it at first either and was thinking about an additional management printer. I immediately voiced suggestions for other things that might be printed like more comprehensive store reports, when they interrupted. "No, No, No! There isn't any hardware! We are printing these things by rotating the image 90 degrees on the cash register printer and using special adhesive label print stock. It's only microcode." Wow, we had another announcement for the upcoming SMI show in Dallas. The chain would load their label format using the communications port and supply label stock with the appropriate backgrounds preprinted, but the item information and price content could be entered at the store. It looked great for creating replacement labels on the spot when labels got damaged.

Marsh Supermarkets had been told about the new IBM 3661 functionality. Marsh was a good IBM customer for mainframe computers, but the store-level was a different story. As the company most prominently identified to be the first to scan a U.P.C. symbol on a Wrigley's Juicy Fruit Gum package using an NCR system in the late spring of 1974, I wanted to see them become interested in IBM. I went to Muncie, Indiana to meet with Clyde Dawson and others and listen to their requirements. By the end of that week we had folded the generally applicable requests from Marsh in with the rest of the open customer requests and were in discussions with George Schenck and Len Felton, who now managed the business management and enhancement process for Store Systems within the Systems Communications Division.

The following Wednesday I was able to have a fairly definite lunch with Karolyn Galyua and other A&P trainers about changes we were prioritizing within the IBM 3661's accounting system. We had come a long way, but they still saw more things that needed to come.

Sales people were bringing us into many probably tangential opportunities. In Boston we reviewed the requirements for Zayre's and presented our capability to them.

Executive Store Visit

Marvin Mann surprised me with a call. John Opel, then President of IBM, was in the building and wanted to visit the IBM 3661 test store. Marvin asked that I take him over. We got in my car and drove to the store. All the way over as we chatted, I was very aware that this was the man who three and a half years earlier had increased more than $50,000 what I thought had been our agreed upon price of the IBM 3660. John was a financially oriented executive, so I was trying to tie down in my head every industry financial measurement I could remember. I started a characterization of industry operating margins long before we reached Six Forks Road. When we got to the store, John did not want to make any fuss. Fortunately, the Store Manager, Harvey Mitchell, was there and I introduced John Opel to Harvey Mitchell as an IBM executive from New York. I can't say it made any impression on Harvey. We returned to the IBM building, said goodbye. Later telling Marvin what had happened, Marvin was amused that I thought I could change John Opel's mind in any way.

I took a week's vacation around the time of Easter that year. Both my wife's mother and my mother were now living in Florida. We were able to spend a few days with each before starting back from Ft Lauderdale the day after Easter.

IBM 3661 Product Changes

Much of the additional functional requirements provided additional information at store level. In IBM's original architectural philosophy, merchandising information like on-going gross profit tracking would be done at the region or headquarters site from information received from the stores. While good in theory, it required the chain's MIS staffs to do some programming when they were already overloaded with other projects. Conversely, the competition's POS systems would provide this information at store level. Merchandisers visiting their stores were intrigued by looking at all kinds of data particular to the store they were in. Jewel Tea in particular liked to see the gross margin by department for each department in the store. They typically had about 10 or sometimes more departments. This was the kind of requirement that we would consider had more universal appeal and we'd incorporate it into the next release which soon would become known as "Function Richer." In mid April, I did a day trip to Chicago to review the gross margin functionality with Jewel.

The other activity absorbing my time was the creation of the system that would be used at FMI. The Super Market Institute was changing its name to the Food Marketing Institute. From 1977 on, the previous SMI show would be known as the FMI show. We would be demonstrating at the show the latest functionality and any special function that had been delivered on a specific request basis, but would be generally available in a future release. I physically picked up terminals and controllers from our manufacturing department which had moved from our IBM 602 building to its own facility at Research Triangle Park a year or more earlier.

This was going to be an interesting show. The Key Entry system portion was very prominent with a focus on the expanded in-store function, an architecture that ensured a very high reliability and availability and a cute demonstration where we entered a supermarket executive's name and printed a store shelf label with that name on it.

Not only did these shows provide the opportunity to talk with our prospects and customers, but we also talked with vendors. We had noticed the increase in the use of front end scales and were very interested in talking with scale manufacturers. Hobart and Toledo scales had been the most frequent scale with our checkout registers, but National Semiconductor's Datachecker division had gotten a lot of marketing traction using a new checkout scale from National Controls, a company in Marin County, CA north of the Golden Gate Bridge, that used load cells. This enabled the scale to settle much faster than the Hobart or Toledo scales. I scheduled a meeting with NCI on Tuesday and the following day with Hobart and Toledo. Both of them recognized the competition from National Controls, but could not respond with load cell scales of their own.

Direct Market Support

After FMI I continued on to the San Francisco Bay area to talk about special function requirements that Lucky Stores was looking for with the sales team in Oakland. I got to see my brother's house in Tiburon, CA for the first time. Months earlier he had left Procter & Gamble to join the San Francisco office of Foote, Cone, and Koenig to manage the Clorox Account. There was a brief conversation with the Safeway Store Systems team, since I would stop in Houston on the way back to present IBM Key Entry function to Safeway's National Division Managers Meeting being held there.

IBM Employee Training Class

At the end of May, I was in Poughkeepsie at Dick Weaver's request to introduce the IBM Point-of-sale business to new IBMers in one of their training classes. It was an educational experience for me, too. In an attempt to include some material specifically germane to new employees, I recounted the story Joe Woodland had told to me years earlier, where a Chain Store Vice President had felt our product couldn't be justified, if we had to have a controller for each store. She knew how much their Corporate Controller earned and that much for every store was more than they could afford. I was bringing it up to show how IBMers have to be careful with our terminology which often has multiple interpretations. While the class was gently laughing at the situation I heard in the undercurrent, "Sheeesh, why does it always have to be a dumb woman?" This was not a good response for persons hoping to have an IBM management career, and frankly, I was quick to add that it only happened to be a woman this time. Sometimes it felt there were 5 ways to get it wrong for every one way to get it right.

IBM System Benefits

The following day I organized a one day task force by calling four senior sales representatives on the East Coast to Raleigh to reconsider the benefits of scanning. IBM had conducted a review of benefits in 1976 and there had also been a Canadian sponsored review. Our group identified 23 areas where IBM had recently expanded function and could claim additional benefit. All participants agreed to test the validity of these additional benefits with their own customers and report back. In a de-facto way, I was accepting responsibility for documenting and analyzing benefit claims as they evolved. This organized itself more and more until the subject was a big part of my activity.

Direct Market Support

Valerie DeMuro of SAMI came to visit in early June to discuss factors about SAMI's consideration to purchase front-end data. SAMI had been exceptionally helpful years earlier, and I provided all the information she could use. The following Monday it was appraisal time again. Paul White, as my immediate manager did the appraisal and my rating did not change. I was still ranked as a "1" performer. I always presumed that Tommy Tomlin was the actual evaluator. I left that afternoon to speak at a Grocery Executive Class in Poughkeepsie and to collaborate on presentations for A&P in New York.

We were moving toward presentations and information exchanges between A&P and IBM at the highest levels. The account team in Cranford, NJ was working on details like specific checkstand designs and physical characteristics of register components: keyboard, printer, display, cash drawer, and at the same time, documenting the list of changes that had been delivered to the existing A&P stores with IBM systems, looking at corporate wide ROI and other analysis that could be presented to the A&P CEO. I provided detail function input and some benefits input to these. At the same time I was working with the IBM Data Processing Division on an advertising program. On June 16th I also met with representatives from Progressive Grocer about the concept of in-store TV commercials. A week later I'd be back in at DPD headquarters to go through the first of several dress rehearsals for the presentation to the top management at A&P.

Page 208 Spreading the Barcode

Store System Applications

At the end of June, I traveled to Giant Stores in Washington, D.C. to discuss the prospects for developing a Meat System using backroom scale inputs, checkout data, and possibly additional meat purchasing information. It gave me an opportunity to catch up with a college roommate that was back living with his parents in the Washington, DC area after his wife had unexpectedly passed-on. This was squeezed in between two trips to the New York area to work on the A&P presentation.

Direct Market Support

The first New York area visit was to the Cranford, NJ branch office. The Cranford NJ Branch Office was very unique among IBM offices. The standard IBM facilities often were a rectangular building with windows somewhat reminiscent of the 80 column IBM card. Completely different, the Cranford branch had been designed by Frank Lloyd Wright and was made of pre-cast concrete in a ripple design with very rough surfaces on both the inside and outside. Tall narrow windows were squeezed in between the castings. Inside it felt dark and cavernous with groups sitting in sections around the floor, and I remember a slight echo if you raised your voice.

The second visit location was also interesting. There was an IBM Field Engineering regional parts location on NJ-17 just west of the Garden State Parkway. Inside they had a very nice large conference room with walls about 4 feet thick protecting the room from the rest of the building. The walls inside the conference room were comprised of alcoves with pull down shade rollers at the top of each alcove behind a cornice. After we completed our work we were told that we had been meeting in the very first headquarters for the Strategic Air Command, the facility they used when it was formed. I went back and checked the walls, doors, etc. more closely.

IBM Store Applications

Mid July found me in Oakland to consider the benefits of scanning with the Lucky Stores team. I got to see my brother again. Lucky had tested some creative uses of Store Systems Data that allowed them to pick more synergistic mixes of products for weekly promotions and to determine the effect on unit movement of certain store rearrangements. IBM had Dr. Henry Steele working with Grocery Accounts to develop these more sophisticated uses for data from scanning stores. He had created and participated in a number of merchandising tests that would find their way into the standard list of scanning benefits.

Over time the applications built on the types of analysis that Henry was doing led to the biggest benefits of U.P.C. symbol scanning. In one test they learned that ads featuring a specific brand of peanut butter had the expected impact of also increasing jam and bread sales, but were surprised to find it also appeared to impact cracker sales. They measured the impact of putting the featured peanut butter on an end aisle display (where it sells much more) versus leaving it in its regular in-aisle location. They measured the specific impact of featuring Ketchup on sales of hot dogs. Detailed store-level item-movement information collected over almost any time period that you chose, opened up whole new categories of merchandising for supermarkets. For example, it was possible to measure the impact of one brand's acceptance on other brands. Within the Ketchup category, the different impact to featuring Heinz, or Del Monte or Hunt's could be measured. Henry Steele's Lucky store test was measuring what I had only hinted about at the Quaker Oats Sales Meeting years earlier.

Another interesting observation was that featuring certain items increased total store volume. And some of these items seemed to have a "linger" effect that kept store volume slightly higher even after their week in the plan.

Now, I imagined what could a supermarket chain do, knowing the sales quantity impact of each item in specific merchandise plans as well as its impact on other items carried in the store for each of its stores individually. Then add in the knowledge about gross margin and handling costs. I imagined thousands of hours of "What If?" questioning, on big, big mainframes to crunch all the product interaction variables needed to provide a profit optimized merchandising plan for any chain, week after week. This would sell a lot of IBM computers in all parts of the grocery chain.

Direct Market Support

Later, I traveled to Minneapolis to participate in a review of the IBM 3661's capabilities and status with executives at Super Value. This was a valuable trip for increasing rapport with Super Value. They became invaluable for collecting information, documenting benefits, and considering product requirements within the next 9 months.

Shopper's Fare

Late one week Tommy surprised me. He called me into his office and after I closed his office door at his request and sat down, he suggested we go off and form a separate company to open our own supermarket. We wouldn't resign from IBM. Initially I couldn't see how IBM would allow us to remain employed and said so. But Tommy didn't see any conflict of interest between marketing cash registers for IBM and running a supermarket. I still wasn't convinced, so Tommy offered to double check with higher management. He told me that every Sunday he played golf with Bo Evans, the IBM Vice President in charge of our Business Unit and all the rest of the Systems Communication Division. He would ask Bo about it over the weekend. That sounded authoritative enough to me. So I agreed to wait for the outcome.

The next Monday I put my head in his office door, and when he saw me he said Bo hadn't seen any problems. So I agreed we should start thinking about it, and that's where it stayed for awhile. It was early August and I had another Meat System meeting with Giant in Washington, D.C. before continuing on to New York City to continue preparing for that top level executive briefing for A&P.

IBM System Benefits

The following Monday we had a staff meeting review of benefits as we knew them and system functionality. At the end Marvin Mann was sitting in Tommy's office and he made another of his offhand remarks that meant work for me. This time he said to Tommy, "I thought we were going to have Bill update the Supermarkets Benefits Presentation." Tommy agreed that I should do it. While it fit in with the concern that had prompted my one day task force on benefits, I had plenty on my work list with the meat system, IBM 3661 functional additions, and the still in the future, executive presentation to A&P.

But this did sound interesting and I could depend on the IBM Store Systems field force to assist. At the time IBM had far fewer installed electronic point-of-sales systems compared to all the companies offering in-store electronic systems. Our competitors had focused on getting key entry systems installed while we had not until recently been functionally competitive, and further IBM had focused on U.P.C. Barcode Symbol scanning. If you looked at stores that were actually scanning, the situation was dramatically reversed. Since IBM had focused so strongly on scanning, we had a commanding lead in the number of scanning stores installed. That meant that it was principally IBM customers that had the first-hand information about the impact of scanning on the bottom line. Generally through their managers, I put out the word to all the Supermarket Store Systems Representatives, asking their customers to identify and document any savings or other quantifiable benefits they could attribute to installing a scanning system. Then I promised to follow up with them in a couple of weeks.

IBM 3661 Product Changes

Meanwhile we worked with development on a FAST, Future Accounting System Technology announcement. This would allow for a more flexible response to future accounting information requests. FAST was only part of the second major release of new function planned for the IBM 3661 Key Entry System.

Direct Market Support

The next few weeks were divided between many finalization meetings on functional enhancements that would be committed to and sessions to develop the presentation charts leading up to an executive to executive meeting between A&P's CEO and John Opel, the President of IBM at IBM's headquarters in Armonk, NY. I was asked to stay in an adjacent room in case some question came up when the breakfast meeting happened.

Afterwards Dick Holleman, the Store Systems Marketing Manager and Len Saltman, the Store Systems Representative to A&P, shared some of the discussions with me. The most interesting question was posed by the A&P CEO to John Opel, that in the face of such limited success, would IBM stay in the Store Systems POS market? John responded that IBM "was very patient." He pointed out that IBM pioneered MICR printing, but it had taken eleven years before MICR finally caught on. He assured the A&P executives that IBM was in this market to stay.

IBM 3661 Product Changes

Two days later I was back in Raleigh laying out charts to present all this new function to the field sales people. Function Richer was revealed by a hypothetical walk through a supermarket where the store manager observes and uses the new information being reported.

IBM System Benefits

I was starting to get feedback results regarding the benefits survey that I had initiated two weeks earlier. It was a mixed bag. Generally, the known benefits we commonly believed at that time were being re-affirmed. No supermarkets had really done an exhaustive study to determine all the benefits achieved. Most stores had two to three benefits which they had used to justify scanning at their locations, but once the store install had been approved and become operational they were not very interested in looking for and documenting additional financial benefits. The specific benefit areas were different from chain to chain, and the size of the benefit also varied between chains.

It looked like documenting benefits was going to become a challenge. A few representatives simply didn't want to push their customers on this subject. I pushed on them, but they were more interested in pushing back at me than getting an answer. I just dropped those. Where there was still hope that I'd get some input, I told them I'd be back in touch in another week or two.

Shopper's Fare

Tommy Tomlin and I reopened conversations about starting our own grocery store. He had discussions with Milton Pearlmutter of Supermarket's General and had been promised use of the Super Value store location software, recognized as the best in the industry. Like most things where real estate is involved, a big part of success comes from: location, location, location. The Super Value program was excellent in qualifying and quantifying the factors that made some locations better than others.

I was concerned about not knowing enough about variable weight systems and told Tommy that we should try for a different type of store, one that didn't sell meat or produce. Actually, there was a retailing experiment going on near my mother's place in New Port Richey, FL where Jewel Tea had advertised they would open stores called JewelT. These stores only sold non-perishables from cases arranged around the floor.

Not being experienced in starting companies, we probably didn't do everything in logical order. For example, we hired a lawyer to incorporate before we had finalized the format, location, or about anything else. The firm would be known as Shopper's Fare. I hadn't realized that the Raleigh News and Observer printed all the weekly corporate filings every Saturday until Ralph Vodika, a program manager in development, stopped by my office on Monday to ask what Tomlin and I were up to.

Two others were involved, Rich Rand who worked in our Market Support area, I knew to be very industrious and had covered Skaggs as a sales representative. He had an excellent work ethic. The other was a stock broker, Jim Bien, who asked me if he could be part of the deal when he heard about it during an informal discussion.

Direct Market Support

But in the meantime there was a roll out of additional function and a fall kickoff to complete. It was now customary for the Market Support Center to schedule a review of the market and updates on the IBM products two or three times a year. Five or six Market Support Center personnel became a traveling roadshow at branch and unit meetings scheduled around the country. This one started with a session in Cranford, NJ on a Thursday. The following Monday we were in Los Angeles, CA and proceeded from there to Oakland, CA. We had planned to leave directly from Oakland for Chicago, when that meeting was unexpectedly canceled

IBM System Benefits

I guess time in transit is a waste of some people's time, but for me, it provides some of my more creative moments. While zipping around I had time to think about the benefits project and arrived at some approaches. The first insight was that in the original benefit presentation which was based on the "standard $60,000 per week" store in 1973, the results appeared too theoretical to many industry executives because it wasn't their average weekly store sales. They didn't see themselves as standard and, of course, over time the average weekly sales had risen considerably from inflation and increased store size, if nothing else. I decided I would normalize everything by expressing all values as a percent of a store's weekly sales instead of a specific dollar amount. Retailers were accustomed to thinking in that context, and then people might be willing to apply the value to a wider range of store sizes. The presentation would not become outdated as soon because of inflation.

I had a habit of taking out a pad of paper and breaking it into four or six squares to create a presentation. I'd sketch out each chart in a rectangle. Whole presentations would get created on six to eight pages. This time, after the title chart, I started playing with a quick review of industry statistics. This eventually became the start of a new benefits presentation.

The most creative and useful insight came from an idea from the President's Class I had been in over a year earlier. In the original benefits analysis and presentation of four years ago when the IBM 3660 was announced, the benefits information was a documentation of the various areas that were positively impacted by switching to a scanning system. Only a cursory mention was made of the cost. Shouldn't the full corporate financial analysis that companies report for their investors benefit be applied? This includes benefits, costs and investments.

After I returned to Raleigh and started assembling the cost and benefit information that had come in through the representatives from existing customers, I called Dave Clutter, one of the instructors in my President's Class, to ensure I had the formulas correct. Using judgment, I apportioned benefits based on the level of automation, ranging from stand alone electronic cash registers with no communications to connecting them using a daisy chain. Data Terminal System functionality was the model for determining what capabilities and costs the stand alone ECR systems would have. The next level was electronic systems that had central controllers. NCR 255 and Datachecker were the models for capabilities and costs these systems would have. Lastly we had non-communicating scanning systems and communicating scanning systems which had the largest level of benefit. These were modeled after NCR and Datachecker for non-communicating systems and NCR, Datachecker, and IBM systems for scanning systems. When all the numbers were crunched, each of the alternatives enhanced profit, but scanning – communicating systems were a spectacularly a better investment.

Scanning Benefits Presentation

As this was coming together, IBM was approached by the Industry Consultant, Tom Wilson of McKinsey and Co., to participate in an October Food Marketing Institute panel put together by Willard Bishop, another consultant in the industry, We decided it was the opportunity to unveil the

Spreading the Barcode

benefits update. I was scheduled as the opening presentation on the second day of a two day conference. When I walked into the room in the Holiday Inn City Centre in Chicago on October 13th, it looked like the whole FMI Scanning subcommittee and more were in the room. There was Bob Cottrell from Kroger, and others I'd met through the years. It looked like a Who's Who of the industry.

Below is the presentation they saw in 1977. Each chart is followed by notes or talking points that would be mentioned by the speaker at that time. below it.

This presentation and what happened subsequently had a dramatic impact. The presentation made a credible case for a justifiable financial investment in scanning at the checkout. Different from other projections, these figures were from observations at supermarkets that were actually scanning at the checkout. They were not engineering projections. As such it may have been more credible to supermarket operators.

It marked the beginning of an explosive growth in scanning systems. In the second chart you can tell that at that time this the presentation was first made in the fall of 1977, less than 200 stores in all of North America using a U.P.C. barcode scanning checkout had been installed, and it was four years after the announcement of the U.P.C. symbol. But only two and a half years later, in the first quarter of 1980, over 2000 new scanning stores would be added quarterly. The industry began installing more than 10 times as many stores every three months, than they had in the four years prior to this analysis becoming available. The change came when the industry understood and believed the benefits.

Chapter 10 Revitalizing the Market Page 215

Chart 1

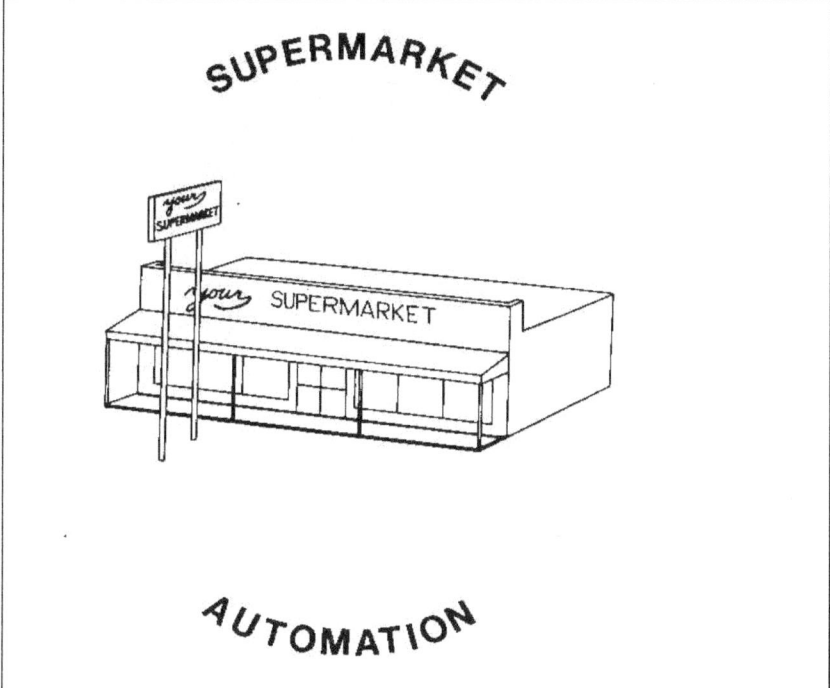

This was the Introduction title slide.

This will be a review of the status of U.P.C. scanning in supermarkets with reference to the benefits being achieved. The data presented is a result of a survey of supermarkets of a variety of size and types that are using IBM equipment today from across the United States and Canada.

Page 216 Spreading the Barcode

Chart 2

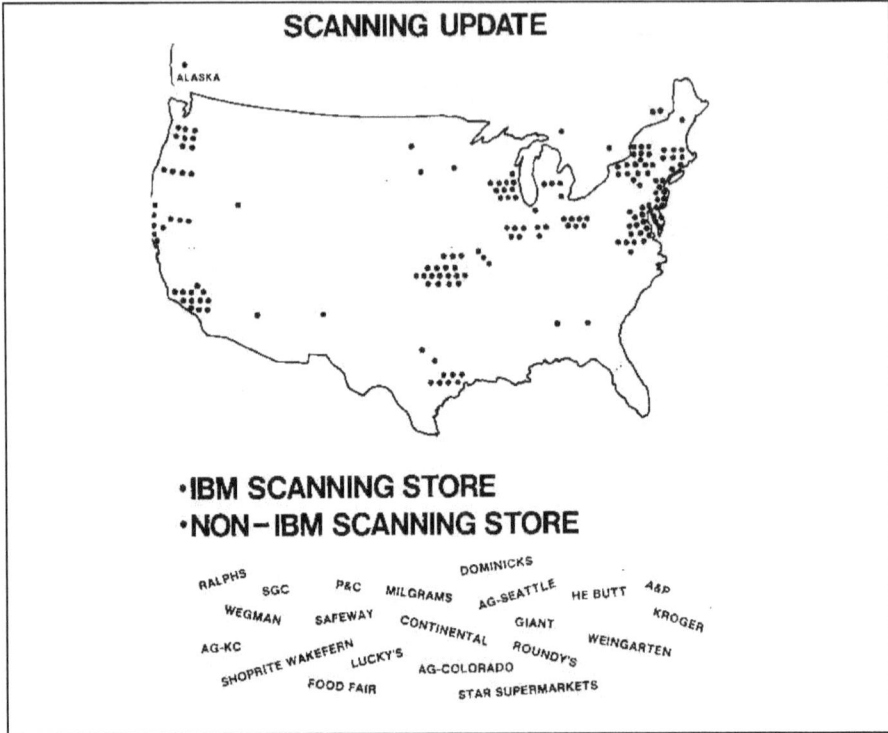

Comments made:

Some of their names are listed here. IBM has surveyed its customers and summarized what we discovered. The significant thing about the chart above is that it identifies every location that had U.P.C. scanners in checkouts the summer of 1977. FMI published a monthly listing that included every known installation. In a rare departure from its common practice to not provide install base information, IBM did report along with the other vendors when a scanning store went live with U.P.C. scanning. The store's name and city was added to the list. Each dot on the image above identifies a store that had scanning checkouts in the summer of 1977. Not really very many stores for being three years since that first U.P.C. was scanned in a Marsh Supermarket and almost four years since IBM had announced the IBM 3660 U.P.C. Scanning Grocery Checkout System.

Chapter 10 Revitalizing the Market

Chart 3

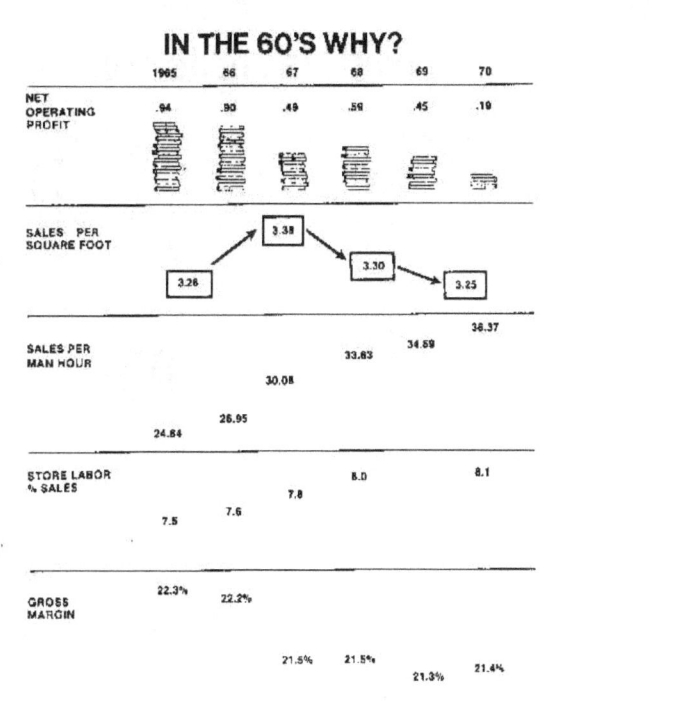

Comments made:

Current Grocery Industry Trends

During the 1960's Supermarkets experienced:

Declining net operating profits

Erosion of an initial increase in sales per square foot

Although there were some increases in sales per man hour,

Increasing wages actually resulted in higher labor costs as a percentage of sales

The net result was a decline in Gross Margin for the Industry

Page 218 Spreading the Barcode

Chart 4

INDUSTRY REACTION

DISCOUNTING

PRICE EMPHASIS
LESS EXTRAS, STAMPS, GAMES

LARGER STORES

EXPAND PRIVATE LABEL

INDUSTRY STANDARDIZATION

Comments made:

Industry Response

The industry attempted to combat these negative trends by:

Discounting and removing previous games, gift trading stamps, and other customer service add-ons to create a price leading image.

Closing smaller stores and opening larger stores that supported more sales per unit.

Introducing Private label product in most grocery categories that provided a larger manufacturing margin while priced below comparable national brands

and Standardization, finding a way to reduce distribution costs by standardizing brand-size identifications.

Chart 5

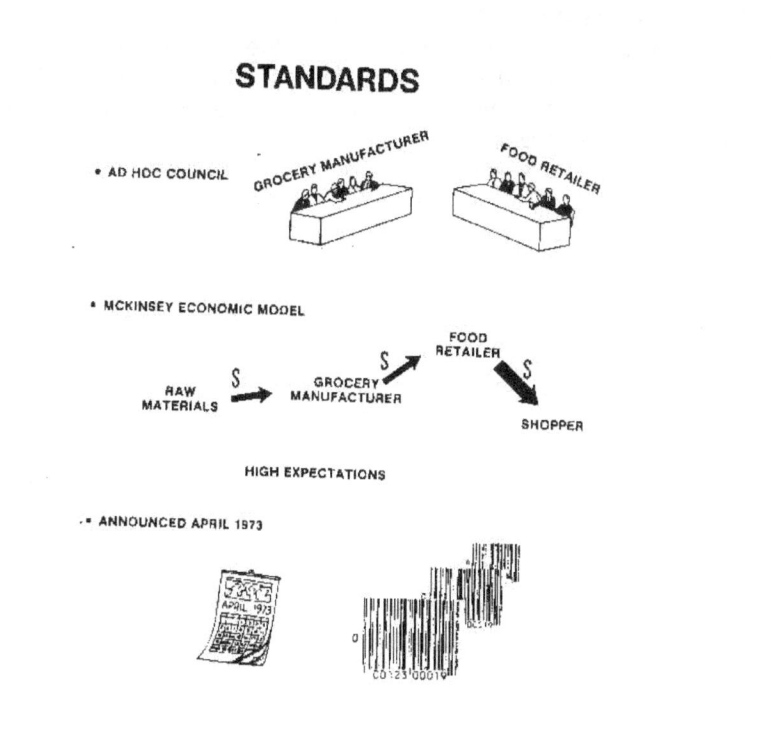

Comments to be made:

Steps to Standardization

Standardization resulted when the industry

Formed an "Ad Hoc" Committee of 5 Grocery Manufacturers and 5 Grocery Retailers

Ad Hoc committee contracts with McKinsey & Company to form Study group. Prospective equipment suppliers participate in detailed cost analysis of entire distribution chain from farm to grocery manufacturer, to retailer to customer.

Result of study shows that standardization would raise the cost to manufacturers, but that would be more than offset by savings in the retail areas of the distribution chain resulting in a lower cost to the final consumer. Benefit expectations were high.

> Prospective equipment suppliers make several proposals for specific symbol standards which are used by the symbol selection subcommittee to create a standard of their own that was announced in April of 1973.

The announcement that it was a standard of the committee's own creation was designed to limit concerns from the other symbol proposal submitters. According to a conversation I had with Barry Franz after the '73 announcement of the symbol, it was 95% the IBM submission and 5% tweaks by the committee in non-consequential areas so that they could announce they had not selected any one vendor's symbol proposal.

Chapter 10 Revitalizing the Market

Chart 6

HIGH EXPECTATIONS

$60,000/WEEK SALES

	ANNUAL BENEFIT	% SALES
FE PRODUCTIVITY	27600	.885
LABOR SCHEDULE	9360	.3
UNDERRING	7200	.231
PRODUCE SCALES	3120	.10
STORE ACCOUNTING	2808	.09
ROUTINE ORDERING	5280	.169
PRICE MARK/REMARK	9572	.31
REGISTER REPLACEMENT	2964	.095
ORDERING TERMINAL	660	.021
CHECKER TRAINING	780	.025
CHECK AUTHORIZATION	2600	.083
TOTAL	79,680	2.426% SALES

Comments to be made:

High Original Benefit Expectations

We started with high expectations (Note here we start expressing everything in percentages of sales, since most grocery chains think in those terms):

Front End Checkout Labor Reduction – the largest benefit

Improved Store Labor Scheduling

Less cashier under ring

More accurate produce scale weighing

More automated Store Accounting

Automated routine ordering

No Price Marking/Remarking for changes

No purchasing mechanical registers

> No Ordering Terminal
>
> Simpler Checker Training
>
> in-lane Check Authorization and more accurate
>
> The total pro-forma benefit was projected to exceed 1.5% of sales. This is exceptional when the fact that the before tax profit the previous year was about 1.3% of sales. But over half the benefit was derived from a projected reduction in check out labor, which we know didn't occur to anywhere near that projection.

It's interesting that several items in the base case do not even appear in the 1977 survey. We no longer looked at a training benefit; in fact training may have been more necessary with scanning. We no longer took repurchase of equipment as a benefit. And we no longer believed in an automated re-order of stock.

Chapter 10 Revitalizing the Market Page 223

Chart 7

EARLY RESULTS

- HIGH COST TO SUPPLEMENTAL MARK
  GROC MFG, PKG, PRINTERS

- PRODUCTIVITY NOT APPARENT
  CHECKSTANDS, WORK METHODS,
  IN-STORE DISCIPLINE,
  SYSTEM FUNCTION

- REACTION TO PRICE REMOVAL
  LEGISLATIVE ACTION
  SHOPPER EDUCATION

WHERE DO WE STAND NOW!

Comments to be made:

Getting benefit results in the initial scanning installations was very difficult. First, there were very few items that had the symbol included in their brand packaging, forcing the scanning stores to apply expensive supplemental symbol labels to most packages or to key codes or prices. The industry had to rethink its checkstand design, and it took several iterations before productive designs emerged, Store management was unprepared to instill necessary discipline in scanning techniques, and elements in the scanning checkout equipment did not operate at the speed required for the task.

Price removal benefits became questionable as retail clerks encouraged consumers to fight price removal and some legislatures proposed laws mandating continued item pricing in grocery stores. A lot of shopper education was required.

But that was 3 years ago, where do things stand now?

Page 224 Spreading the Barcode

Chart 8

CHECK OUT PRODUCTIVITY

	% SALES
ORIGINAL PROJECTION	1.185%
EAST	.4 - .607
MIDWEST	.49
WEST	.46 - .63
AVERAGE	.43

Comments to be made:

Front End Checkout Productivity

IBM recently surveyed stores with electronic checkouts across the country to attempt an update on the original pro-forma projections based on actual experience. Here is where things currently stand in various benefit areas:

Checkout productivity gains have been far less than the original projection of 1.185% of sales. Although it varies from store to store, productivity gains have only be .43% of sales on average across the country.

Chart 9

CHECK OUT PRODUCTIVITY

SCAN & BAG
- MORE PRODUCTIVE METHODS

- KEY ELECTRONIC
  - 5-10% INCREASE IN $/HR.

- LABOR SCHEDULE
  - GREATER IMPACT THAN ORIGINAL ESTIMATE
  - ALLOWS ACHIEVEMENT OF PRODUCTIVITY BENEFIT

Comments to be made:

Checkout Productivity

Several things contribute to the current state of productivity: IBM has noticed that it is necessary to scan and bag to achieve higher productivity. Scan then bag is only marginally faster.

Impressive productivity gains with electronic keying systems have been attained through well-disciplined and enforced checkout training.

But significantly, all checkout activity is time-stamped in checkout systems which lets any electronic system level store achieve store wide improvements scheduling people in for work, resulting in improved productivity results.

Page 226 Spreading the Barcode

Chart 10

PRODUCE

	% SALES
ORIGINAL PROJECTION	.10
EAST	.07 - .218
MIDWEST	.15
WEST	.12 - .24
AVERAGE	.16

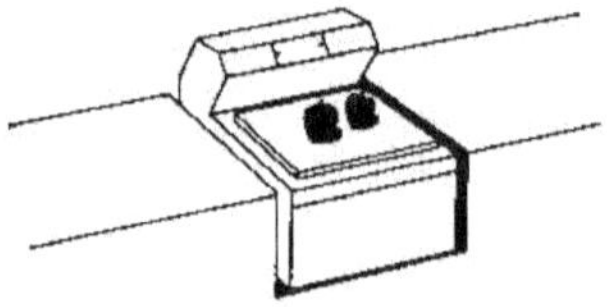

Comments to be made:

Produce Checkout

The results of keying or scanning produce have been much better than originally projected. We found it ranged from a low of .07% at one store in the east to a high of .24% at a store in the west. Overall the average was .16%, significantly higher than the .10% originally projected.

Chapter 10 Revitalizing the Market   Page   227

Chart 11

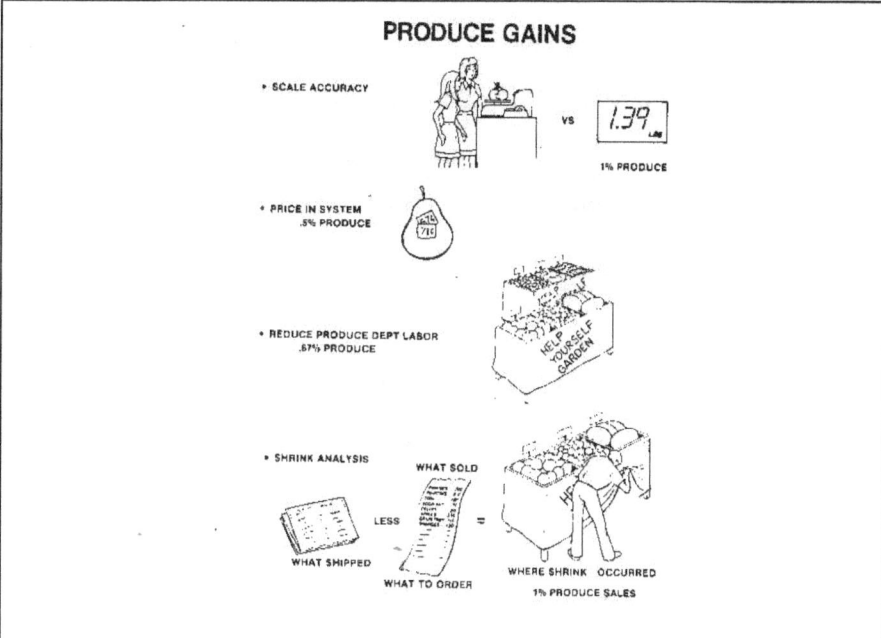

Comments to be made:

Produce Gains

Produce gains arise from several affects:

Scale weight accuracy has resulted in a 1% of produce sales increase in revenue, using a product code lookup instead of price marking catches miss keys resulting in an additional .3% of produce sales gain,

Better labor management possible with more detail on timing of produce sales results in an additional .67% of produce sales gain and

the ability to target specific products helps improve high spoilage items resulting in a .7% of produce sales gain

The impact of this at your whole store is naturally affected by the amount produce sales contribute to total store sales.

Page 228 Spreading the Barcode

Chart 12

NON-PERISHABLE SHRINK

ORIGINAL PROJECTION	.231
EAST	.25 - .39
MIDWEST	.25 (1-1.6%)
WEST	.1 - .21
AVERAGE	.232 (1 - 1.6%)

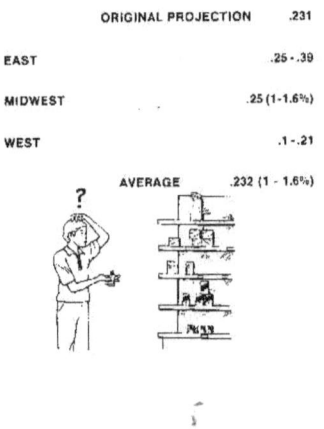

Comments to be made:

Non Perishable Shrink

Non-perishable shrink came in just about where it was projected, although there were wide store to store differences

Chart 13

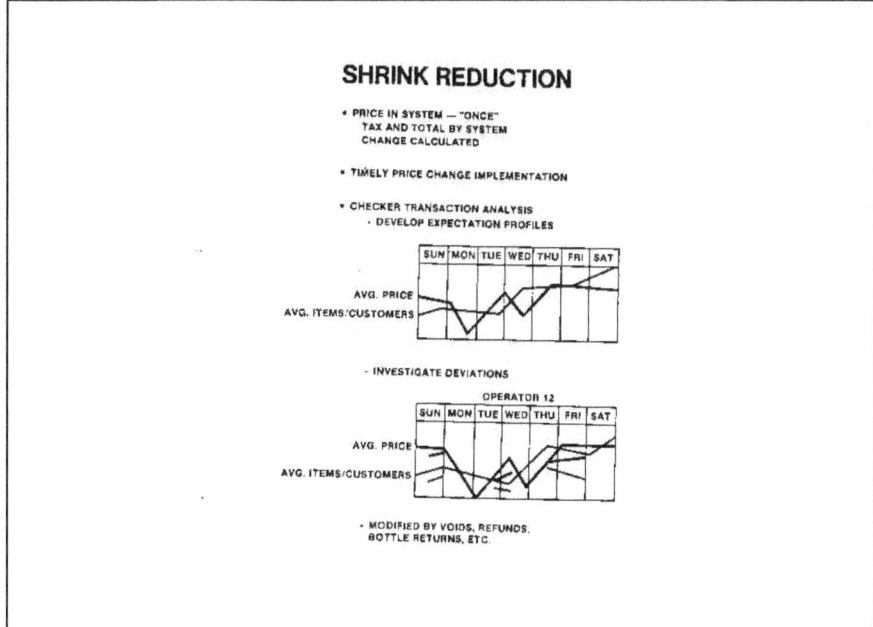

Shrink Reduction

Shrink reduction results from

The prices are in the system, removing problems of miss marking and misreading prices on individual items. The change due each customer is calculated automatically

Price changes are implemented in a timely fashion from centralized schedules.

Detail checker average price expectation profiles can be developed, then actual average price profiles can be compared to find training problems or worse a checker under charging for their friends (sweet hearting).

Bottle refunds, over rings and other corrections are specifically identified

Page 230 Spreading the Barcode

Chart 14

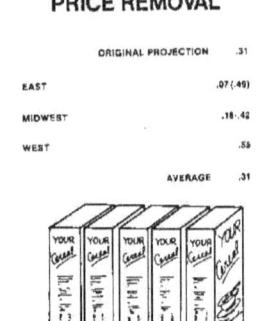

PRICE REMOVAL

	ORIGINAL PROJECTION	.31
EAST		.07 (.49)
MIDWEST		.18 - .42
WEST		.55
	AVERAGE	.31

YOUR CEREAL .15 PER OZ. $.82

Comments to be made:

Price Removal

Price Removal has been a benefit most have found difficult to achieve due to consumer resistance. But for those stores that have successfully removed prices, the benefit has been almost double what was originally anticipated.

Chapter 10 Revitalizing the Market   Page   231

Chart 15

PRICE REMOVAL

- TOTALLY REMOVED
  .18 - .55

- PARTIALLY REMOVED
  PRICE MARK LEGISLATION
  .07

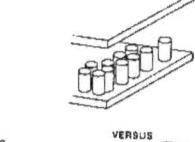

- REDUCED WORK
- FASTER STOCKING

VERSUS

- WAREHOUSE STORES
  MINIMUM 1% IMPROVEMENT TO GROSS

Comments to be made:

Price Removal

The price removal benefit includes the cost of price labels and the labor to apply price labels

It allows for faster stocking of shelves. The cases unload more uniformly, so they can be restocked quicker.

Warehouse stores claim a 1% total savings from price removal since they do not remove product from the shipping cases.

Page 232 Spreading the Barcode

Chart 16

IN-LANE
CHECK AUTHORIZATION

	% SALES
ORIGINAL PROJECTION	.083
EAST	.011-.022
MIDWEST	.012
WEST	.015
AVERAGE	.015

Comments to be made:

In-Lane Check Authorization

System level products have check authorization data bases that speed up checkout settlement by avoiding having the customer going to an office window for check approval. Although a modest cost benefit, it greatly improves relations with the shoppers.

Chapter 10 Revitalizing the Market Page 233

Chart 17

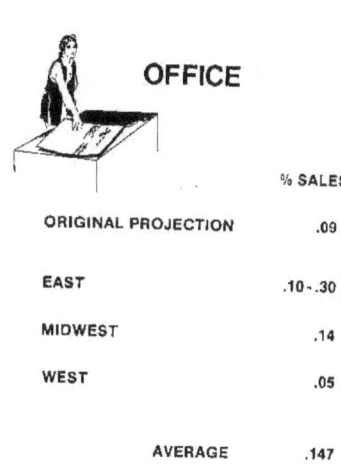

	% SALES
ORIGINAL PROJECTION	.09
EAST	.10 - .30
MIDWEST	.14
WEST	.05
AVERAGE	.147

Comments to be made:

Office Savings

We were surprised to find that office savings were about 150% higher than originally projected

Page 234 Spreading the Barcode

Chart 18

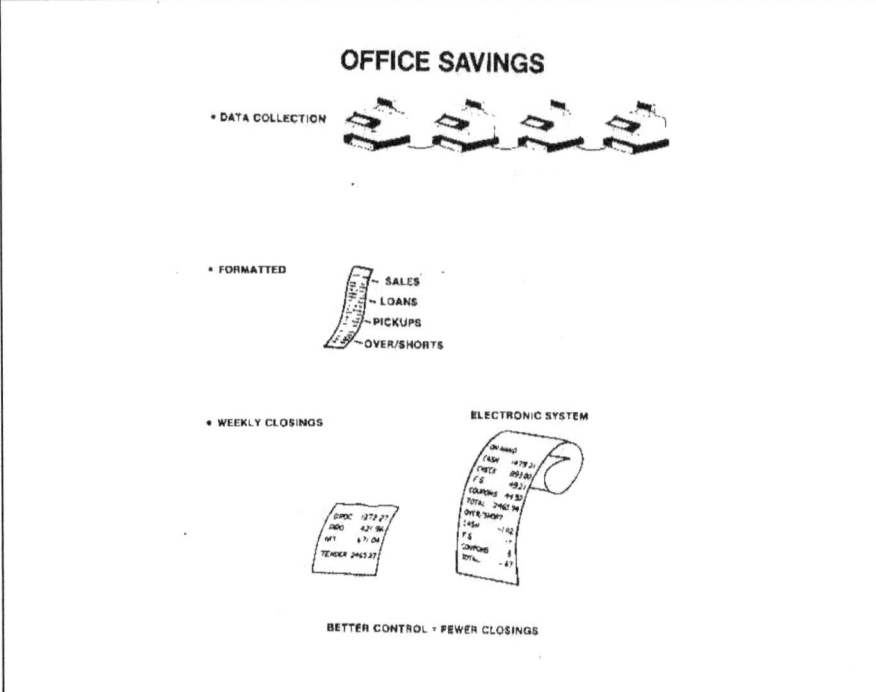

Comments to be made:

Office Savings

Office savings arise from savings through:

Automated data collection. The Head Checker no longer has to walk out to each checkout lane to read the register values

Clearly formatted reports allow the head cashier to find and reconcile numbers more easily

Data for weekly reports are generated automatically, removing the occasional arithmetic error

Chart 19

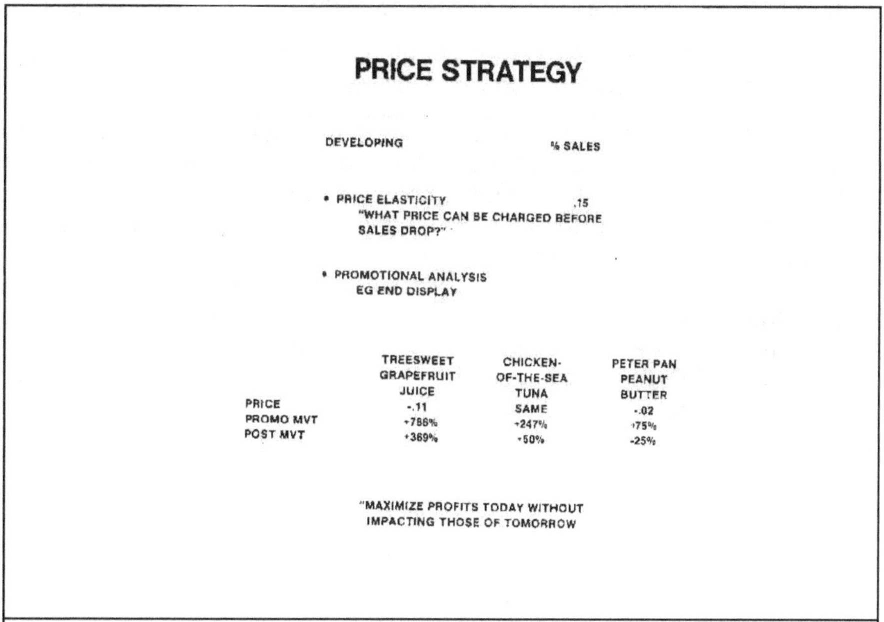

PRICE STRATEGY

DEVELOPING   % SALES

- PRICE ELASTICITY   .15
  "WHAT PRICE CAN BE CHARGED BEFORE SALES DROP?"

- PROMOTIONAL ANALYSIS
  EG END DISPLAY

	TREESWEET GRAPEFRUIT JUICE	CHICKEN-OF-THE-SEA TUNA	PETER PAN PEANUT BUTTER
PRICE	-.11	SAME	-.02
PROMO MVT	+786%	+247%	+75%
POST MVT	+369%	+50%	-25%

"MAXIMIZE PROFITS TODAY WITHOUT IMPACTING THOSE OF TOMORROW"

Comments to be made:

Price Strategy

Now we come to some observed benefit areas that were not considered in the original benefit analysis.

The first of these is improvements in a store's price strategy. The best example of this would be a test run at Ralph's Grocery in Los Angles. Ralph's had been selling a half gallon of Ralph's Orange Juice for 83 cents next to Birds-Eye at $1.05. The price of the Ralph's Orange Juice was raised 3 cents to 86 cents and "unit" volume, recorded by the scanner increased 2%. They raised the price on the Ralph's Orange Juice an additional 3 cents to 89 cents and unit volume went up again an additional 1%. When they raised it a third time 3 cents more to 92 cents, unit volume dropped 1%. We are not saying why this happened, just noting that it did happen.

A different California chain store used the detailed item movement to learn how products sell as they are moved to different parts of the store. It became apparent some product sales were increased much more when moved to an end aisle display than others. As a result the end aisle display program was significantly changed.

Products are promoted for a variety of reasons, but the expectation is that general sales will go up as a result of the promotion, and the product selected for promotion will benefit from the promotion after it concludes.

Page 236 Spreading the Barcode

> Scanning store item movement has permitted some interesting analysis shown here that indicates some products benefit much more than others.
>
> The message is: detailed item movement can help you to maximize today's profits without stealing from the future.

Over the years, by far the greatest benefit has been the detailed sales information data that U.P.C. scanning provided, although we didn't conceive of all the ways this checkout information has been employed. Scanning appears to have redirected retail marketing, and to some extent vendor marketing as well, from blind panels investigating carefully crafted statistical subsets of the market, to taking the market as a whole, denominating the tools to stratify the market for targeted programs, and generally putting all the tools in the sellers camp. It ended up being more valuable to retailers and vendors than all the other benefits discussed here. But in the 1970s, very few understood that.

Chapter 10 Revitalizing the Market   Page 237

Chart 20

INCREMENTAL SALES

	% SALES
ORIGINAL PROJECTION	—
EAST	.34 - .70
MIDWEST	.54
WEST	.62 - .94
AVERAGE	.631

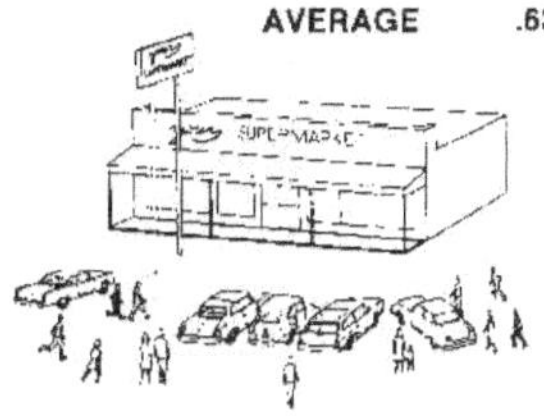

Comments to be made:

Incremental Sales

This benefit was a surprise that we did not anticipate. We don't know why it happens, but in most cases the volume of sales in a store goes up after a scanning system is installed. This is a very healthy benefit, .631% of sales on average. That is because these are the most profitable sales you can make. You have already paid for the advertising, store manager, rent, electricity and so on. The net profit on additional sales is much higher than on the original base.

Page 238 Spreading the Barcode

Chart 21

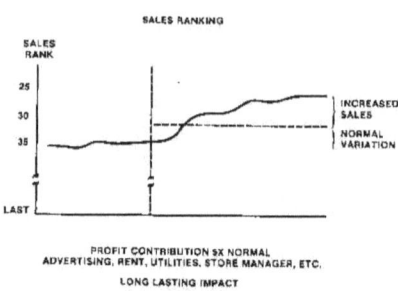

Comments made:

Incremental Sales

Generally within about 5 weeks of starting to scan, store sales will start up and level off on average 10-12% above the pre-scanning level. We haven't had any drop off reported.

Chapter 10 Revitalizing the Market

Chart 22

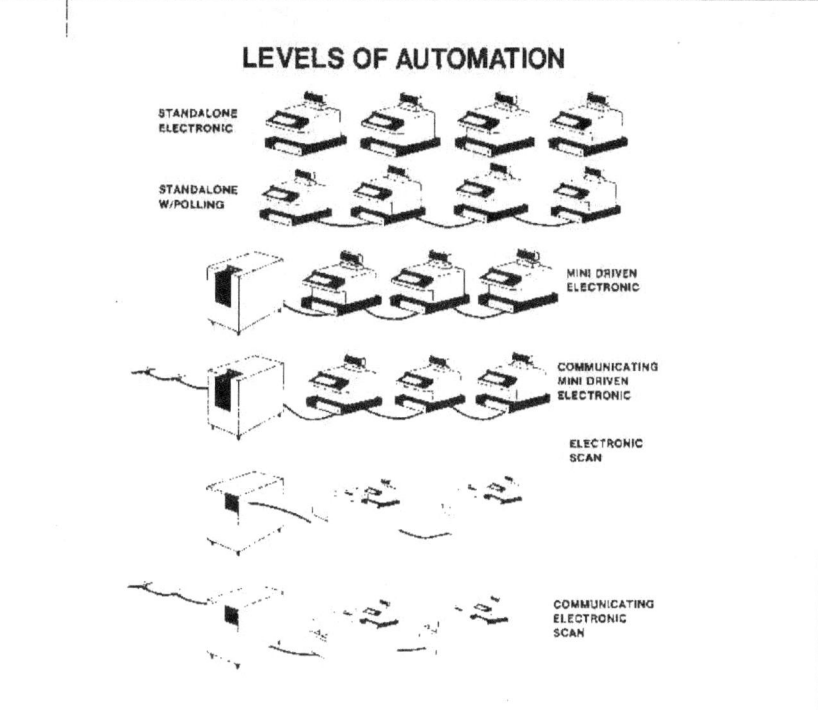

Comments to be made:

Levels of Automation

Before we sum up the benefits, let's consider the many checkout alternatives open to grocery stores today. There is more than one type of automation.

At the simplest level there are stand alone ECRs, essentially an electronic equivalent of the electro-mechanical cash register.

Next we have the inter-connected ECR. These machines are able to share subtotals, but generally have limited data storage for price lookups, etc.

The first system level is the minicomputer ECR. These can handle a large PLU file, check authorization files, etc. At this point I'd like to factor in another new technology that is now available, the ability to electronically transfer information from the store to a regional or headquarters location to assist them with their operations. So the next level is a communicating ECR (You won't be surprised that all IBM key entry systems are of this type.)

The next technology jump is to add scanning, which provides detailed item

Spreading the Barcode

movement capability.

and at the highest level the communicating Scanning system such as the IBM scanning system.

Chapter 10 Revitalizing the Market   Page   241

Chart 23

	STAND ALONE ECR	COMMUNICATING MINI	COMMUNICATING MINI SCAN	COMMUNICATING SCAN
READILY ACHIEVABLE				
PRODUCTIVITY	.12	.12	.12	.18	.18
NON-PERISHABLE SHRINK	—	.05	.003	.232	.232
PRODUCE	.10	.05	.05	.15	.15
PRICE REMOVAL				.10	.10
OFFICE		.05	.05	.05	.05
16% INCREMENTED SALES				.63	.63

100%

MANAGEMENT DIRECTED				
PRODUCTIVITY		.06	.06	.38	.38
PRICE REMOVAL				.45	.45
OFFICE		.09	.097	.097	.097
CHECK AUTHORIZATION		.02	.015	.015	.015

70%

INFORMATION				
LABOR SCHEDULE		.05	.05	.09	.09
NON PERISHABLE SHRINK*		.91	.91	.94	.94
PRODUCE				.10	.10
PRICE STRATEGY*				.15	.15

40%

| GROSS POTENTIAL | .22 | .495 | 1.525 | 2.264 | 3.554 |
| FACTORED POTENTIAL | .22 | .443 | .895 | 2.001 | 2.513 |

ORIGINAL PROJECTION   2.425   2.426

*UNDER DEVELOPMENT

WHAT DOES IT MEAN

Comments to be made:

Benefits Summary

This is a summary of the previous listed benefits. Each of the benefits in the summary is achieved today at some scanning store. There is no store that is achieving all the benefits, but every benefit included is being achieved by some store somewhere.

Since we collected details about how the benefits occur, we can and have appropriately assigned partial benefits to stores with less than a full communicating scanning system capability. For example the electronic scale accuracy benefit occurs for all systems, the benefit from better pricing and PLU lookup depends on having an adequate PLU capability, etc. So partial benefits are awarded.

It is also true that some benefits are more easily achieved. Some benefits require coordination between different parts of the chain to achieve, Price Strategy for example; Store Managers do not generally set the item prices. This benefit requires communication of in-store information to regional or headquarters personnel responsible for pricing. To reflect this, we have applied a factor to benefits in the summary: Easily attained in-store

Spreading the Barcode

benefits are 100%. Benefits that might require a higher level of discipline, manager sophistication, etc but are still principally contained within a store are factored at 70%. If the benefit requires coordination with personnel beyond the store to attain, it is factored to 40%.

If you can follow along at the bottom, you see reported the Gross Benefit summation for each level of automation and the factored level. Note that because of all the additional significant benefit areas that have been achieved, the factored level scanning benefits is greater than the original projection even though achievement on the specific benefit areas has generally been much less than what was originally projected. What does this mean?

Chart 24

NETTING EXPENSES

	STAND ALONE ECR	COMMUNICATING MINI	COMMUNICATING MINI	COMMUNICATING SCAN	COMMUNICATING SCAN
DEPRECIATION	.054	.100	.162	.161	.205
MAINTENANCE	.035	.159	.169	.109	.109
INSURANCE & TAX	.008	.015	.015	.091	.096
HOST DP PROCESSING			.035		.036
T.P. EXPENSE			.015		.023
TOTAL EXPENSE	.096	.285	.396	.361	.468
GROSS BENEFIT	.22	.443	.895	2.001	2.513
NET BENEFIT	.124	.158	.499	1.54	2.045

Comments to be made:

Cost/Investments

Before we can know the true bottom line impact, we need to net out the expenses of each level of automation. In this we use Depreciation (covers cost of acquisition), Regular Maintenance, Taxes and Insurance, Headquarters Application Programming expenses to use the data, and the telecommunications costs. Summing the costs and netting them against the Gross Factored Benefits, we get net benefit that range up to slightly over 2% of sales for a communicating Scanning System.

Page 244 Spreading the Barcode

Chart 25

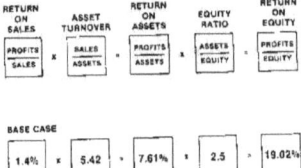

Comments to be made:

Profitability Model

Now rather than just consider this in traditional payback or return on investment terms, let's look at how this impacts the financial operation of your business. To do this we're using this economic model: Return on Sales times Asset Turnover equals Return on Assets. That number times the Equity Ratio equals the Return on Equity. If we put industry average numbers in for each term it works out to slightly under 20% Return on Equity for the Supermarket Industry. Of course you can substitute the numbers for your company.

This is idea came from attending the IBM President's Class a year earlier.

Chart 26

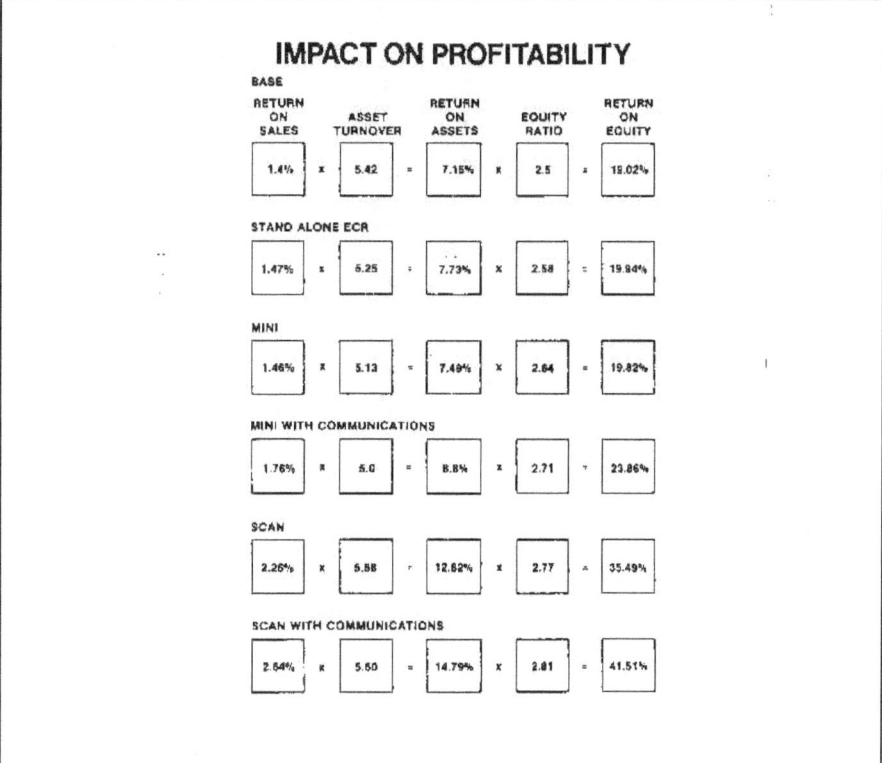

Impact on Profitability

Applying the net benefits from the levels of automation to the model, it shows us that benefits don't really start to jump until there is communication of information out of the store and used for staffing, pricing, merchandising. When scanning is added there is another significant jump so that communicating scanning stores can potentially more than double the industry average return on equity. The return to shareholders stays in the 19 -20% range until communications takes it to almost 24%. But U.P.C. scanning makes it jump to more than 35% and adding communications can raise that to 41.5%.

Page 246 Spreading the Barcode

Chart 27

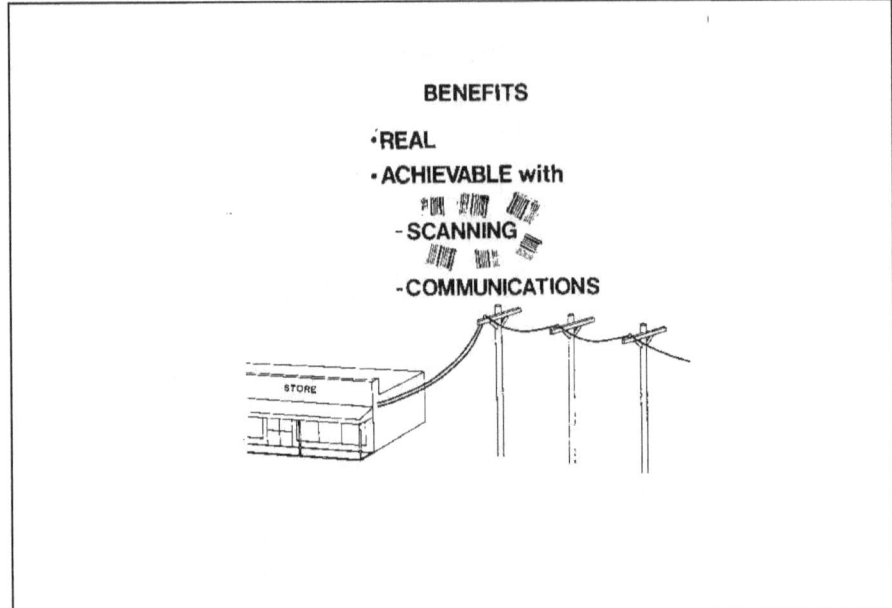

Comments to be made:

Summary

In summary automation can greatly enhance financial results. The benefits are real and can be most significantly achieved when communications and scanning are part of the system.

The presentation was well received. The message seemed to have been communicated that scanning was a very profitable investment. After the presentation I had lunch with friends, Ron Nuti, the POS Coordinator from Dominick's, and Henry Morris whom I'd come to know from the meat project at Giant Foods. We were joined by two gentlemen from Burroughs checkstand, Don Ernsberger and Dan Hurley, and by Lou Koewler from Toledo Scale. We talked about the compatibility of the scanners and other register components with checkstands. There were only a few questions about the benefits presentation, mostly on the make-up of the stores and types of merchandising plans that the chains that were included used. I took this to mean there were no significant surprises, but they were still going to want to shade the conclusions based on differences between the stores in the study and their own stores. On the airplane ride home that afternoon I recalled the business games we had played to learn principles of running a business seven years earlier in the "Marketing in the Seventies" course IBM put on for all field Marketing Representatives. Would it be possible to create a gaming environment to consider the benefits of U.P.C. Symbol scanning? I decided I'd call Dave Clutter again sometime in the next few days.

The best evidence of the acceptance of that presentation came the following day in Raleigh when Tommy Tomlin told me he had just received a call from Tom Wilson, the McKinsey & Company consulting partner responsible for McKinsey's contract with the U.P.C. Council. Tom Wilson asked Tommy to tell me that my presentation had been adopted as the official benefit analysis of the U.P.C. Council. It was now the official justification doctrine of the industry and as such would either lead people to switch to scanning checkouts or stay with key entry solutions. In hindsight it was probably most significant that unlike the prior studies, it pointed to the value of the information scanning systems provided to their marketing and management managers and reduced dependency on physically achieved and other in-store benefits. It way underestimated the informational value, but it recognized that most of the value was in the information. This would drive an industry historically run by high school graduates to incredible new levels of sophistication.

IBM 3661 Product Changes

But for me, first, there was a review of the new Key Entry function being prepared for release. The original IBM Scanning system was still essentially unchanged, but the close and responsive working relationship between the Key Entry engineers and Marketing people was resulting in the IBM 3661's third significant functional release in twelve months. Nothing makes a bigger impact on the sales force than a product that is continually re-inventing itself into a more comprehensive solution, demonstrating responsiveness to customer input.

The opportunity to see Dave Clutter in person came up sooner than I had thought possible when the team covering Woolworth Stores asked if I would listen to functional requirements Woolworth had, before considering proposing the IBM 3661 for some of their stores. So seven days later I visited them in the Woolworth building in New York City to start the documentation of their requirements.

IBM System Benefits

Then I drove up to DPD Headquarters at 1133 Westchester to talk with Dave Clutter. After the briefest review of what had been done with the Benefits Presentation, Dave was more than enthusiastic to assist. I would learn over the next few months that one of the frustrations of Dave's job with the President's Class was that he really never got feedback. People talking to customers get all kinds of feedback. Although Dave's class did have a feedback form, that's not the same as getting a sales order to confirm you communicated well. I might have been the first student of Dave's that had come back to implement the material he was teaching in something that would directly help IBM sales people sell. Dave was stoked! We spent an hour or so on approaches and decided to build an interactive model. We thought we could install it on IBM's internal marketing network known as HONE, Hands On Network Environment. I spent the night in White Plains and we met further the following morning.

Before leaving I walked around to the Distribution Marketing area and discussed the idea with some of the staff there. I think I asked Ed Igler if he knew of any SE's in the field that might be able to help with programming such a tool. People indicated they would check around. It was only a few weeks before I learned there might be an SE in Toronto that knew how to program in APL and was available to assist.

The following week I disclosed to the affected IBM Store Systems representatives the new IBM 3661 functional changes that met their specific customer's requirements. By the end of the week I had also briefed George Schenck, the development business manager, about the requirements I had received from my visit with Woolworth in New York City and our updated benefits analysis.

Valerie DeMuro from SAMI, chaired a Guide Distribution Industry project meeting in Atlanta the first few days in November where I presented the results of our benefits update. But most of the next few weeks were spent finalizing with development the field product requirements and talking with other headquarter marketing people about the functional enhancements we were about to deliver.

IBM 3661 Product Changes

We had released "Function Rich" and we had released "Function Richer." This would be "Function Richest" because except for all but the most unique customer requests, they were now all included in every IBM 3661 Key Entry systems' microcode. We felt we could offer IBM customers the widest possible choices in functionality, and as we started planning for how this would be presented, we picked up on the then memorable TV advertisement from Burger King about "having it your way!" That would be our theme when we initially announced this enhancement package to a national Store Systems Marketing Managers meeting being held at DPD headquarters, 1133 Westchester, White Plains, NY. Alicia Maxwell, Jim Sanderson, and I devised a little skit about someone making decisions installing a new IBM 3661 system. I had gone to the Burger King in Cameron Village, Raleigh, NC the evening before traveling, identifying myself as an IBM employee with my business card, explaining that I needed a prop for an announcement skit, and asking to borrow from them one of their Burger King hats. They may have looked at me weirdly, but it was only for a second and they agreed and handed over the hat.

The timing of the meeting was fortuitous since I had also been asked to meet with Woolworth people who were focusing on the WoolCo Mass Merchandiser business at their offices in Lake Ronkonkoma way out on Long Island, New York. I remember it was a very long drive out from La Guardia, and I assumed I'd gotten lost several times before I finally arrived. We had a good meeting confirming most of what I had picked up from my meeting in New York City weeks prior.

Friday, the following morning, was the presentation skit to the Marketing Managers. We had kept out of the meeting room and generally out of sight until the time on the program scheduled for the announcement. The meeting's moderator told the group that we had decided to do a skit to tell about what was coming rather than a presentation. The hat was inside my shirt with one button undone so I could get to it. According to the script ,Alicia Maxwell, playing the customer, was telling me that she supposed I was going to force her to compromise on how she ran her store because of limitations on things my system could do, Then I reached inside my shirt, pulled out the hat, and putting it on my head announced, "Why no, you can have it your way!" I heard Ralph Converse erupt into laughter behind me and it sounded real good. Pulling a stunt like that can be really good or you could end up playing the fool. The rest of the announcement went real well. I was on a 1:40 pm flight back to Raleigh and turned the hat in for dry cleaning that afternoon. It was back to Burger King's Cameron Village store by Monday.

The announcement while received well on the surface by the field marketing and systems representatives, soon produced an interested and strong backlash. Marketing Representatives while happy to see the progress in IBM 3661 Key Entry system functionality, were more than disappointed there was no equivalent announcement for the IBM 3660 Scanning system. Some mentioned that they didn't want any more function on Key Entry until the IBM 3651 Model 60 system got a refresh. Some strong criticism for "all" the progress being applied only to the Key Entry system was conveyed to management. Why was IBM not expanding the capability of the IBM 3660 Scanning System? The emotions were quite strong about this, and the large system eventually had to respond to it.

IBM Systems Benefits

The name, Howard Katz, an SE starting his career in Toronto, Ontario, Canada was suggested as someone who loved APL and could help with developing the benefits tool. We made arrangements for him to fly to La Guardia the first Monday in December of 1977. I met him and we discussed what this was all about while driving up the Hutchinson Parkway to 1133 Westchester to meet with Dave Clutter. Over the next day and a half we outlined a program that would allow Marketing Representatives to show how conversion from mechanical registers to any form of electronic registers would change their prospective chain's balance sheet. In keeping with the

Page 250 Spreading the Barcode

presentation, all calculation data is carried in percentages of sales, not raw dollars.

Users started as a 100 store, hypothetical chain but the number of stores could be adjusted. We included a store income and balance sheet information based on the most recent industry averages as presented in Chain Store Age, but the numbers could be modified here too. We identified the benefits as a percent of sales, but allowed the user to modify them and we also allowed for a lag factor to be set independently for each benefit. For example, the electronic scales produced their benefit from the first day of operation, but it might take some time to instill the discipline necessary to get the front-end checkout benefit or take time to collect the data necessary to achieve some of the merchandising benefits. Costs would be applied at the install date. Next the user stated an install rate for the type of system being modeled, e.g. 1 per quarter, 3 per quarter, 10 per quarter. The model would then produce pro-forma results projected ahead quarter by quarter for as many quarters as you requested.

Howard was asking the right detailed questions, and Dave and I were answering. Dave's knowledge of corporate finance and measurement practices was invaluable. I provided the industry swag and overall concept. I felt very strongly that we were starting something really unique and useful.

Chapter 11 Store and Forward Expanding the Market

When I returned that first week in December, 1977, Tommy Tomlin had a new task for me. A new product was being considered, a single register terminal model that could operate alone and would replace all the existing connected register products, the IBM 3663 Supermarket Terminal and the IBM 3653 Retail Terminal. Additionally, this register could contain a small disk drive allowing it to operate as a limited function controller. This was something very new for IBM DPD store products. The Key Entry system required an IBM 3661 Store Controller, the Scanning system required the IBM 3651 Model 60 Store Controller and the retail system required the IBM 3651 Model 50 Store Controller.

Tommy indicated he wanted to talk to me because the development division, SCD, did not then have the manpower to do what IBM referred to as a Phase 0 study. Phase 0 was the first of six expected phases every IBM product went through.

Phase 0 documented that there would be a credible business case for the customer to purchase the product that IBM could profitably develop and manufacture. Phase 0 was completed before any real development activities could began.

Phase 1 occurred when working prototypes had been achieved. Models had been built and the product could start an internal test or alpha test procedure.

Phase 2 was after a successful alpha test. IBM could safely say it was working in the laboratory, manufacturing and field service divisions would be aware of it and it could be priced, a First Customer Ship month determined, and it could be announced.

At Phase 3 all development activity was not only successfully completed but completely tested in every relevant configuration, a full regression test. The product would be shipped. Phase 3 was often achieved on the very last day of the month which had originally been announced as the first customer ship month. Sometimes we thought we might need 25 hours that day, but in actuality very few products and none that I knew of, ever missed that date. People would work incredibly long hours to be sure to achieve shipping in the month first customer shipment was promised for.

Phase 4 was known as the mid-life kicker, a re-engineering to extend its profitability in the market usually a few years after Phase 3, it extended the original product development investment by taking advantage of technology enhancements that occurred in the interim.

Phase 5 was End of Life, the withdrawal of the product from the market

Store and Forward Phase 0

I was being asked to coordinate the task of determining and documenting a defensible business case for the product. The major portion of that was documenting how many prospects for the product existed and that they had a viable buying proposition, i.e. a good business justification for the prospect to buy considering their business and the competition for the product from other vendors. I would have two advisors from SCD that had done this before and about seventeen specially chosen DPD marketing people to help with the analysis. Internally the product was known as the Store and Forward product because of the option on the register for a floppy disk and a communications connection. It would later be announced as the IBM 3680 Store System. The register with the internal disk would collect information from all other connected registers much like the IBM 3661 and use its communications to upload this information in response to a call from an external site. Like all the existing controllers, it stored the microcode that booted the other terminal registers in its system.

We officially kicked off the project on December 13, 1977 with about a dozen DPD personnel in the Retail Blue Briefing Room. The remainder of the DPD marketing people would not become involved until later parts of this Phase 0. After the customary NDA signings and warnings about not discussing what they might know from this activity, the two SCD advisors went over the process. The initial objective was to size the market from a macro and a micro viewpoint. In this instance the "market" was really comprised of many different types of retail outlets and so it was segmented to get more specific analysis. The segments had to be about retailers that were organized into chain store firms. We were not interested in retail industry segments where every retail outlet was a separate buying decision point. There had to be a reason to centralize information from many different outlets.

By design each segment ended up reasonably homogenous. A reasonable person should recognize any outlet within the segment as belonging in the same category. Our objective was to learn the segment's size, the buying decision process, and how well our store and forward solution met the requirements of prospects in that segment. There was no product even started yet to illustrate what it might become, but the advisors listed the things the product should probably be able to do on the white board. At that point signs went up on the doorway banning non-authorized people from entering the room.

Next we had to understand the justification process the prospective customer would apply and measure our product against it. Then, document the business case the prospective customer would use to consider a proposal for the IBM product. From this we could make some estimates of the numbers of the product that would be purchased. Then the development people could determine if IBM could build and sell a product the customer could justify.

Chapter 11 Store and Forward Expanding the Market Page 253

Even with my close to five years experience at the Market Support Center for Store Systems, I wasn't going to be told all the cost figures internal to IBM.

In the next few days we all learned to do a macro and micro structure of the market. The SCD advisors brought in the 1975 US Economic Census books they had purchased. From this it was relatively easy to determine the numbers of enterprises, retail locations, and employees in each of fifteen defined market segments. SCD also had some trade publications for many of the segments which had annual industry surveys in them. That expanded our information a lot. A mad scramble resulted when some DPD people pointed out additional trade publications the advisors had not heard of. Many of these publications got telephone orders for reprints of their annual surveys to be expedited to our offices in Raleigh.

For each segment we used the US Economic Census to define the numbers of establishments from a macro view. Then we used trade publications that printed annual industry reviews to identify the most significant companies in the segment by order of size. For each segment a firm among the top five was identified which we would later ask to visit and collect more detailed information to develop case studies on their store operations. The case studies would come next year. The DPD staff worked out the numbers on each industry so that we had good sizing information by the end of the year.

I spent time with engineers and SCD business managers trying to understand their costing algorithms and kibitzing on functionality. Dennis Kekas, the hard working repairer of the broken A&P store accounting systems assumed a significant role in the Store and Forward hardware design. I went to his office because I wanted to resolve a major challenge to checkstand design and manufacturing, the size of IBM cable connectors. In general IBM was still using large rectangular connectors like those used to connect tape drives and printers under the floor in a main frame computer room to connect simple things like the dot matrix display, register printer, keyboard, etc. This was a big problem in checkstand design and it seemed to me it could only get worse in the many more varied environments where the Store and Forward system was targeted.

I was complaining to Dennis that we needed to get the connectors slimmed down. He reached around and pulled the little plastic RJ-11 connector off the back of his touch tone telephone and waved it at me asking if I thought he should get the connectors down to that size. Well yes, in fact I thought that would be great. Dennis did improve them. Later I saw that the existing large rectangular 1 x 1 ½ inch connectors were gone. In their place were round ¾ to 1 inch diameter connectors used by the Federal Systems Division. They were going to feed through tight corners in checkstands much easier.

Shopper's Fare

Vacation occupied the last two weeks of 1977 spending one week each with

JewelT attempted a trial concept store on Route 19 in New Port Richey, Florida

my wife's mother and my mother in Florida., Considering Tommy's and my Grocery Store project, I took my camera into the JewelT box store in New Port Richey and played tourist taking pictures to show him and the others how it operated. Earlier in December I had spent hours on Saturdays, driving around Raleigh and nearby towns looking for available buildings without much success. I wasn't concerned about the building looking too modern. In my mind a slightly older building would suggest that "we were spending less on facilities so we could charge less." The objective of a box store is to be priced less on the non-perishable items than the regular grocery stores. By not having spoilage we could still earn a profit selling non-perishables at slightly lower prices. In hindsight I was probably demonstrating that I knew some things about how to operate a grocery store, but not necessarily how to market it.

Chapter 11 Store and Forward Expanding the Market Page 255

In JewelT stores non-perishable product was merchandised by cutting open the top and side of the shipping cartons, stacking the cartons on wooden tables, and hanging a very competitive price from a wire over the cartons.

Store and Forward Phase 0

The first section of the Phase 0 document was completed in early January. It defined market sizes, all the larger companies in each segment, the basic financials, and challenges each of the industry segments faced according to their trade journals. Now we needed to get closer to each industry segment, get first hand knowledge by talking with the people operating a business in each segment.

For each segment a representative leading company was chosen and the IBM host marketing team was approached and asked to contact his customer to assist in a business analysis. Nothing was said about any particular product, but they were told that IBM wanted and needed to better understand their type of business in greater detail at the retail level and would like to visit with them for generally two days. The best way to consider our approach was to think of it as if we would be preparing a Harvard Business School Case Study. The DPD staff visited the accounts and collected the information.

Small Grocery – Super Value	Drug Stores – SuperX
Hardware Stores – Moore Handley	Shoe Stores – Edison Shoes

Page 256 Spreading the Barcode

Fast Food Stores – Burger King	Convenience Stores – U-Tote-M
Jewelry Stores – Zales	Book Stores – Christian Book Store
Liquor Stores – ABC Stores in Florida	Card and Stationary Stores - Hallmark
Clothing Stores – The Limited Stores	Automotive Accessories – NAPA
Small General Merchandise – Dollar Stores	Handicrafts – Tandy
Tires, Battery, Accessory - Firestone	

There was a common occurrence in most of these studies. Two headquarters people would come in from Raleigh and be joined by at least one local IBM representative. The discussions were rarely about data processing, but rather about how that company operated its retail businesses, staffing, cash control, merchandising, security customer demographics, and more. Often this was the first time the local IBMer had really delved into his customer's business operations, and it usually really intrigued them. It became commonplace to walk out at the end of one or two days and hear the local sales representative declare that now that he understood his customers business, he was going to leave IBM and open a (fill in whatever type of store we had just visited). Generally IBM sales people knew that they were well paid and thought themselves somewhat unique. It's amazing but it came as sort of a surprise that there were many other very profitable business models too.

In mid-January I went to Cincinnati to visit SuperX Drugs again and then on to Minneapolis to visit with Super Value. Both were very open with their information, but I had known SuperX and Super Value represented new terrain. Super Value was the largest wholesaler supplying independent grocery stores in the United States. They provided grocery products for resale, but they also provided a wealth of services also. For example, they would help people with accounting or pick locations for their stores. It was their store location model that Supermarket's General had promised to let Tommy use.

During this visit the Super Value CFO was showing us the accounting documents for several of their client retail grocers. Another Super Value service was to provide accounting services and tax return assistance to client companies. The CFO described how this particular store owner had started with one store in a small town. It grew and he expanded to another town. The CFO showed me where two of the owner's cars and a van were being depreciated as store property. Clearly there were many more benefits to being a business owner than just the profits from the business. He made copies of a range of representative store statements for our analysis. Both

Chapter 11 Store and Forward Expanding the Market Page 257

SuperX and the Super Value stores saw value in better store scheduling and improved shrink and cash control. SuperX also had the requirement for handling prescriptions which wasn't in many grocery stores at that time.

Shopper's Fare

The next weekend I didn't drive around Raleigh, Durham, or Chapel Hill looking for store sites for my project with Tommy. I started looking in Wendell, Zebulon, Fuquay-Varina, and Pittsboro, the little towns. But Tommy had been busy too. He'd been talking with Harris-Teeter of Charlotte, NC. We were invited to visit them at their headquarters and he and I declared a personal holiday and drove to Charlotte, NC.

Harris-Teeter was interested in our plans, offered to be our supplier, and even was interested in having us locate next door to one of their markets. This surprised me, but they indicated it would be synergistic to have a low price non-perishable store next to their store. They felt the combination would attract more customers in total. And they offered to show us other tricks of the trade.

IBM Systems Benefits

In late January I attended the Midwestern store system's Branch Kickoff meeting to present the supermarket benefits presentation again. At that time I announced to the branch that there would be a tool available at some point so that Marketing Representatives could sit with their customers and prospects and see the impact of Point-of-sale investment on their Grocery Chains. Several of the Marketing Representatives were quite interested.

Howard Katz was making progress on coding the APL simulation model and came down to Raleigh to show it to me. But before we got started, he had something else he wanted me to see. He logged himself onto the HONE system and started some program that typed out "You're walking down a trail.

"You see a grate with some keys next to a lock…"

I just sat there. I had no idea what it was, so I quizzically asked Howard, "What is this?"

He just asked me, "What do you want to do?" Well we went back and forth because I had no idea there were computer games on big mainframes like the HONE system was, but the next thing I knew I had opened the grate and entered a cave.

At that point Howard pulled out this large map he had drawn on two pieces of taped together flip chart paper that diagramed what he knew about the cave. This was my introduction to "Adventure," one of the early computer games. Howard explained how you walked from room to room fighting beasts and

Page 258 Spreading the Barcode

collecting treasure, carrying things until you were overloaded and had to leave things, then maybe retrieve them later. I couldn't believe that things like this existed on IBM computers; it was so far from business. I was later to find out hundreds of different games were on IBM machines at that time. This was mostly because the HONE system, although only internal to IBM, was in its own way, very much like the Internet. It was loosely controlled, any and every field sales or systems person had access, and it went to all IBM marketing locations.

After Howard had administered my introduction to computer games, one of the future applications of computing, we got back to the project. I was such a straight-arrow. I could see the value of a game to sell IBM Point-of-sale. But games to explore caves seemed a bit frivolous at the time.

Howard also had a suggestion for the name: S.P.I.F.I., the Supermarket Point-of-sale Investment Financial Impact program. That was a better name than any I'd thought of, and we adopted it. A few days later I mentioned it while talking with Dave Clutter on the telephone, he liked it too.

Store and Forward Phase 0

In February I did my first Store and Forward Phase 0 business case-study investigation by traveling to Birmingham, AL to visit Moore Handley, at the time the largest hardware chain in the country. We conducted the interviews using open questions starting with "What are the biggest challenges in operating your stores?" It was an interesting visit with a very different business operation from the food and drug store outlets I had more familiarity with. It was interesting to learn they had two different starting times, early each morning for contractors who paid differently from consumers and required a credit management capability, and about mid-morning the store opened for regular consumers who paid with cash or credit card. I collected my notes and returned to Raleigh to write up the results. A week later I got a box of fan folded paper which was a printout of every store's monthly store statement in the Moore-Handley chain. The new requirement for Moore-Handley type of operations would be systems to assist with handling contractors and special types of customers.

A second interesting case study was conducted with U-Tote-M, a convenience store chain based in Houston, TX. I met Al Smith, an SE who, in addition to programming, could teach you a lot about pig farming around Ft Worth, TX. I learned a lot between meetings with U-Tote-M management. We met with operational staff from the Regional Vice President down to the zone manager and, of course, store personnel as well as financial and security people. I was surprised that the CFO wasn't terribly concerned about shrink since a modest amount of shrink helped to keep wages down. The zone manager we talked with had a police scanner on the shelf behind his desk because he wanted to be able to get to the store at the same time as the police.

While talking with the Vice President of Operations about his biggest challenges, he commented that he couldn't find good people. I empathized with that, indicating IBM was challenged by the same thing. He then volunteered that there had been discussion about taking over one of the large, now mostly vacant hotels in downtown Houston, putting up chain link fences, and raising their own employees. My pig farming associate had an appropriate humorous come back and I had a hard time keeping myself on track.

But the most interesting event during the day was when the Fort Worth SE, I, and the IBM Marketing Representative that covered U-Tote-M were talking with a mid level operational manager. The SE covering U-Tote-M came and pulled the Marketing Representative out of the meeting. We caught up with the Representative about 45 minutes later and were told the reason. The representative had sold U-Tote-M a distributed data collection and processing machine called the IBM 3790 to assist operations and finances on a district level. Over ten of these were scheduled to be installed, but I think only one had been installed up to that time and the programming was still being developed.

So as the second machine was going in, they ran the store reports and every single store showed in excess of 20% shrink, more than double what normally occurred. U-Tote-M immediately began taking administrative action. By the time the IBM SE was made aware of the results, more than fifty of that division's store personnel had been terminated. The SE, of course, suggested they immediately stop, since it was probably a programming problem, which it turned out to be. These people needed to be rehired. But, the U-Tote-M people told the IBMers to just keep it quiet.

Several requirements were documented. A system to handle vendor deliveries made directly to the store would be very useful in this type of outlet. Also, we needed to provide quick access in the instance of robbery and quick accounting after the robbery was all over. In spite of the CFO's comments, I continued to favor shrink control as a key application. They suggested a store access control option where the doors would not open before a specified time and would lock at a specified time like a bank vault. Power management was high on U-Tote-M's list of things to manage in the store. Although gas pumps were common, I don't remember much interest in making them part of any store level system. Al Smith accompanied me back to Raleigh to help write it up.

International Support

In the middle of February, first thing one morning as I was getting some papers in order, Tommy put his head in and told me to get my passport updated. "What?" I replied. I didn't have a passport. "Well go get one and charge it to the company." he replied. "Wait, what's up?" I came back. "Never mind," he replied "just get a passport."

I'd seen this before. When Jim Lightner had managed the spectacular announcement and healed from his gun shot wound, he was rewarded with a trip to Denmark.

I was a pretty brash person in those days, well maybe I still am. I followed Tommy back to his office and told him I wasn't interested in a trip to Europe. If management thought I'd been doing a good job, promote me to Marketing Manager, the classic next step for a direct marketing type person. Tom had previously suggested I should move to development where he felt I'd have a strong career, but I held out for the classic path. In hindsight, that was an amazing position to take in light of how well my following his and Bill Carey's suggestion had worked out with the IBM 3661 store test. But, I did go get a passport and told him after I had it.

Store and Forward Phase 0

The next case study was very different but also in Texas. One of the retail store system SE's from New York City accompanied me to Dallas to talk with Zales. In the two days we were in Dallas, we spoke with operations people, financial people, security people, and real estate people. And being Zales, we also spoke with specialists and heard about the process of acquiring diamonds. We were educated about the role of De Beers who were the world's largest diamond cutters and Zale's own diamond center in New York City. Special Zales' requirements included the control of special order jewelry, and general inventory management. Zales has an exceptionally valuable inventory that is easily pilfered. The SE came back to Raleigh, and unlike the other DPD people who rented cars and stayed in a hotel, she rented a van in which she lived in the Building 602 parking lot.

International Support

Tommy told me why I needed a passport. I was being asked to go to Tokyo, Japan for a week to work with the IBM sales team helping organize a special store study at the largest department store in Tokyo with hopes of justifying IBM Point-of-sale. Then I would go to Australia for four days to brief the CEO's of the country's largest chain stores including Woolworth on the status of the U.P.C. based on experience with source marking and scanning benefits. The last day of the second week I was to spend with chains in New Zealand.

I was really, really brash. So I told Tom that if the Director wanted to avoid feeling guilty about under recognizing me, let him promote me. I didn't need a boondoggle. Today I can't believe I really behaved this way, but I did. Tommy was unbelievably good about this response and didn't react at all.

Instead about two weeks later the Director of Distribution Industry for IBM Japan came to my small office in Raleigh, NC and personally asked me to come to Tokyo to help with the store study. What could I say, I agreed to go.

IBM Store Systems Benefits

In late February I got a call from Howard Katz's Manager in Toronto. She asked me how he was doing, and I gave her an honest, excellent report. Then she indicated they wanted to give Howard an award for this effort at the branch meeting at the end of the first week in March and felt it most appropriate if I came up and be part of it. I readily agreed.

International Support

In the interim I found out, the Japan trip really was part boondoggle. While in White Plains at the start of March to discuss the benefits model activity and progress on the Store and Forward product, it became known that I was going to make the trip to the far east. My friends in White Plains came forward with gifts and advice. They offered me a several hundred page reference book titled the "Business Man's Guide to Japan." I made a comment that I'd like to see Perth, AU and there was only a moment's hesitation before the organizer replied, "Perth? (pause) Perth's ok. We can do Perth!" Then I was advised that the company doesn't like its employees to fly more than 12 hours without a break, so I should plan a stop when returning from New Zealand. This person had found Fiji was nice. He even had a recommendation for a hotel and told me about many interesting people that he'd met in the pool. "Oh, and the company doesn't really understand how the International Date Line works, so stay in Fiji an extra day." was his final observation. The exact date wasn't set, but obviously this was supposed to be fun.

Before leaving that day I was in Paul Palmer's office, the Director of Distribution Industry Marketing for DPD, and Paul asked me, "What do you want to do?"

"I want to put a computer in every home in America," I replied. For several years I had been visiting anything that remotely looked like a home computer store. On trips to the west coast I'd stolen 30 to 45 minutes to visit IMSAI in San Leandro, CA. I'd seen the Apple and the Commodores. This was a very interesting subject to me.

I may have been answering a slightly different question than Paul was asking, but he responded, "Wow. You've got to talk to...." and he set up a meeting for a few weeks off.

IBM Store Systems Benefits

I also stopped by and saw Dave Clutter while in White Plains. Work on the benefits tool was progressing nicely. Dave enjoyed seeing the material taught in the IBM President's Class get to the field in such a visible way. We also talked about other ventures he was considering. Using his understanding of finance he was starting a side business to rent surplus trailers as temporary storage. I thought this was pretty creative. He'd get some clients that needed short term storage e.g. a service station holding a sale on tires, buy a trailer that had seen its end of life as an over the road vehicle, and lease it out.

Store and Forward Phase 0

I left late that night for Nashville, TN to do another business case for the Store and Forward product. This time I was meeting the Christian Bookstore, identified as the third largest in the bookstore industry. I knew the Marketing Manager from years earlier, so he and his Marketing Representative both accompanied me. It was a very congenial call, and I learned about the special information needed to succeed in the retail book business. There are new books coming out all the time. Some are hot, for a while, and some are not. Books have a faddish characteristic. Publishers make the first printing just slightly larger than the number of books that they will distribute in their initial push to the trade. So if the retailer can be first to identify those books that will be hot, there is a short time period to make a second buy from the initial inventory left at the publisher and get delivery before the book loses its initial appeal. If you re-order too late, the order is filled from the second printing which generally arrives later after the book's lost that initial high acceptance. We went through the retail store statements and he compared his firm to Walden Books, the industry leader. As we walked out and my friend prepared to take me to the airport, he commented, "I need to leave IBM and start a book store!"

I was fully absorbed in completing the Store and Forward project. Marvin Mann and I reviewed our findings from the case studies with an eye to any functional hardware or software changes that needed to be made. Rather then collect them into a single document I talked frequently with engineering managers and business planners about adding small features like a slot in the front of the cash drawer to allow people to insert credit receipts without having to open the drawer.

I took Marvin through the various ways that different segments of the Store and Forward market potential could benefit from our product. It was clear there was a much wider range of business information required, less commonality between prospects, than when our prospects were just grocery and department stores. IBM might need to open up the programming of the system to someone closer to the end user to allow it to better fit each prospective customer segment.

Chapter 11 Store and Forward Expanding the Market

IBM Store Systems Benefits

The first Monday in March I was at the Toronto branch office meeting. Howard's manager kept me sequestered so that Howard did not know that I was there. That branch had a special recognition of a specific technical person known as "The Systems Engineer of the Month Award" which included some compensation. She tried to brief me about its history but I confess I was more focused on what I had planned to say about what Howard had accomplished. When the meeting started I was introduced and walked out from behind a curtain. Howard was beginning to catch on. I spent most of my time talking about the significance and impact that Howard's work would have on IBM's success in the Grocery Point-of-sale industry. I believed it would be very, very significant. I wanted his peers to know that what he was accomplishing went far beyond that branch, and I was delighted to hand him the envelope with the special check. When I got off stage his Systems Engineering Manager noted that I had not mentioned that he was to be the "The Systems Engineer of the Month" but she would take care of it.

When Howard and I finally got together after the meeting, the first thing he told me was that he was the "Systems Engineer of the Month" and he was very happy about it. This illustrates the significance that special recognition played in motivating IBM personnel above their compensation. I don't know if at that time, Howard saw the same significance that his tool would have once it was up on HONE, but he understood the significance of that recognition.

IBM Recognition Event

When I returned from Toronto I was told that I had been invited to attend the 1977 Achievement Forum at the Fontainebleau in Ft Lauderdale, FL. I realized this could be combined with a Central America vacation. Two years earlier a guide in Mexico City had suggested I should go to the Yucatan to satisfy my interest in Central American Indian cultures. I had been entranced with a visit to Teotihuacan and now wanted to understand the Mayan culture better. My wife and I could take a week's vacation in the Yucatan and Cozumel before the Forum, then I would go to the Forum while my wife stayed with her mother nearby in south Florida.

IBM Product Changes

The Store Systems field people were still upset that nothing had been done to implement all the software changes in the IBM 3661 code in its big brother, the IBM 3660 U.P.C. Scanning system. They used their opportunities to express their concerns with Paul Palmer, Tommy Tomlin, and others. Then considering the variety of environments the new Store and Forward product would need to fit, management began considering opening up the

Page 264 Spreading the Barcode

programming to the customer. This had been taboo. We had originally believed that chains feared leaving the application open to their own programming staff.

One morning Jim Sanderson, Gene Frazelle, and Louis Preet were at my office door. Tommy had told them that IBM was considering letting the customer be able to program the cash register. They were each opposed. They felt it caused too great a security risk to let anyone within the customer be able to change the code in an IBM 3660 or the IBM 3661 system. Most people have heard stories about the unethical programmer at the bank that put all the rounding error from the interest calculations in his own account. What might be done to embed a sweet-hearting scheme where giving his friends an automatic discount might be programmed into the normal operation. While I understood their viewpoint, I also saw the other side.

Tommy had given the dissenters two days to define their arguments, and then he scheduled a meeting to hear them out. We met in the Red Briefing room, but the arguments presented were the same ones that had been presented before. After about 45 minutes Tommy announced that he had heard all that they had to say, but now a decision had to be made. Based on not hearing any new arguments to convince him otherwise, IBM would open up the programming in all the systems.

First, they would incorporate the additional function produced for the IBM 3661 system into the IBM 3651 Model 60 Controller and then release it as customer configurable microcode. That was that! Jim, Gene and Louis still agreed on only one thing, the discussion was over. We were going forward with a programmable system.

Personal Machines

In mid March I was asked to visit with an IBM stealth group in offices located behind a non-descript grey door on the fourth floor of the Sears Building in downtown White Plains. This was the visit Paul Palmer arranged as a result of our conversation in his office about computers in the home.

When I entered the building there was no mention of IBM in the Buildings Lobby Directory and leaving the elevator there wasn't a single mention of IBM at that floor's lobby. The door was gun metal grey with a small glass window with wire in it to make it difficult to break. When I looked through a window, all I could see was a bare wall. I rang a bell and after identifying myself, I was let in. This was feeling very clandestine.

At the time I could have been considered one of the most retail knowledgeable persons inside IBM. This was a group that, after I signed their NDA, indicated they were exploring IBM's entry into consumer level marketing.

Chapter 11 Store and Forward Expanding the Market

They asked me what I thought should be stocked in IBM retail stores. I told them they shouldn't have IBM retail stores because people would want to see a variety of computing alternatives. I'd already seen SOLs, IMSAIs, SWTech, and other personal computers. I felt IBM would win in a side by side, without knowing any thing about what the IBM computer would be.

I was asked to review a market research questionnaire. The questionnaire dealt with a hypothetical IBM television set that was also a computer. It dealt with questions about TV's that kept track of menus and balanced your checkbook. I remember asking them how they happened to select a TV as the subject, and they told me they thought the public would accept the high price tag, in the $1000-2000 range, and it was electronic. It sounded reasonable.

On the flight back to Raleigh I was surprised to find Lee Dixon on the same plane. Lee was the optics expert for the scanner. I asked him what he'd been doing and he indicated he'd been to Fishkill under a NDA. I told him I'd been to White Plains under a NDA also. We talked obliquely a little further and soon discovered that we had both signed the same NDA. This meant we could talk with each other. That's when I found out that in Fishkill he had seen the console TV with an IBM logo on it.

Recognition Event

A week later my wife and I started our Yucatan vacation. I've always had an interest in history, and learning about Middle-American cultures was great. We saw three significant Mayan city ruins and several roadside ruins. It was interesting to observe the current Maya and reflect on the grandeur of their prior civilization. I only embarrassed myself once when after a guide learned that I worked for IBM he told me he was going to teach all of us how the Mayans did arithmetic. He was sure I would excel at changing values from one number system to another; today we use base 10, while the Mayans used base 20 in a two tiered fashion. When he called on me I totally messed it up.

Ed Salonus, my old sales partner from Kroger was also at this Achievement Forum. We had some good conversations.

Page 266 Spreading the Barcode

Chapter 12 Moving On

I was back in the office on the second Monday in April 1978, but I had travel plans to Minneapolis to validate Point-of-Sale benefits with Super Value and then get Marketing Practice's concurrence with what we displayed on the screens in the S.P.I.F.I. tool. Tommy called an unscheduled staff meeting that morning to introduce a new manager to the Market Support Center and his group including me. He was a tall, mid-thirtyish man by the name of George McGregor. In his opening remarks George indicated he wanted to meet with each of his new staff and would publish a schedule. When the schedule came out I was at the end of the list and scheduled an hour before my flight to Minneapolis.

To make it even more challenging, he then fell behind schedule. I was allowed off the "on deck circle" 30 minutes before my flight. But remember I don't leave early for the airport. I actually thought I'd just have to leave when his door opened, but I was still there when he asked me to come in and sit down. He opened with, "Well, what can I do for you?"

It came across a little disingenuous and I responded, "Well, frankly it's more what I can do for you, since I've been around here almost 5 years and have functioned in most of the roles of this organization. But I have a flight in less than 30 minutes from now so we should continue this later." He suggested it was important to talk with him and possibly I should take a later flight. But I was meeting the Super Value CFO at 8:30 am the next morning and didn't want to appear tired from a late arrival. He relented, but as I left I returned and told him, "If you want to do something for me, get me promoted." Then I went and picked up my material in my office. As I left to go to my car, I noticed he was already into my personnel folder.

The Super Value people were happy with our S.P.I.F.I. tool. Super Value had the highly regarded store locater tool. I was hoping they would recognize IBM for this POS implementation impact tool. Marketing Practices had little if any difficulty with our screens, so things looked very positive. Howard Katz could get the tool up on HONE. We wanted to capitalize on this at FMI. With everyone signed off it looked like IBM was going to take the unusual step of obtaining a hospitality suite at FMI at the Fairmont Hotel in addition to the exhibit booth and installing a few terminals on leased lines to demonstrate S.P.I.F.I. at both sites. Gene Frazelle coordinated the FMI show that year

1978 Food Marketing Institute Show

At the FMI Show I spent much of the time in the booth with the S.P.I.F.I. terminals. Although it's difficult for people to get a full experience using the tool within the short time they will devote while walking through the show, many were aware of the benefit study and were interested in the results.

Chapter 12 Moving On Page 268

Then I was told Tom Wilson wanted to meet with me in the hospitality suite at the Fairmont. When I arrived Tom had Jim Oddy of Jewel Tea, and Al Haberman of First National Stores in Boston, with him. They got a brief overview of S.P.I.F.I. and Jim Oddy started making adjustments to the model on the screen. He was intrigued. When Haberman had his turn he indicated he wished he'd had S.P.I.F.I. 3 years ago when his firm was financially challenged. The four of us spent about an hour trying different strategies, asking and answering questions. It was a solid validation for the value of the tool.

Promotion

Near the end of the show, George McGregor took me aside to tell me he had arranged for me to interview for a Marketing Manager's position in Louisville, KY. I was very pleasantly surprised. My return tickets to Raleigh were altered to go to Louisville and interview with the Branch Office Manager, Gregg Ulligan. Afterwards I felt good about the interview, and I called George from the Louisville airport to tell him how it went. By the time I was back at my office in Raleigh, George had talked with Gregg and told me he thought I had the job. And I did.

When I returned to my office I tried to play it cool and not say anything. In less than 60 minutes, Jim Sanderson was at my office door telling me about an unannounced brief staff meeting in the red room. When I said I'd be along in a minute, he became insistent which was a little odd. I got up at a normal gait and walked to the room to find the staff was there, but no management. As I sat down, Jim pushed down the front white board to reveal one behind it with a big "Congratulations Bill!" on it. So much for low key.

Wrapping Up

The next two or three days were very emotional for me. I was leaving a group that had become the center of my life. Slowly I went through my desk separating out things that were personal from action files and background files on source marking, 3660 and 3661 function, and benefits analysis. I left card caddies with over 300 cards from packaging and printing people at grocery manufacturers across the country. (Six months later when I wanted to recover the phone number from one of the cards, I found they had all been sent to Valhalla, the massive data retention site where IBM was required to store all documents for the court case. It would cost $500.00 to retrieve any document. A card wasn't worth that much.) I sat down with George and Tommy to decide who would get S.P.I.F.I. up on the HONE system and published to the field.

And, of course, we had to think about Shopper's Fare. The most expeditious resolution was to un-incorporate, which we did and returned almost all of the money each investor had put in back to them. Later I was to discover Tommy retained the corporation for himself.

Promotion

I started in Louisville the following week with the understanding that I had to return to participate in an end of May tour across the country explaining the S.P.I.F.I. benefits tool to the store systems field personnel. I added a day to that trip to fly, at my expense, from LA to San Francisco and spend the night with my brother before heading back to Raleigh for the weekend. Store Systems was paying my expenses for the business part of the trip so George McGregor had to sign the expense report. When that happened I asked him about the trip to Japan and he asked me if I wanted a career or a trip. I knew I wanted a career, and that was the end of the conversation. I learned that Gene Frazelle did go to Japan late in June, participated in doing the in-store study and then returned directly to Raleigh.

Later in June Jim Sanderson hosted a promotion party for me at his house. It was a great evening and now I have my own "Time – Man of the Year" painting.

The following January the IBM 3680 system, the store and forward system, was announced. Several months afterward the Market Support Center had another update briefing which I attended as a Marketing Manager. During the session a Market Support Center manager pulled me aside and privately shared with me that first day orders for the IBM 3680 had exceeded 140,000 units. That was spectacular and I felt really good about that!

My adventure with cash registers and assisting in opening up this new business area for IBM was over. To Ralph Converse, Larry Goodwin and all the others I worked with at that time, "It was truly an incredible experience, wasn't it!"

Chapter 12 Moving On Page 270

Chapter 13 Epilogue

There are things that organizations can learn and things we personally can learn from this experience. I have my opinions about these, but I also know I was in the midst of the forest as close as any lumberjack could be, so I may not be the best to tell the outline of the forest in total. Better would be to let more of the involved people participate in that process. An Internet mail list and web site to allow registered users to add their own experiences has been established. It allows many of the other people that participated in this industry program from all companies to contribute their own stories and observations. You may see the website at http://www.idhistory.com/discussions. The mail list links are from the navigation sidebar on http://www.idhistory.com Anyone mentioned in this book and anyone who has a role in getting the U.P.C. to be the universal program it became, will be welcomed as a registered user and allowed to contribute to the site.

My initial observations first for the high tech organization:

Easily the first thing to be learned is how difficult it was to announce a product that was dependent on an external infrastructure which didn't yet exist. IBM had previously experienced such success in announcing new technology to new markets; it may have blinded the original staffs to this Achilles-heel called "source-marking." But in the 70s there wasn't much infrastructure for most new technological markets. I believe IBM became accustomed to creating the infrastructure along with the product. It had tremendous resources and was probably one of very few companies that could announce a product requiring a missing industry infrastructure such as source market grocery goods and possess the patience and strength necessary to fix the situation. The computer industry of the 1990s and later probably would not attempt such a bold effort. The Retail Food Industry is in debt to IBM for that. How different checkout might be if everyone had just waited for the more propitious time to come instead of taking the reins and working to make the change then. What economics would have occurred without our activities? You have to ask: When would the Grocery Manufacturers have given up space on their packages to put on barcodes without the educational program undertaken by IBM, McKinsey, and a very few others? Would they have waited for more scanning stores to drive the need? And how many grocery chains would have endured the excessively costly effort to in-store label with a symbol that scanned? Likely none would have before the concept had languished so long that no organization would still believe it would ever happen.

Spreading the Barcode

The second lesson is that there is much more to being successful than just having the best engineered systems product. In fact, having the "easiest for the customer to accept" market strategy probably trumps product excellence.

The third lesson for the organization would be to work closer with the real prospective customers. Initially, we were very focused on technology, but although we had excellent technology, we didn't have the user reports in the grocery store office that the grocery industry wanted. Sales greatly expanded with the Function Rich to Function Richest releases. In 1980 I was surprised to learn about a grocery retailer that had fourteen communicating systems from one of IBM's dominant competitors. Attempts were made to communicate with these systems nightly, but they were never successful in reaching all fourteen stores. Yet years earlier IBM systems seldom, if ever, failed to establish communications. Too bad IBM didn't have all the right information on the department sales report. Great technology, but IBM didn't include the customers' higher priority requirements. Pay most attention to what your customer expects from your product.

The fourth lesson is to shorten the communications link between the real user and the real developer. Without even intending to, each link in the chain from the user to the developer provides their own bias and prioritization of the information. Shortening the links in the case of the IBM 3661 and having a local real life test case made everything different.

The fifth lesson would be determination, persistence, and patience. These characteristics enabled IBM to continue on when other companies with less self-assuredness might have reconsidered. It took six years for the scanning rocket to lift off. From less than 200 installed scanning stores in the summer of 1977, two and a half years later in the first quarter of 1980, more than 1750 stores installed scanners. The benefits were there, but people had to be directed where to look for them. Only the persistence and determination of IBM would keep looking for them after four lackluster sales years.

What were the characteristics that allowed, and almost required, IBM to make this effort:

Vision. IBM and its employees projected the impact of how the products they developed would change their customers and the world. They saw change as their mission as much as making money.

Creativity and Intelligence. IBM was so prominent in the 1960's and 1970's that the most capable people wanted to work there. Almost everyone was allowed the freedom to innovate. In the early 1970s IBM encouraged and celebrated what they called "Wild Ducks," people who productively innovated what they did or how they used IBM products.

As Dr. Henry Steele noted in the Preface of this book, over and above the job the people participating in this program, particularly those in the program early, were committed to changing the way the world shops.

Epilogue

At the same time, management and we ourselves recognized the human characteristics we all share. Not everything turns into successes, and everyone doesn't applaud when we do something. But, we could allow for some amount of failure and try to improve our approach as a consequence of it.

Every day was a new beginning. We only carried yesterday's rejection of our product as data to act on today. We still believed strongly in each other and in jointly finding the better way.

We measured ourselves by what changed and happened rather than how people felt about us or talked about us. We tried to stay objective. Feeling good about ourselves came as a consequence of what happened.

Had the Industry waited for the infrastructure to evolve before pursuing scanning, would it have evolved? The interaction between symbol marking and developing equipment to read the symbols was a chicken and egg situation where each side could have ended up waiting for the other side to make their side a reasonable business opportunity. But in the 1970's, companies like IBM saw the opportunity was not just increasing their own products, but the expansion of the computing technology into new application areas. Twenty years later by the 1990s most companies would elect to wait for the infrastructure, making it much less likely that any transformations as major as the U.P.C. would occur.

Because IBM pushed not only themselves, but worked to sell the whole industry, retailers, grocery manufacturers, and the printing and packaging companies, the U.P.C. Symbol technology became part of the infrastructure and was so successful there has not been a technology sufficiently more productive to replace it even into the 21st century.

Our personal usefulness builds on our prior experiences. Whatever we are trained to do or invent on our own that works, is picked up and used again later where appropriate.

But sometimes we don't really see the true impact. In hindsight, the creation of the U.P.C. Barcode revolutionized the amount of information available about consumers in almost any sample size. The entire consumer marketing, sales, and distribution techniques have evolved and continued to change as we find more uses for knowing who is likely to buy what and when they are likely to buy it. None of the people mentioned in this book knew how impactful the information collection capability would be at that time when it was established. The rework of the Benefits Pitch in 1977 hinted at the value, but immensely underestimated the true value. In fact, the information uses turned out to be much more valuable than the original labor, shrink, and other saving benefits, for which the program was developed. As time goes on, more and more sophisticated uses for the information available from U.P.C. scanning will be developed.

Page 274 Spreading the Barcode

Glossary

I suppose jargon is the consequence of a techno-geek life. I'm indebted to Art Cornwell for suggesting maybe the best solution would be a glossary at the back of the book. I hope this helps.

Term	Definition
Baud	A telecommunications term to designate how quickly bits are put onto a communications line. There are some technical nuances that make it different for certain types of characters, but it safe to consider a baud as a bit per second. Thus 2400 baud is 2400 bits per second.
Bit	The smallest unit of anything. Each core of the System 360 computer stored one bit, either a 0 or a 1 indicated by the direction it was magnetized. It was usually represented by a small b as in 2400 b/second.
Byte	A term that came into common use with the IBM 360 to represent the most commonly addressed characters. A byte was 8 bits in an IBM machine. It is usually represented by a capital B as in 512,000 B.
DPD	Data Processing Division of IBM, the Sales and Marketing arm for large and complex computing Systems
DSD	Direct Store Delivery is a term used to designate those items sold in a store that are delivered directly from the vendor as opposed to being received at the chains warehouse and reshipped to the store. Commonly these were items like baked goods, beer, crackers and cookies, potato chips and similar products.
EAN	European Article Number, an evolution of the original U.P.C. to allow for a greater number of vendor codes by defining country codes.
ECC	Error Correction Code commonly program routines that use mathematical formulas to correct errors when a bit is erroneously changed from a 1 to a 0 or a 0 to a 1.

Page 276 Spreading the Barcode

ECR	Electronic Cash Register is a slightly ambiguous term since sometimes it was used to reference all electronic system alternatives, but specifically it referred to electronic versions of cash registers that operated independent of each other or at most might be wired together to pass register sales summary totals between themselves.
FSD	Federal Systems Division of IBM, the group within IBM that engineered, manufactured, and sold products exclusively to the Federal Government. Some of their products might later be available for sale within DPD or other IBM sales organizations.
GSD	General Systems Division of IBM, the sales, marketing development, and manufacturing arm for entry level systems and small computers from IBM.
Hexadecimal	A number system, just as decimal is a number system. Hexadecimal is a base 16 number system and was used with the IBM System 360. The possible values were 0,1,2,3,4,5,6,7,8,9,a,b,c,d,e,f.
K	A binary quantity. One K is 1024 usually bytes but also possibly bits.
Mini	Mini is a general term used to describe smaller than mainframe, multi-user computers. They are roughly file cabinet size and include the storage, processing, and communications capability within themselves. They generally needed a terminal for a person to use them.
MSC	Market Support Center, a group of people typically at a single site, focused on a specific market area or product, and were a second-level resource for sales and systems engineers in the field.
NDA	Non Disclosure Agreement. A legal agreement where parties who sign legally agree not to disclose anything considered to be proprietary to any other outside parties. Generally they should define what is to be considered proprietary, include some period of enforcement like 3 to 5 years, and escape clauses to end continued enforcement should the information become public knowledge by some other means.
NIRI	Net Installed Revenue Increase is a primary,

Glossary Page 277

	commissionable measurement received when a salesman has IBM equipment installed and is netted against the price of any equipment that is being replaced.
NSRI	Net Sales Revenue Increase is a primary commissionable measurement received when an order is deemed to be firm in the customer's mind and is net of any equipment that will be replaced at installation time.
On-line	The system that is actively connected and exchanging information with a remote site.
PSC	Production Schedule Confirmation: the time at which the IBM Branch Office certified to manufacturing that the order would be accepted by the customer with no further modifications. If there were any modifications or worse a cancellation, the Branch Office would be charged for the changes. Customers were customarily asked to put their intention in writing at the PSC time.
RAS	Reliability, Availability, Serviceability was a term used to identify product characteristics that reduced the amount of time a computing system was not available for use to the customer because of failures.
Regression Test	A quality assurance procedure where each added function is tested to prove it operates correctly with each combination of features. For example, if there were three options there would be one test with nothing turned on. Then three tests with each of the options. Then three tests with unique combinations of two options turned on. Then a test with everything turned on. It's clear this becomes more complex for larger numbers of options.
RJE -Remote Job Entry	Remote Job Entry terminals generally were fixed function devices able to read cards, punch cards, print at a reasonable line rate, and communicate to and from a remote computer generally in a 1200 baud or faster.
SCD	Systems Communications Division of IBM, the group focused on engineering products for communications based applications which would include Communications Control normally located

Page 278 Spreading the Barcode

	near a main frame down to the remote systems and individual terminals that connected to them and were sold by the Data Processing Division.
SDD	Systems Development Division of IBM, the development group that engineered all products. During the time this covers, it was split into multiple different development divisions each focused on different segments of the computing and communications market. SCD was one of these.
Sloop	Supermarket Loop refers to the communications protocol both physical and logical used between the Supermarket controller and the register terminal. It's probably best to consider it as a modified "Token Ring" since it physically was a dual loop with a token (or choo-choo as we described it) pushing out responses from the controller ahead of it and gathering requests from the register terminals behind it.
Spool	A common term in Data Processing that refers to creating a file to insert a stream of some type of data. Often used to refer to a print file where all records are lines to be printed.
Store Systems	The separate overlay sales organization created by IBM within the Data Processing Division to sell systems for all types of retail stores.
SE	Systems Engineer, a technical salesman paired with one or more salesmen (Marketing Representatives). The SE typically created the demonstrations, ran the bench mark comparison, and did the detailed analysis.
Time Sharing	A technique for sharing access to a computer which was pretty much made obsolete by the advent of the PC. Prior to personal computers the common way to provide cost effective use to individual persons was to share a large computing resource by connecting to it from remote terminals. Each user felt like he had the whole machine but, in fact, if there were 200 users, each user only got roughly 1/200 of it before the machine went onto the next person.
Troika	A term out of Russian culture to define a group of three that functions as an administrative or

	governing body.
U.P.C.	Universal Product Code – a Product Identification number created from a category number system value (0-9), an assigned Vendor Number and the manufacturers own assigned product ID number. Over time there have been some extensions to allow for expansion to the rest of the world.
U.P.C. Symbol	A graphical representation of the U.P.C. using barcodes to incorporate the category number, the vendor number, item code number, and a checksum digit. Now it's commonly referred to as "the barcode"
Wild Ducks	A term to describe and even encourage creative thinking in employees. IBM told its people that they were encouraged to think about things from different perspectives and experiment with non-traditional, but more productive approaches.
Work Sampling	A time study technique where you identify what activity is happening at a regular short interval. In large samples, the number of occurrences of an activity will tell you the percentage of the time required for that activity. Dividing the total number of observations into the total observation time and multiplying by the number of observations of each activity, calculates the average time necessary for each activity.

Page 280   Spreading the Barcode

Index

A
A Programming Language,APL....91, 128p., 137, 248p., 257
Adams, Ron....12, 21, 37, 50p., 57p., 61, 65, 70
Akers,John 67, 88p., 99p., 167
Altomare, Fred..................v, 179, 199
Anker Cash Registers...................28
Antonelli, Doug 78, 91
Arcnet..174

B
Babka, Frank..............................94
Beal, Teri....................................88
Beal, Tony..................................87
Berland, Harland.......................182
Bischoff, Joe....10, 13, 30pp., 45, 47, 49
Blair, Dick...................26, 57, 60, 99
Bliese, Russ..........................70, 99
Boie, Adrian...............................132
Brothers, Stan...........................182
Burger King.....................248p., 256

C
Carey, Bill. v, 44, 60, 72p., 78, 81pp., 88pp., 95, 97p., 102p., 107, 117, 119p., 122, 125, 131, 133, 135, 141, 143, 146, 152, 154, 158pp., 167, 169p., 176p., 179p., 182, 184, 192, 194, 199, 202, 260
Carr, Bill....................................167
Cary, Frank............49, 135, 152, 195
Caver, Mike................................19
Chapman, Clay....................52, 54
Checker Training......148. 150p, 180, 182p., 222
Checkstands.....26, 37p., 64, 87, 97, 105, 116, 147p., 150, 194, 207, 223, 246, 253
Christian Book Store...........256, 262

Clutter, Dave......213, 247, 249, 258, 262
Cogdill, Jerry.............................160
Coin Dispenser..........................87.
Colonial Markets...............78, 80, 82
Compton, Anne..................126, 155
Computer System Training 4pp., 14p. 19, 206
Consumer Reaction 138p., 179, 223, 230
Converse, Ralph........iii, 72p., 81pp., 87p., 95, 100, 109, 134, 143, 162, 249, 269
Cottrell, Robert..........26, 47, 64, 214
Customer Education.......2, 8, 12, 13, 179

D
Datachecker.......134, 142, 160, 166, 198, 206, 213
DeMuro, Valerie.................207, 248
Distribution Codes Incorporated (DCI)....................102, 110, 144
Distribution Number Bank (DNB) 102, 110
Dixon, Lee...................124, 202, 265
Dominicks...43, 145p., 148pp.,161p., 166, 246
Doremus, Bob.....72, 82, 100p., 133, 139, 191
Doyle, Gary......22, 31, 34, 45, 48, 61
Drew, Jerry...........................31, 34

E
Electronic Cash Register (ECR). 213, 239, 277
Electronic Scales. 132, 162, 206, 250
Ellis, Lloyd.................................172
Ernsberger, Don.......................246
ESIS.......27, 38, 134, 141, 147, 165, 174pp., 202p.
Evans, Bob....................63, 161, 209

Evans, Glen..................................65

F
Farmer Jack.............................107
Felton, Len..............................204
Fernandes......................165, 169p.
Ficken, Jim................................31
First National Stores............145, 268
Fitzgerald, Russ...........................4
Flying Neutrons..............40, 52p., 55
Flynn, John............................176p.
Food Marketing Institute (FMI)...140, 167, 202, 205p., 213, 216, 267
Forberg, Richard....................132p.
Franz, Barry....................62, 131, 220
Frazelle, Gene.............264, 267, 269

G
Galyua, Karolyn............180, 184, 204
Gee, Cal...................................121
Getz, Marion...........................192p
Giant Foods......101, 119, 138p., 145, 150, 161, 165p., 174p., 199, 210, 246
Goliber, Dave...............160, 165, 170
Golub Markets......160, 165, 170, 175
Goodwin, Larry......iii, 72p., 81pp., 87, 95, 98p., 105, 109, 269
Grand Union............................187
Great Atlantic & Pacific Tea Company........10, 179pp., 190pp., 196p., 201, 204, 207p., 210p., 253
Grimes, Paul..............................61
Grocery Manufacturers Association (GMA).................................118

H
Hamilton, Bill...............195, 197, 200
Hands On Network Environment (HONE).......129, 248, 257p., 263, 267p.
Handy......................................94
Hartwell, Jim........................90, 95
Hawranek, Joe...........................89

Hedgepeth.................................94
Higgens, Owen....................40, 52
Hitchings, Sam....................20, 31p.
Hobart Scale...............132, 162, 206
Hodge, Ray....................195p., 198
Holleman, Dick.........................211
Hurley, Dan..............................246
Hurst, Dick...............................163

I
IBM 3650 Retail Store System.....84, 91, 94p., 133
IBM 3651 Store Controller....87, 168, 249, 251, 264
IBM 3653 Retail Terminal............251
IBM 3660 Scanning Supermarket System..ii, 82, 84p., 93, 95, 97pp., 107, 114pp., 118p., 134p., 138, 143, 145pp., 149pp., 161, 167p., 174p., 179, 186, 193, 197pp., 205, 213, 216, 249, 263p., 268
IBM 3661 Key-Entry Supermarket System......143, 167p., 179p., 182, 184, 186pp., 191pp., 201p., 204p., 209pp., 247pp., 251p., 260, 263p., 268, 272
IBM 3663 Supermarket Checkout Terminal...87, 149, 180, 189, 192, 251
IBM 3666 U.P.C. Checkout Scanner 79, 87, 173
IBM 3680 Retail System......252, 269
IBM 3735 Terminal..........59p., 65pp.
IBM 3741 Terminal........................70
IBM System/3..........................37, 62
IBM System/360....2, 7, 10p., 14, 20, 22p., 25, 30, 34p., 63, 67p.,92, 276p.
IBM System/370.....30, 35pp., 59, 68
IBM Training..2pp., 9, 13, 30, 68, 71, 91, 93, 142, 206
Igler, Ed 28p., 50, 62, 72, 142p., 154, 248
Intermec...............................131p.

J

Jablonover, Alec..........................182
Jewel Tea Company..38, 188, 202p., 205, 212, 254pp., 268
Jordan, Harry........................23p, 35

K

Katz, Howard........249, 257, 261, 267
Keane, Peter..................................18
Kekas, Dennis.........189pp., 202, 253
Keyser, Dave................26, 57, 60, 99
King Soopers...............................100
Kroger Company..........ii, 9pp., 17pp., 28pp., 34pp., 43pp., 57pp., 63pp., 67p., 70, 72p., 75, 80, 83, 91p., 99pp., 103, 119, 135, 142, 145p., 148, 150, 160pp., 184, 214, 265

L

Laser..58, 79, 108, 111, 123pp., 202
Laurer, George...v, 83, 94, 104, 124, 135
Ledbetter, Willie 90, 95
Lightner, Jim...........72, 82, 97, 100p., 114p., 133, 191p., 260
Lucky Stores.............99p., 206, 208p.
Lunkenheimer, Erik.........147pp., 165, 170p, 174p, 177, 184
Lyles, Dean................................133

M

Macior, Ken................................182
Magruder, Bill.............57pp., 61, 64p.
Mann, Marvin........62pp., 88, 93, 117, 120, 125, 133, 142, 177, 188, 205, 210, 262
Markov...94
Maxwell, Alicia.........................248p.
McEnroe, Paul 84, 94, 117, 131, 189, 196
McGregor, George.................267pp.
McKinsey & Company..83, 138, 159, 166, 169, 184pp., 213, 219, 247, 271
Memorex............................44, 67p.

Index   Page 283

Mitchell, Harvey. 181, 183, 188p, 205
Molloy, Harry..............57p., 60, 64pp.
Moran, Bill...180, 182, 185, 189, 196
Moran, Milo................................197
Moreno..94
Morissey, John.............................93
Morris, Henry.............................246
Mosser, Jan. 100, 104, 122, 124, 141
Murray, Brendon........................188

N

National American Wholesale Grocers Association (NAWGA) 107
National Association of Food Chains (NAFC).......................97pp., 109
National Cash Register Company (NCR)..22, 28p., 37, 85, 134, 141, 160, 164p., 168, 174pp., 186, 195, 198, 204, 213
National Semiconductor (NSC)....82, 134, 142, 160, 166, 198, 206, 213
Nuti, Ron.......................149pp., 246

O

Opel, John....................99, 205, 211
Operation Mark-it 137, 140, 152, 157, 162

P

P&C..186p.
Palmer, Paul. 89, 122, 133, 135, 142, 188, 261, 263p.
Pendl, Bill. 2pp., 7pp., 13p., 19p., 25, 31p., 45pp., 49, 63, 65, 67p., 72p.
Pitney Bowes...............84, 99, 202p.
Powell, Joe........................162, 167
Preet, Lois..................................264
Price Chopper......160, 165, 170, 175
Price Marking...58, 71, 83, 130, 138, 221, 223, 227, 230p.
Procter & Gamble (P&G).......2pp., 9, 17pp., 21, 25p., 40, 50, 62p., 113, 117, 129pp., 155, 163p., 199, 206
Provetero, John..........................182

Q

Quaker Oats.............146, 153p., 209
Questad, Larry....72, 81p., 96, 99pp., 125, 138, 140, 142, 144, 159, 174, 191, 193

R

Rafferty, Jim.....................126, 150p.
Rand, Rich....................................212
RCA.......27p., 37p., 57p., 62, 64, 80, 83p., 103, 141
Rippe, Herb..........................51, 145
Russell, Larry........................83, 159

S

S.P.I.F.I..........................258, 267pp.
Safeway.....10p, 28, 70, 72, 91, 99p., 197, 199, 206
Salonus, Ed.......v, 44pp., 48, 61, 63, 67p., 73, 192, 265
Saltman, Len....180p., 184, 188, 211
Sanderson, Jim. .139, 168, 248, 264, 268p.
Savir, David................83p., 104, 106
Schenck, George.................204, 248
Schrotel, Stan................................18
Schwartz, Will....................52, 68, 70
Selling Areas Marketing Inc (SAMI) 125, 129, 154, 207, 248
Selmeier, Dick. .v, 95, 114, 129, 155, 206, 208, 269
Shaw, John............86p., 91, 95, 98p.
Shehorn, Bobby...................146, 153
Shipp, Mac 65
Shoprite Fooderama....................186
Sloat, Bob.....26p., 37, 47, 57, 60, 99
Smith, Al....................................258p.
Source Marking...57, 97, 102p., 106, 109, 119, 121p., 125p., 128pp., 137, 140, 144, 146p., 151p., 154, 157pp., 161pp., 165, 179, 199, 260, 268, 271
Spectra Physics..........................125
Spiller, Ed............................28, 71p.
Star Markets.....187, 196, 199, 201p.

Steele, Dr. Henry. iii, 170, 208p., 272
Stevenson, James 71
Stop & Shop.......72, 145, 148, 160p., 165, 170, 175, 177, 186
Store Loop...................128, 175. 279
Strubbe, Jack..........................18, 63
Super Market Institute (SMI). 139pp., 166pp., 179, 191p., 204, 206
Super Value.209, 211p., 255pp., 267
Supermarkets General (Pathmark) 101, 121, 131, 133, 137, 150, 152, 161, 165, 175, 182, 202
SuperX Drug Stores 12, 17, 21p., 37, 46, 50p., 57pp., 64pp., 69p., 255pp.
Sved, Paul. 71p., 145, 148, 170, 175, 201

T

Tarrant, Dick................133, 139, 142
Toledo Scale....131p., 162, 206, 246
Tomlin (M.G,) Tommy........69, 89pp., 94pp., 102, 117pp., 126, 133, 180, 182, 199, 202p., 207, 209pp., 247, 251, 254, 256p., 259p., 263p., 267p.
Trembley, Fred..........................45pp

U

U-Tote-M Convenience Store.....256, 258p.
U.P.C. Benefits.63, 83, 93, 105, 179, 207pp., 256p., 260pp., 267pp., 272, 274
Union...138
Unisys (see also RCA)..................62
Universal Product Code and Symbol ipp., 28p., 62p., 79, 83p. 87, 94, 97pp., 101pp.,108pp., 118pp., 121pp., 135pp., 142pp., 151pp., 157pp., 169, 173, 179, 186, 197pp., 202, 204, 208, 210, 214pp., 236, 245, 247, 260, 263, 271, 273p., 276, 280

V

Verckler, Dave..............................181
Vick, Gordon 10, 17, 19p., 23, 28, 30, 33, 36, 39p, 44, 49p., 60, 63, 72, 75, 78, 81, 83, 90, 94, 143, 174, 191

W

Wade, Harry.........................195, 198
Walker, Ron. 17, 21, 25, 30p., 39, 50, 60p., 72, 184
Warnier, Dave........................3p., 19
Weaver, Dick.................................206
Wegman, Bob...........147, 150, 165p.
Wegman's Markets 145, 147, 149pp., 157, 160p., 165p., 170p., 174pp., 184pp., 191, 199
Wetterau..............................143, 158
White, Paul..........................202, 207
Willard, Phil.......................................3
Williams, Dick..................................v
Wilson, Tom Jr.. .159, 166, 169, 177, 184, 213, 247, 268
Winn-Dixie.........................187, 194p.
Woodland, Joe. .78pp., 83p., 101pp., 106, 108p., 111, 114, 120p., 124, 131, 206
Work Sampling....172, 174, 185, 280
Wratten #26.........................123, 163

Z

Zales Jewelers....................256, 260
Ziegler, Jerry................................182

www.ingramcontent.com/pod-product-compliance
Lightning Source LLC
Chambersburg PA
CBHW032036150426
43194CB00006B/298